A POPULAR HISTORY
of the
CATHOLIC CHURCH

A Popular History
of the Catholic Church

by Philip Hughes

MACMILLAN PUBLISHING CO., INC.

NEW YORK

Nihil Obstat: Patricius Morris, S.T.D., L.S.S.
                Censor deputatus

Imprimatur: E. Morrogh Bernard
                Vicarius generalis

                Westmonasterii
                die 12a Octobris 1946

Macmillan Publishing Co., Inc.
866 Third Avenue, New York, N.Y. 10022

Macmillan Paperbacks Edition, 1962
Eighth Printing 1979

Printed in the United States of America

To
John A. Agnew

Contents

1. PRIMITIVE CATHOLICISM: ST. PETER TO CONSTANTINE   11
   The World in Which the Church was Born. Gnosticism. Marcion, Montanus, and Mani. The Apologists. The Christian Daily Life. The Roman Church. Origen. First Expansion of the Church. The Persecution.

2. THE CHURCH UNDER IMPERIAL PROTECTION, 313–711   35
   The Conversion of the State. The Problem of the Catholic Emperor. The Arian Crisis. Nestorius and the Council of Ephesus. The Council of Chalcedon. The Problem of the Monophysites. Justinian. The Monothelite Heresy. The Council *in Trullo*. Primitive Monasticism. The Greek Fathers.

3. THE CONVERSION OF WESTERN EUROPE, 313–755   68
   Donatism. St. Augustine. The Barbarian Invasion. St. Martin, St. Patrick, St. Benedict. Conversion of the Franks. The Irish Missionary Monks. Conversion of Spanish Visigoths. St. Gregory the Great. Conversion of the English. St. Boniface.

4. THE ASSAULT ON CHRISTENDOM AND THE RECOVERY, 714–1123   92
   Mahomet. The Iconoclast Heresy. The Origins of the Papal State. Charlemagne. The Breakdown of Civilisation. Cluny. The Hildebrandine Restoration. The Eastern Schism.

5. CHRISTENDOM TRIUMPHANT IN THE WEST, 1123–1270   116
   The Revival of Learning. The New Orders of Cîteaux and Prémontré. Expansion of Christendom. The Crusades. The Menace of the Emperor. Innocent III, the Albi-

genses, Dominicans, and Franciscans. The Struggle against Frederick II. The Averroist Crisis, St. Thomas Aquinas.

6. THE DECLINE, 1270–1517   143
New Perils from Within. The Defeat of Boniface VIII. The Struggle with Louis of Bavaria. The Black Death. The Avignon Papacy. The Schism of the West. Popes *versus* Councils. The New Devotional Life. The Renaissance. The Secularised Popes.

7. THE REVOLT OF THE PROTESTANTS, 1517–1648   175
Luther. Calvin. England. The Catholic Reformers. Trent. Paul IV. The Counter-Reformation. The Menace of the Catholic Prince. The Thirty Years' War.

8. THE REVOLT OF THE CATHOLIC KINGS, 1648–1789   207
France and the Huguenots. The Revival in France. Jansenism. Gallicans and Quietists. Deists. The War on the Jesuits. Febronius and Joseph II. The Apparitions of the Sacred Heart, the Passionists and Redemptorists.

9. THE ASSAULT OF LIBERALISM, 1789–1878   237
The Spirit of the Period. France. Germany. Italy. New Orders, Saints, the Vatican Council.

10. THE MISSIONARY CHURCH   257
Latin America. India and the Far East. Africa. The Catholic Revival in England. The Irish.

11. THE CONTEMPORARY SCENE, 1878–1946 268
The Aims and Achievement of Leo XIII. Pius X. Benedict XV. Pius XI. Pius XII.

CHRONOLOGICAL TABLES   295

INDEX   315

Recommendations For
Further Reading

For a fuller treatment of the elements of this great subject, the History of the Church, the following works are suggested:

I. GENERAL WORKS:

D'Arcy, M. C., S.J., *The Life of the Church.*

Hughes, Philip, *A History of the Church.* Vol. I for Chapters I and II; Vol. II for Chapters III, IV and V; Vol. III for Chapter VI.

Barry, Mgr. W., *The Papal Monarchy: 590–1303; The Papacy and Modern Times: 1303–1870* (Home University Library).

Pastor, L. von, *History of the Popes: 1378–1799* (so far, a score of volumes of the English translation have appeared, bringing the history down to 1740).

Leman, A., *The Church in Modern Times: 1447–1789.*

MacCaffrey, Mgr., *The Church in the Nineteenth Century.*

Premoli, A., *Contemporary Church History: 1900–1925.*

II. SPECIAL SUBJECTS:

Bardy, G., *The Church at the End of the First Century.*

Amaun, E., *The Church of the Early Centuries.*

Cambridge Summer School Lectures, *The Pre-Nicene Church.*

Butler, Abbot, *Benedictine Monachism.*

Batiffol, Mgr., *Primitive Catholicism; St. Gregory the Great.*

Duchesne, Mgr., *The Early Days of the Papal State.*

Jarrett, Bede, O. P., *St. Dominic.*

Cuthbert, Fr., O. M. Cap., *St. Francis.*

Guiraud, J., *The Medieval Inquisition.*

Hawkins, D. J. B., *A Sketch of Medieval Philosophy.*

Salembier, L., *The Great Schism of the West.*

Gardiner, E., *St. Catherine of Siena.*

Grisar, H., *Luther.*

Brodrick, J., S.J., *The Early Jesuits.*

Cuthbert, Fr., O. M. Cap., *The Capuchins.*

Ponelle and Bordet, *Life of St. Philip Neri.*

Soderine, E., *Life of Pope Leo XIII.*

Bazin, R., *Pius X.*

Rope, H. E. G., *Benedict XV.*

Hughes, Philip, *Pius XI.*

1

Primitive Catholicism:
St. Peter to Constantine

THE STORY of the first beginnings of the Church is to be found in the pages of the New Testament. For the Church is the society of the believers in Jesus Christ, of those who accept His claim to be God incarnate, His mission to redeem mankind and to make known to it the fulness of God's revelation. To such believers He offered a new supernatural destiny, and the means to achieve it. He offered a doctrine about God and a means to know that doctrine surely. The means whereby the believer would learn that doctrine and attain that destiny was the society He called into being. It was as a member of that society that the believer would be saved, and in a very real sense the society would, once He ceased to be visibly, bodily present on this earth, continue His work among men.

The task before the historian of the Church is simply this—to say how the divinely founded society has fared in the two thousand years or so since it entered on its mission, how far its field of action has expanded, how far its mission has been helped or hindered, by whom and by what natural circumstances. How has the society itself developed internally? How far has it changed? How far has it remained the same thing? To-day it is a body of three hundred million members. It includes among its members every known race, every nationality, every social class. It is a highly organised society, with its beliefs set out in a scientifically ordered theology, and its moral life similarly related to its beliefs, while an elaborate code of law safeguards the detail of its organisation and the procedure of its corporate life.

Every Church History has to show, in some way and to some extent, how all this has developed from that initial group of believers, "about an hundred and twenty" (Acts i, 15), who, after Our Lord's Ascension, "persevering with one mind in prayer" (*ib.* i, 14), awaited in the upper room at Jerusalem the coming of the Holy Ghost. Every Church History has to deal, then, with two thousand years of complex human activity. To do this in even the most summary fashion will need, if all the facts are to be more than merely listed, and every personage of importance to be so much as sketched, several volumes. So slender a book as this must be content to be either a vast choronological table or to give no more than a very general impression of leading events, of tendencies, and of the personalities that shaped them and were shaped by them. It is the second alternative that has been chosen, with full consciousness of the omissions this must entail, and of the risk the narrative must at times run of being a caricature. There is, of course, no space at all in such a book for the discussion of different points of view, nor for the reasoned defence of the point of view the author himself has taken. The book simply offers itself as an introduction of the most elementary kind that will relate as parts of an organic whole "the main events which directed the course of the current or were regarded as specially symbolic of each passing age," [1] and that will roughly estimate the effect on the general development of the chief of the many great personalities with which the history of the Church has been enriched.

The sources from which the historian must reconstruct the story of the primitive Church are, from the point of view of his task, far from ideal. There are no diaries, memoirs, or correspondence of the chief actors, no dossiers of official papers, no systematically filed records, certificates, and statistics. There are the summary lives of Our

---

[1] G. M. TREVELYAN, *British History in the Nineteenth Century and After* (1937), vii.

Lord we call the Gospels. There are letters from various Apostles to different communities of believers, and, in the next two centuries, a none too voluminous collection of polemical, apologetical, and expository writings. But nowhere, save in the Acts of the Apostles, is there, for nearly three hundreds years, anything that can be called a contemporary historical record. The precious facts, very often, are no more than the carefully gleaned *obiter dicta* of the theologian and the controversialist, of the unbeliever and the heretic too, no less than of the Catholic writer.

It is not surprising that most of the events known to us are what may be described as "literary events"—the appearance of new theories about the meaning of doctrines or about right conduct, their acceptance or condemnation, their effect on already accepted beliefs—rather than events that centre round revolutions in administration or the clash of rival policies and personalities. One great exception there is indeed to all this, the event, recurring continually through the first three centuries, and in every part of the Church, of the Catholic accepting death and torture rather than forsake his religion. It is the martyrs who are the leading personalities of this early Catholicism, and they abound, but again only a handful of the vast multitude are known to us even so much as by name.

The martyrs apart, the early history, so far as we know it, is a history of struggles where the leaders are largely anonymous, life and death struggles none the less, the struggle, for example, to keep the revealed truth clear of the fashionable movement to amalgamate all religious truths, or again to keep it clearly distinguished from the theories by which individual Catholics endeavoured to explain its obscurities and to reconcile its antinomies, the struggle to prevent premature "explanations" of doctrine which would have explained the doctrine away.

Meanwhile the Church continued to grow. It spread from Palestine to Asia Minor, to Greece, to Italy, to Egypt and to Africa, to Gaul and to Spain, to Germany and to Britain, but after the generation of the first missionaries, we scarcely ever know even the names of the pioneers in these countries nor the circumstances in which the faith was introduced there. The fact of expansion and conversions is there before us. At a given date there are churches

in these lands, recognised as the Church of Christ by believers in the lands where the Church had a prior existence, but a baffling anonymity hangs over all else.

There is the same vagueness, when we seek for details
of date and personality, about much of the early development of the internal organisation of the Church, and, to
take a particular example, about the first beginnings of so
characteristic an institution as the organised life, publicly
authorised, of those consecrated to God by a vow of vir-
ginity. At the outset of our survey of the history of the
Church we must not, then, expect the impossible. Least
of all must we expect a study of History to do what the
teaching Church alone can do, i.e., give us a full knowledge of the revelation made through Jesus Christ Our
Lord. The history of the Church confirms the teaching of
the Church. It can never supply for it nor take its place.
It is not, and cannot ever be, the chief means of our
knowing that teaching.

The first important fact to realise about the world into
which the Church was born is that it was a world where
interest in religion was universal. St. Paul, writing to the
Galatians, speaks of God as sending His Son "in the fulness of time," and history can connect this text with the
fact of a world-wide movement of religious change that
began about the time of Alexander the Great (died 323
B.C.) and was reaching its high-water mark about the
time Our Lord was born.

This movement can be summed up briefly by saying
that everywhere men were beginning to be explicitly
aware of the brotherhood of mankind and to turn to religion for confirmation of this, and for rites that would
deepen their awareness of the fact. Religion was being
called upon to play a new social rôle in the life of man.
It was not any longer expected to be only a matter of
rites duly performed to placate gods or win their favour
or to give validity to the acts of social life. It must be
aware of human misery, of man's anxieties and uncertainties—above all of his uncertainty as to his own origin and
his final destiny. It must take account of that endless
struggle in the heart of every man between his ideal self
and the ceaseless counter-cravings of a lower self. It must
face the fact of his frequent falls and in some way give

him an assurance that these will not, ultimately, destroy him. The new development begins, then, to associate religion and morality—and this for the first time. Simultaneously with this slow transformation of religion by the association with it of moral ideas, another force was at work—the tendency known as Syncretism. The gradual reduction of almost the whole of the known world to the political power of Rome had brought about new possibilities of knowledge. Old barriers, such as State frontiers, disappeared, and the whole world becoming one State, its different cultures and its myriad religions began to interact and to fuse as never before. Everywhere men were now in a position to study religions and to compare the differences of rite and legend and the elements all had in common. Soon the chief divinities of one heathen system began to appear in the Olympus of another system, and their legends to be similarly transferred.

The new religion of Christ Our Lord, from the moment it moved outside the Jewish *milieu* in which it first was preached, was thus immediately brought up against the influence of world-wide religious activities. In every city there were philosophical mystics and moral teachers ready, with their host of disciples and adepts, to see affinities between their own beliefs and the teaching of the new arrival. Moreover, once the Church began to make converts from this class it was but natural that these would be attracted to the task of converting their former associates, and that they would endeavour to present Christianity to them in the only language in which it could be understood, i.e., through an adaptation of the terminology of their own old philosophico-religious beliefs.

In all this activity, in these first contacts of the Christian mind and the Pagan philosophical mind, there was obviously much room for misunderstanding and for serious mistakes. And the ruling authority in the Church had, of course, no precedent to guide its action. It was the first time that such things were happening, and the Church must act according to its nature.

The story of these first crises and their resolution is told most simply in describing the Gnostics, the other heretics, and the Apologists of the first three centuries.

Gnosticism is the name given to a religious movement

older than Christianity, whose origins lie in that fusing of religious ideas and practices which went on continuously during the last two centuries before Our Lord and the two which followed. Long before the movement began to affect the religion of the Church it had attacked the paganism of the classical world, and Judaism as well. It was only a matter of time before it would make its appearance in the new Christian world also, to menace the new religion with what it had done to the others, dissolving away all that was definite and distinctive in them, softening their outlines and whatever core of religious and moral principles they possessed.

Gnosticism, as the name implies, purported to be a way to the knowledge, or rather the vision of God. It proclaimed its teaching, its rites, and its practical prescriptions to be divinely revealed and to have been transmitted and preserved through some mysterious tradition. It offered itself as an infallible means of salvation, operating usually through magical rites and formulæ, and it offered itself not to all men, but—and this was one secret of the movement's attraction—to the select band of the initiate few.

The basis of the Gnostic teaching was the idea of a fundamental antagonism between the world of matter and the world of spirit. Matter was evil, spirit alone was good. The Supreme God was not only, therefore, purely spiritual but He had not, could not have, any contact with the material. The creation of the material world was the work of some lower God, Demiurge, or, in some of the Gnostic systems, the angels. One of the most striking features of all the Gnostic teaching is the careful, genealogical elaboration of these successive emanations by which the Supreme God is linked with created reality. The teaching about the antagonism of matter and spirit, and of the evil nature of all that is material, had very diverse consequences in Gnostic moral teaching and practice. The Gnostics fell inevitably into extremes. Either they lived without any restraint, for the flesh, being matter, is something unworthy of serious consideration, or practised an unnatural asceticism, since, matter being evil, the flesh is a thing to be shunned and even marriage is sinful.

The historical fact of the life of Jesus Christ and His death offered no great obstacle to the Christian-Gnostic systems. His body, they taught, was only a body in appearance, since matter is always evil. And, of course, His death was not a reality but a show. The earliest traces of Gnostic attempts to amalgamate with the religion of the Church are to be found in the warnings of the New Testament.[2] There was not any one single system of Gnosticism, but it is not untrue to say that ideas such as these were common to all the Gnostics and fundamental in all the systems. So the Gnostic boasted that all that was to be known he knew. He was the heir to all the religious traditions, he possessed the key to all the mysteries, and was master of all the cults. Because of his knowledge, the Gnostic knew himself to be saved. He was no longer the victim of material things but supremely free. And he was, of course, the supremely qualified teacher of the truth about God and His Creation.

Now despite the seeming farrago of fantasy and raving which Gnosticism may present, it had a very evident, if superficial, relation to the religion of the Church, for the Gnostic was concerned to offer a solution for the problems that universally trouble mankind, the meaning of evil, responsibility for sin, the chances of salvation, the truth of the soul's immortality. These disciples of Gnosis saw in Christianity yet more raw material to be absorbed into the great corpus of their beliefs, and converts from the various forms of Gnosticism endeavoured to use the Gnostic philosophies as a rational explanation of the Christian mysteries. The natural result was the appearance, in the course of the second century, of a new, Christian Gnosticism, and soon, everywhere, this new kind of Christianity began to show itself, and to win to itself, apparently, many of the educated classes by its promise of an intelligent explanation of what they believed.

The Gnostic's ultimate justification of his assertions was his own personal possession of a special knowledge, and it is most interesting to note that to this earliest effort to subordinate the Faith to a private explanation of it, the Church replied by insisting that it is the very nature of Christianity that it is a thing transmitted by the believer

---

[2] Cf. especially Colossians, Ephesians, Timothy I and II, II Peter, Jude.

as he has himself received it, that the Faith is not a thing to be refashioned by any human intelligence, but something to be safeguarded by the Church's authority against any such refashioning. The opponents of Gnosticism were the bishops of the churches where it showed itself, and their single weapon against the subtle danger was the assertion that Gnosticism was at variance with what they themselves had received. Christianity thus shows itself, in its first meeting with doctrinal controversy, as a religion that is, essentially, strictly traditionalist.

There is one great name that has been preserved of these episcopal adversaries of the Gnostics, that of St. Irenæus of Lyons (died about 202). He was by birth an Eastern, a disciple indeed of St. Polycarp, bishop of Smyrna, who was himself a disciple of St. John the Apostle. Irenæus spent some years of his life at Rome and then he became a priest of the church of Lyons and, upon the martyrdom of its bishop in the great persecution of 177, bishop of Lyons. His most famous work is the one generally called *Adversus Hæreses*, but whose original title was *An Exposition and Refutation of what is falsely called Knowledge*. It is an elaborate survey of Gnosticism as the saint knew it, a denunciation of its dogmatic and moral errors. More than this, it is important because, by the way in which the particular problem of Gnostic errors is dealt with, the author has produced a model line of argument applicable to test the truth of all theories that call themselves Christian, a line of argument that has, necessarily, been followed ever since by the Church in its contests with doctrinal rebels. If only for his pioneer work in stating this now classic test of Christian orthodoxy, St. Irenæus of Lyons must rank as one of the leading figures in the Church's history.

The Gnostic's claim to correct and supplement Faith by his superior esoteric knowledge is worthless. For, so runs the argument, the doctrines which knowledge puts forth are not Christian because not true. If anyone wants to know with certainty what is true in religious matters, he has only to find which of the churches possesses a line of bishops going back to one of Our Lord's Apostles. What these churches teach as something handed down to them from the Apostles is true. What is in contradiction with this is necessarily false. To go round the world looking for such apostolic churches is a laborious task. It is simpler, and it suffices, to find out the teaching of the Roman Church, founded by the glorious apostles Peter and Paul. "For with this Church all other churches must bring themselves into line, on account of its superior authority." The test of Christian orthodoxy is the teaching of the Roman Church.

Gnosticism never utterly died out. It is not fantastic to say that a Gnostic undercurrent has persisted through all subsequent history, and its spirit informs movements still alive. But never, from the time of St. Irenæus, has it threatened to take hold of the Church.

Two other movements contemporary with Gnosticism, and which were a cause of great anxiety since, like Gnosticism, they aimed at a radical transformation of Christianity, must be noticed. Like Gnosticism, also, they drew many away from orthodox Christianity. These are the movements called, from the names of their founders, Marcionism and Montanism.

If the Gnostics often put us in mind of the Modernists of the last generation, it is Luther whom Marcion recalls. For Marcion, the son of a bishop (born about the year 110), left the Church to organise outside it a return to what he considered the Gospel's primitive purity. For Marcion there were two Gods, the lesser of whom was the creator of the visible world. It is this god, Demiurge, who, jealous of his own creature man, expelled him from Paradise and thereby began the history of human sin and misery with which the Old Testament record is filled. The Jews were this God's chosen people. Salvation is from the good God, who sent Jesus Christ to save men from the bond of Demiurge, and who was Himself really God but man in appearance only, for matter is essentially evil, and so He could not take a body that was a reality.

There is, then, a fundamental opposition between the Old Testament and the New, and Marcion is very anti-Jewish. His great hero is St. Paul—the greatest of all the disciples of Jesus Christ. St. Paul's writings are the great guide. Unfortunately, according to Marcion, they have suffered much at the hands of the Judæophile Christians who persecuted St. Paul alive and dead. Much of St. Paul's writings, as they had come down to the Church, Marcion therefore refused to accept, and, applying as a test his own notions and theological theories, he brought out a revised version of St. Paul (and indeed of the New Testament) from which he cut away whatever did not square with his system.

Marcion had a genius for organisation. He made many disciples and, following the model of the Church, organised them into churches throughout the Roman world, and provided them with a ritual and a moral code of impossible rigour, based on the notion, which he shared with the Gnostics, that all matter is evil and that the disciple must liberate himself from servitude to matter, i.e. from the use of matter as far as possible.

Montanus, who appeared in the second half of the second century, does not appear as an innovator in matters of belief. His one personal contribution to the life of the time was the fixed conviction that the second coming of Our Lord was at hand. The event was to take place at Pepuza —near the modern Angora—and thither all true followers of Our Lord should make their way. His authority for the statement was an alleged private inspiration, and the new prophet's personality and eloquence won him a host of disciples, who flocked in such numbers to the appointed spot that a new town sprang up to house them. Nor did the delay of the second advent put an end to the movement. On the contrary, it gave it new life and form as a kind of Christianity of the *élite*, whom no other authority guided in their new life but the Holy Spirit working directly upon them, and who practised a rigorous asceticism of much the same kind as the Marcionites and some of the Gnostics.

The Montanists were very numerous and, naturally enough, it was only a matter of time before they came into conflict with the bishops universally, for with these special protégés of the Spirit episcopal authority counted for nothing. The greatest feat of the movement, perhaps, was its capture of Tertullian, a convert African jurist of genius, a polemist of the first order, gifted with the clear ferocity of Swift and a literary style that recalls Tacitus. Tertullian is the first Latin theologian, and the impress of his genius is still discernible in the technical exposition of Christian doctrine. The secession of his gigantic personality must have been a frightful blow to the Church, which henceforth he attacked with all the savage skill he had for years put forth against her foes.

There is nothing spectacular, to the general reader, in such a chronicle as this, but already we are seeing the appearances of types that will never cease to reappear throughout two thousand years: Catholics who propose to explain Catholicism by synthesis with the intellectual life of the time, Catholics who look back from the difficulties of the moment to the happy time of a far-off golden age of primitive faith, Catholics who turn from an official teaching that does not encourage their personal likings to an alleged private inspiration that sets them apart from the ordinary discipline. In one sense Church History is a web where threads such as these do but cross and recross.

Fifty years or so after the first developments of Montanism a curious religion appeared in Persia that was a fusion of Christian and Pagan and Gnostic elements. Its founder, Mani, had the deliberate plan to unite in a new religion the best elements of all the old. As Manicheeism some of his theories were destined to survive all attempts at repression—Pagan and Christian alike—for a good thousand years, and to be, during all that time, an ever-recurring danger to the peace of the world. A time would come in the fourth century when the boast of Mani was to be momentarily fulfilled and from Morocco to China the Manichee church would flourish.

Mani, who styled himself "Apostle of Jesus Christ," claimed none the less to be the final interpreter of Zoroaster and of Buddha, too. The Paraclete had descended on him and revealed all things to him and an understanding of all mysteries. Manicheeism is, in fact, a heresy of the Gnostic type, but organised, as was Marcionism, with the ability of genius. The doctrines included the familiar opposition of matter and spirit, the idea of matter as wholly evil and the curious juxtaposition of an extraordinary asceticism—the refusal to marry, for example—with gross licentiousness. Of the relations between Manicheeism and the Church in the first century of its existence, we know very little. But from the time when the heresy meets us in the early life of one who was its most illustrious capture, St. Augustine of Hippo, we see it ceaselessly in conflict with the Church, until its final rout in the Albigensian Crusade of the thirteenth century.

Something must be said, too, about another aspect of this vigorous intellectual life of these first Christian generations, namely about the first thinkers who endeavoured to set forth in some definite form an answer to the questions: Who is Jesus Christ? How is He the Son of God? And if He is God and the Father of God, how is God one? And if God is one and the Father is God, and Jesus Christ is not the Father, how is Jesus Christ really God? In an age teeming with sects and religious theories, when indeed, to all appearance, religious discussion was a main occupation of all thinkers and publicists, it was not long before the thinking Christian had these problems thrust on him, either from outsiders or from his own inevitable reaction to the *milieu* in which he lived.

The Church did nothing, officially, to provide any theory or formula which would answer such questions. All that came from authority was a faithful and continuous repetition of the traditional belief, there is one God, Jesus Christ is truly God, Jesus Christ is truly man. The private individuals who worked out explanatory theories, by the aid of logic and philosophy, and especially by the aid of analogies found in Platonic teaching, not infrequently stumbled into error. Some—the so-called *Monarchians*—saved the truth that God is one by sacrificing the truth that Jesus Christ is really God. Really He was but man, and He was God, they explained, only by a special and unique *adoption*. Others presented Him as God indeed, but only in a secondary *subordinate* sense. Yet again other theories explained the Trinity as three modalities or rôles or functions of the one sole God.

The Church is not assisted in its teaching office by systematic new revelations to its hierarchy, nor are these officers, the bishops, guided by positive inspiration. The means at their disposal are human means, namely their own knowledge and their knowledge of the tradition. In their rôle of guardians of the tradition they are preserved from error. They will never say a truth is traditional which is not so, nor that a truth is contrary to the tradition when it is really in accord with it. It is in a negative way that, throughout these early theological controversies, the Church first acts. The thinking activity of Catholics proceeds, and at intervals an official condemnation of one theory or another is made. Then, at the opportune moment, the long discussion ripens into some explanatory formula which is patient of one interpretation only, and that orthodox. The Church accepts this, makes it her own, and uses it henceforward as a vehicle of positive teaching.

In these second and third centuries the Church is acting in the watchful, negative way. The ground is thus cleared for the positive, new construction of the definitions of the great Councils which fill the fourth and the fifth centuries, to which constructive work the Church comes unembarrassed by any temporary alliance with the instability of merely human theorising.

It remains to add a word about the work of the group of writers we call the Apologists. These were the first Catholic "intellectuals," converts from Paganism and the Philosophical religions. The whole aim of their writings was to defend Catholicism from the hundred calumnious imputations everywhere believed to be true and to show it as the ideally reasonable thing, as the crown and perfection indeed of all that was best in the world to which they themselves had once belonged. Naturally, the aspects of Catholicism of which the Apologists treat are those in which it seemed to them to present some resemblance with the beliefs of those whom they wished to placate or convert, or again they stressed those doctrines which seemed to respond to the terrible craving of the pagan soul for reassurance about its immortality and about the possibility of purification from sin. The truths most particularly stressed by the Apologists are then the existence of God, the nature of God, the immortality of the soul, the possibility of salvation, the Christian ideal of holy living, and the fact of the superior morality, and indeed of the sanctity, of so many of the Christians, irrespective of age, sex, social rank, or profession. Several of these "apologies" are addressed directly to the emperor himself, for even in the height of the persecution these writers did not lose hope that the beauty and reasonableness of the Christian doctrine and life would, of itself, win the sympathy of whoever could be brought to know it. So St. Justin made his philosopher's appeal to Marcus Aurelius, and Athenagoras to Commodus. The best known of all these writers is St. Justin the Martyr, of whose works there survive two apologies addressed to the emperors and the famous *Dialogue with Trypho the Jew*. St. Justin was a Greek born in Palestine, who had travelled all over the East, ever in quest of new and better philosophical teaching. He was, in fact, a philosopher and lecturer by profession, and after his conversion, which took place about the year 130, he established himself in Rome where he opened a school in which the doctrines of the new religion were explained and given a reasoned proof. Finally, a rival heathen philosopher, Crescentius, denounced St. Justin as a Christian and, with some of his disciples, he was put to death.

All this time we have been concerned with what is, no doubt, a very special aspect of primitive Christianity, the life of Christian thinkers, "intellectuals" as we should say. What of the ordinary believer? Unfortunately for us he never set down the detail of his story. We have no early-Christian Pepys, but must reconstruct the ordinary religious round as best we can from between the lines of what literature has survived.

The Church, from the first moment it is revealed to us in the New Testament record, is organised in a multitude of "churches," one church to each city. In each church there are two groups, the clergy, who preside over its affairs, offer the sacrifice, administer the sacraments, explain the teaching, and the laity. This arrangement is everywhere secured, with a uniform regularity that derives, obviously, from something that is not just chance. All is according to some single primitive pattern.

The clergy are chosen for their position by the whole local church and they receive their spiritual powers by a ritual (the imposition of hands) from others who have already received these powers and the power to communicate them. There are three main degrees among the clergy. Each church is presided over by a single bishop.[3]

---

[3] I.e. from the end of the first century at any rate; before that date it is likely that the churches were ruled by colleges of bishops, under the surveillance of the Apostles.

The bishop is assisted by priests, for the spiritual administration, and deacons, whose main work is the care of the Church's property, distribution of alms, assistance of its poor, its widows and its orphans—for one of the most striking features of this primitive Christianity is its active organised benevolence. "How these Christians love each other" is one of the earliest spontaneous Pagan tributes to the new religion that we possess.

The various churches founded by an Apostle possessed an obvious unity in their relation to the common founder. For most of the affairs of life they were self-sufficing, but, during the second century, a movement began whose first-fruits are discernible by the middle of the third century and which ended by grouping the churches of a given region round the church of the principal city or metropolis. From this time onward we begin to meet the practice that, for affairs of general importance, the bishops of a given region meet in council and their common action is determined by the will of the majority. No doubt these first groupings owed much to the circumstances in which the different churches first came into being, e.g. the daughter churches would be grouped around the mother church that founded them. So Alexandria had a suzerainty over all the bishops of Egypt, and the churches of Italy had a special dependence on the bishop of Rome.

All these Christians, members of one or other of these local churches, felt themselves to be, and were members of the great Church of which all these were cells, i.e. of the Church universal, the Catholic Church as St. Ignatius of Antioch, writing about 107, called it in a phrase that has lasted. All were united in belief, in ritual, and in the regulations that governed their daily life.

Of all these churches one, from very early times, is seen to have a special rôle, regulating the affairs of other churches, and acting as with a higher kind of authority over them. This is the Church of Rome, which the universal tradition already maintains had had for its ruler the apostle St. Peter to whom Our Lord had said: "Thou art Peter and upon this rock I will build my church. . . . To thee will I give the keys of the kingdom of heaven. Whatsoever thou shalt bind on earth shall be bound also in heaven and whatsoever thou shalt loose on earth shall be loosed also in heaven." [4] The precise date at which the Roman Church was founded we do not know, nor the date at which St. Peter first went to Rome. But it is universally the tradition of this primitive Christianity that St. Peter ruled the Roman Church and that at Rome he gave his life for Christ in the persecution of Nero.

We do not know very much about the first developments of this Roman Church. The obscurity which, in these centuries, veils so much, veils this, too, very largely. But comparatively speaking we know quite a lot, and it is significant that whenever Rome does make an appearance she is engaged in this rôle peculiarly her own, the rôle that is never denied her (though her exercise of it is sometimes resisted), the rôle that no other church ever even attempts to claim, the rôle, that is to say, of a general superintendence over all the churches of the Catholic Church.

So Rome is seen under the pope Clement I, about the year 90, intervening in the affairs of the Church at Corinth. About the same time St. Ignatius of Antioch is giving her peculiar position acknowledgement in the famous letters written on the eve of his martyrdom at Rome (107). The tradition as it shows itself in St. Irenæus has already been noticed, and about this same time, under the pope Victor I (189–198), there is a striking exercise of the Roman authority to compel the obedience of the apostolic church of Ephesus in a matter of liturgical observance. Sixty years later there is another crisis, between Rome and Carthage. The question is not disciplinary merely this time, and Rome's whole attitude is again that of a final judge, delivering the law and an ultimatum to secure its observance. Rome's opponent here was no less a person than St. Cyprian, the primate of Carthage, and in 262 Pope Denis is found correcting the theology of his namesake, the bishop of Alexandria.

These interventions are produced, so far, by crises that regard the faith, the traditional doctrine and its practice. It is the doctrine that is all-important. This is the foundation of all the rest. To keep it pure and unalloyed is the Church's chief function. After this the most important

---

[4] Matthew xvi, 18, 19.

Λ

thing is to preach the doctrine, and this is the special office of the bishop.

This teaching was given to the general body of the faithful in the weekly assembly, held every first day of the week, at which the sacrifice of the Holy Eucharist was offered and the whole Church received the sacrament, Jesus Christ Himself really present under the appearances of the bread and wine over which, by the presiding bishop, the mysterious ritual words had been pronounced. These sermons had for their occasion the readings from the books of the Old and the New Testaments made during the service. The text, of the Old Testament especially, was often treated allegorically and from it was drawn the exposition of traditional truth and morality.

Besides the teaching through sermons like these, there was, in every church, the systematic instruction given to the newly converted in preparation for their reception into the Church by the sacramental rite of Baptism. These instructions were spread over a long period, they were both theoretical and practical, and, as the weeks went by, the catechumen was prepared by various special rites and prayers for the solemnities of Easter during which he was baptised.

A third way in which the Church taught was in such catechetical schools as that established by the bishop in Alexandria. Here, in much the same fashion as that used throughout the intellectual circles of the Empire, the Christian *doctor* lectured, not to whatever audience would come to him—as the earlier apologists (St. Justin the Martyr, for example) had lectured in their own private scholastic ventures—but to the Christian anxious to know his faith better or to be prepared to answer the objections daily made against it. Two masters especially of this school of Alexandria have left an imperishable memory, Clement and Origen.

Clement (150–*c*. 215) was Athenian born. He possessed all the philosophic and literary culture of his time and, once converted and established at Alexandria, he delighted his educated auditory—Alexandria was at this time the capital of the Roman Empire's culture—by a scientific presentation of the faith, to the exposition and proof of which he brought all the treasures of the ancient culture

in which is listeners had been bred. Not a single occupation of the day, not one of the phases of that sophisticated
civilisation, escapes his moral scrutiny. For Clement is not
merely an academic, fascinating his clientèle with a
clever display, but a priest leading souls to perfection.

Clement's disciple and successor, Origen (185-254), is
of another order of men altogether, possessed of genius so
rare that to have been his master is, perhaps, Clement's
greatest title to fame. It is indeed a moot point whether
in Origen there was not given to the Church the greatest
mind it has ever known. Scripture study in all its branches,
Theology, Philosophy, Apologetic, Polemics, Sermons,
Moral Exhortations, Letters, the amount he managed to
write is beyond belief. Nor is Origen a mere compiler. He
possessed a most original and speculative mind, and boldly
ventured to advance explanations for every difficulty that
could confront the thoughtful Christian. He was a pioneer,
and in this difficult affair of interpreting Christian teaching to the non-Christian world, and of exploring the in-
terior relation of its own several parts, he had to construct
his own technical language. This was one cause, and there
were others, why Origen fell into immense errors on important points, and though he was never officially censured
in his lifetime—he was indeed a man of saintly life, and
he died a confessor for the faith after enduring fearful
tortures—his writings were to be, in later years, a source
of many bitter controversies. But for the next two hundred
years, until the establishment of St. Augustine's authority,
it is Origen who dominates all theological thought, and in
the East he continued to dominate it until long after that.
For it was Origen's great merit to attempt a systematic
explanation of the whole body of the Christian tradition,
and this is not in any controversial mood but for the sake
of the truth itself.

Christianity spread slowly and steadily, if somewhat
unevenly, once "the days of Pentecost were accomplished."
The first of many decisive foundations was the establishment of the Church at Antioch, the third city of the
Roman Empire, destined to be the first main centre of
Christian life and, for centuries to come, the main source
of all missionary activity in the East. It was from Antioch

that St. Paul evangelised Asia Minor, Macedonia, and Greece, and that Osrhoene—the buffer state between the Roman and the Persian empires—was gained for Christianity in the following century. Thence, a hundred years or so later, Persia first received the new religion while at the same time Armenia was won over by St. Gregory the Wonder-worker. In the middle of this same third century, too, the Christians penetrated into the countries that are to-day Roumania and Southern Russia. When and how the Faith first went to Egypt we do not know. There were Christians there certainly by the time the second century was half-way through, and we have a list of bishops of Alexandria that goes back to the first century. But Egypt does not really enter the history of the Church until the eve of Constantine's conversion (312). By that time, although it is impossible to give anything like statistics, it seems safe to say that Syria and Asia Minor were very largely Christian, the Pagans in some parts being reduced to a half or less of the population, and some towns being wholly Christian.

Curiously enough, the Jewish nucleus from whose activities all this had sprung by this time disappeared from sight. The divisions between those who wished to impose the whole Jewish Law on all the Christians and those who, following St. Paul, denied that this had any longer any binding force, had already weakened Jewish Christianity when the Jewish War of 69–70, destroying Jerusalem, destroyed its material *raison d'être*. The Jewish Church had already shrunk to a poor handful of believers when, sixty years later, Hadrian's repression of the last Jewish revolt and the establishment on the ruins of the Holy City of the new town Aelia, into which no Jew might enter, destroyed it altogether as a church. The Jewish Christians, drifting henceforward about Palestine, ceased to be recognized as Christians by their Greek and Syrian co-religionists. They were now the *Nazareans*, regarded, rightly or wrongly, as heretics and classed, sometimes, as such in the catalogues of ecclesiastical writers.

The evangelisation of the East had thus gone on apace throughout these first three centuries. The case with the West was very different. About the origins of Christianity in Rome itself we know nothing. It is already a flourishing church when, in 56, St. Paul refers to it. Three years later he himself arrived in Rome, a prisoner, for the hearing of his appeal to Cæsar. St. Peter first appeared there, apparently, some three years later, about the time St. Paul, acquitted, had left the city. In the course of the next two centuries there were founded, and from Rome, the hundreds of churches of central and southern Italy.

Roman Africa had Carthage for its Christian capital and though we know the city to have become a centre of missionary activity, again we are ignorant of how itself it received the Faith.

Spain St. Paul had planned to evangelise, and it is probable that he did in fact visit it. But we know nothing of Spanish Christianity until half-way through the third century. Our first knowledge of the Church in what is now France is the account of the great persecution at Lyons in 177, and it is only towards 250 that we hear of churches at Arles, Toulouse, Reims, and in far-off Trèves. Other Gallic cities we know to have possessed churches from the next century, but the west of France was still largely Pagan fifty years after Constantine's conversion (312).

Again, not until the middle of the third century is passed do we hear of Christianity in the valley of the Danube, in Hungary, Austria, or Bavaria, and the first reliable information about the Church in Britain is the appearance of British bishops at the Council of Arles in 314.

This steady, progressive extension of the Church was accomplished despite the divisions and controversies about its doctrines and despite a constant hostile pressure from outside, namely from the civil authority, the Roman Empire. During all these first three centuries, in fact, the Church was always liable to severe persecution, and during the greater part of that time it actually suffered persecution. The basic reason for the attitude of the State can be stated very simply. The Roman Emperor, supreme autocrat of the whole of Roman life, legislator, judge, commander-in-chief, and supreme pontiff, embodied in his person the whole power and being of the State. The State was deified and worshipped with religious rites and so, too, was the emperor. Not to pay this religious homage to the emperor and to Rome was to fail in a fundamental civic duty, to proclaim one's own loyalty as suspect.

Paganism—whatever the variety—had no such thing as a fixed creed of belief. The question of the incompatibility of one form of Paganism with another could not arise. No Pagan could have a conscientious objection to forms of worship other than those which had gained his own personal preferences. There was no difficulty in combining whatever cult he favoured with the cult of Rome and the emperor. In this respect, for the Roman, the Christian stood out as dangerously eccentric. His religion was not a part of his nationality—understood as such, no more than such, and able to be allowed for as such, as the religious prejudices of the Jew were allowed for. The Christian was an ordinary citizen who professed a belief that he declared was incompatible with any other cult. He refused any acknowledgement whatever to the only gods the State knew. To the State he was godless, an atheist, and in a culture and civilisation whose bases were religious he was, necessarily, as dangerous as an incendiary in a town of wooden huts.

Poetic fancy, the piety and gratitude of later generations, indignation against persecutors, have, it is true, combined to cover the facts of the story with a mass of legend. But the story of the Roman persecution is terrible enough, in even the scanty authentic detail that has survived.

Apparently there was never any need for special legislation to inaugurate these persecutions. Let an accusation be laid before the competent authority that a man's religious practice was in such contradiction to the established order, and let that accusation be proved, then he must be put to death as dangerous to the State. This would explain the apparent paradox that—madmen like Nero and Domitian apart—the worst persecutors were the best emperors, strong, capable administrators and reformers such as Trajan, Marcus Aurelius, Septimius Severus, Decius.

The classic description of "the ten persecutions" leaves much to be desired as a summary. It is more accurate to describe the long aggression according to the varying policy of the State.

In the first period the persecution works without any

stimulus from authority, by the ordinary process of existing laws. Then Trajan (98–117), in answer to a celebrated enquiry from Pliny the Younger, at this time governor of Bithynia, states that Christianity is itself a crime, that those accused in due form must be properly tried and, if convicted, punished with death. If they will renounce their belief they are to be set free. But the magistrate is not bound to make search for Christians, nor are anonymous denunciations to be noticed. This régime lasted for the next hundred years and more, and until the accession of Commodus (180–192), the vicious and decadent child of Marcus Aurelius, it was enforced fairly constantly.

In the third period the State takes the initiative. Edicts are published from Rome and a plan of campaign drafted to operate throughout the empire. From this moment the Trajan policy seems to fall out of use. It is possible that it is abolished altogether by Alexander Severus (223–235). The edicts are for special purposes. While they are in force the persecution rages with a violence hitherto unknown, the whole ingenuity of the State being employed to root out those named in the edict and to compel their obedience. On the other hand, between the edicts there are intervals of peace and times even when the Church enjoys the emperor's protection. One emperor, Alexander Severus, has a personal veneration for Our Lord and another, Philip the Arab (244–249), is actually a Christian.

The principal edicts of this third period are those of (i) Septimius Severus in 201 forbidding conversions to Christianity; (ii) of Maximin, in 235, against the bishops; (iii) of Decius against all suspected of being Christians: this was the most terrible persecution so far; in every town and village all the suspects were haled before commissioners and summoned to sacrifice; (iv) of Valerian in 257 against the bishops, suppressing all assemblies of Christians and confiscating the cemeteries where they often met; and then, in 258, against Christians generally. This too, was a well-organised and bloody affair. But Valerian's son, Gallienus (260–268), made peace with the Church, revoking the edicts and restoring the confiscated properties. Henceforth for forty years the Chistians were secure from molestation.

This long peace, which gave the Church the great chance to perfect its organisation and to build everywhere the first churches, was broken, suddenly and unexpectedly, by the edicts of the emperor Diocletian that ushered in the last and greatest of all the persecutions.

Diocletian has a deservedly great name in history as the general and administrator whose acquisition of the imperial title in 284 halted the anarchy which for fifty years had desolated the empire. It was his merit to realise that the Roman world could no longer be governed by any one man—wherefore he named as co-emperor with himself Maximian—and also that the emperor should live where he was now most needed, not in Rome but on the frontier. To each emperor there was assigned a kind of junior emperor—the *Cæsar*—and so when the persecution of 303 broke out it varied in intensity according to the dispositions of the empire's four rulers.

Diocletian was apparently won over to assent to the new attack on the Church by a curious coalition of the moral philosophers, the Pagan priesthood, and the crude, old-fashioned, rural Paganism of his army. Christianity had so developed in the long half-century since Valerian that its adherents were now to be found in every walk of life. The very wife and daughter of Diocletian were Christians.

The measures now adopted were modelled on those of Decius. What was seriously attempted was a war of extermination. The one part of the empire which enjoyed anything at all of a respite was that governed by Constantius Chlorus, i.e. Spain, Gaul, and Britain. These, however, were the least Christian provinces of all, but upon the ancient churches of the East, and especially upon those of Asia Minor, all the furies of hell were loosed for some nine years.

Meanwhile Diocletian and his colleague had resigned, there were successive civil wars among the rivals to the succession, and, on the eve of a battle for the possession of Rome, one of these, Constantine, the son of Constantius Chlorus, declaring his belief in the God of the Christians, had the cross affixed to his standards. His victory

(312) was the beginning of the end and ten months later a joint decision of Constantine and his Eastern colleague, Licinius—the so-called Edict of Milan—ended the persecution throughout the empire, gave to all men the right to worship each in his own way, and to the Church compensation, too, for all the losses of the last ten years.

2

The Church under Imperial Protection, 313–711

THE EDICT OF MILAN, by which Constantine and Licinius ended the last of the persecutions, was not a pro-Christian manifesto but a charter of freedom of worship to all religious men. It was the act of a State that valued every manifestation of religion without officially committing itself to any one in particular. There is nothing surprising in this. Licinius was a Pagan, a recent persecutor, and destined, before he died, to repeat the rôle for a few brief months. Constantine was master of only half the Roman world and even so he was not yet a Christian. Whatever his belief in the God of the Christians, it was scarcely yet faith as the Church understood it. Nor was he to submit himself as a catechumen until twenty-five years later on his death bed, and then it was from a heretic and a most bitter enemy of Catholicism that he received baptism.

For some time yet the Church gained no more than the right to live—not, indeed, an inconsiderable gain. But in Constantine's personal friendliness to the Christians, in his increasing indifference to Pagans, his magnificent generosity to the old centers of Christian piety, the signs of coming changes might have been read.

The Christian clergy were put on the same footing as the Pagan priests in the matter of exemptions from civil burdens. Wills could be made in favour of the churches. The laws against celibacy were abolished, and the punish-

ment of crucifixion. None of these favours were extended
to the existing bodies of dissident Christians, the Marcionites and Montanists for example. And in the emperor's
enthusiasm to preserve the unity of discipline and belief
he showed himself so actively hostile to such new dissi-
dents as the Donatists, that anyone concerned for the
future freedom of the Church might have trembled antic-
ipatingly.

Licinius was defeated and slain in 323, and it was only
when, after fourteen years as sole ruler Constantine died,
leaving three sons to share the empire, that the movement
to destroy Paganism really began. Laws were now enacted
forbidding public exercise of Pagan rites and even private worship (341 and 353). Sacrifices were forbidden
under pain of death. But where the Pagans were numerous and strong these laws remained a dead letter, and
nowhere is there any record, or hint of a record, of martyrs for Paganism. The very emperor who showed himself
most hostile—Constantius II (337–361)—was at the same
time a violent persecutor of orthodox Christianity and
called in the Pagans as his allies!

The successor of Constantius II was the unhappy young
man who has gone down to history as Julian the Apostate.
In his isolated childhood—he was the sole survivor of a
host of relatives of Constantine murdered on the emperor's
death in the interests of his three sons—he had been bred
an Arian. The only Christianity he knew was this desic-
cated caricature, and the Christian life had presented itself
to him as a succession of endless, arid controversies in
which the different sects of Arians strove for the mastery.
From this the Hellenic philosophy cults, to which he was
introduced as a young man of twenty, afforded immense
relief. Henceforth it was to these that his heart was given,
and once safely installed as emperor it was this semi-
magical neo-Platonism, with its promise of intimate contact with the divinity and its practice of mystical exaltation, that he proposed to set up as a State religion.

Everywhere he had the temples reopened, and the
sacrifices began to be offered once more. His knowledge
of Christianity gave him a model on which to reorganise.
Paganism was now to have a creed and a moral law. Its
priests were to practice virtue, to give themselves to prayer,

to become preachers and apostles. Christians he persecuted, and this not by any frontal attack but, sinuously,
by cutting them off from all the culture of the time, forbidding them to teach or be taught, by harassing them
with vexatious regulations and by conniving at the inevitable recrudescence of ancient Pagan hatreds.

How all this would have ended is matter for speculation. Julian was himself almost the sole true votary of the
new faith. But on June 24, 363, he was killed in battle,
after a reign of scarcely eighteen months. "Thou hast
triumphed, Galilean," he is said to have cried, and indeed
all was over. The artificial, pedantic reconstruction
crumbled immediately, to the mockery of all beholders.

Under Julian's successors the empire returned to the
policy of the Edict of Milan, but when, in the west, Gratian (375–383) succeeded to his father, Valentinian I,
and Theodosius (379–395) to Valens in the east, the anti-
Pagan movement was resumed. Gratian refused the title
and office of supreme pontiff, which even the Christian
emperors had so far retained, and proceeded to the "dis-
endowment" of Paganism, suppressing all the immunities
from taxation it had enjoyed and confiscating the revenues
and property of the priestly colleges. Theodosius forbade
all sacrifices of divination and, in 391, closed all the
temples. A further step was the prohibition of even the
private exercise of Pagan cults. Nor were these laws left
unexecuted, and on the death of Valentinian II (392)
there was a short-lived restoration of Paganism at Rome
itself. Two years later and Theodosius had crushed the
usurper, Eugene, who had patronised it. He was now sole
master of the Roman world, and the Senate at Rome
voted the official abolition of Pagan cults.

There were no Christian reprisals following on the victory—St. Ambrose of Milan saw to that. But henceforth
the Roman state was not merely not Pagan, it was definitely Christian. Theodosius is the first really Christian
emperor. He made Christianity the law of the land, gave
its bishops a place in the State, and recognised their
jurisdiction in all the matters that concerned the life of
Christians. The feast days of the Church became public
holidays and Lent a holy season.

The empire, as well as the emperor, was now Christian,

but this very victory brought with it a new anxiety, a problem that was for centuries repeatedly to hinder the progress of the Gospel, causing all the Church's energy to be turned to defend its very life, a problem that still continues to vex and to embarrass Catholic activity. This is the problem of the relation of the Catholic State to the Catholic Church. In its earliest form, as it presented itself to the Catholics of the third and fourth centuries, it was the problem of the place to be given to the personage who was the omnipotent master of the Roman world. His will, his mere whim, was the law for millions and, for centuries, most of his subjects regarded him as semi-divine. Would he now be content, as a Christian, to sit on a bench and be taught his catechism, to receive the Sacraments, cultivate a spiritual life, give liberally to charities, and secure the Church in its property and in its right to protection? Could anyone humanly expect the omnipotent emperor to be a mere subject in the life of this spiritual empire within his own empire? Did anyone expect that he would be no more than this?

The new problem of the lawful rôle of the Christian emperor within the Christian Church lends an additional interest to the events which fill the next three hundred years, the great theological controversies, that is to say. The fundamental traditional mysteries of the Faith are reasserted in carefully chosen technical terms that leave no loophole for ambiguous interpretation, and, secondly, the controversies offer the emperor an opportunity to lay hold of the Church and make it an organ of the State.

The importance of the issues and the wealth of personality in all the leading actors of the drama make this one of the most fascinating periods of all history. Nor were these controversies mere theologians' quarrels. The whole population was passionately interested. All the chief crises of the Arian trouble were accompanied by great popular demonstrations, by rioting and street fighting. At Ephesus in 431 the populace escorted the orthodox bishops to their lodgings, after the definition of faith, with torch-light processions. Again, the aftermath of Chalcedon, as will be seen, was a kind of civil war in the east that only ended when these provinces were lost for ever to the empire in the seventh century.

How embarrassing, and indeed injurious, to the cause of truth the new imperial protection could become was to be shown with a terrible clarity in the fifty years that followed Constantine's conversion. In the eastern half of the empire there began a revival of the heresy that had troubled the Church a hundred years before, the heresy namely that the Second Person of the Trinity, God the Son, is not really God in the sense in which the Father is God. The movement which, in the east, now afforded the emperor his opportunity to control the affairs of the Church, was thus concerned with the truth of a doctrine fundamental to Christian life. If God the Son was not really divine, then Jesus Christ was no more than a creature. And if so, what of His redemptive sacrifice, what of His mission as teacher and founder of the Church?

The heresy was not new. When it had previously shown itself its fate had been that of all the first revolts against the tradition. The bishops, as guardians of the tradition, had condemned it, had warned the believers that this was not Christianity, and ultimately the innovators, expelled from the Church, had formed a dissident body outside it. Never had they succeeded, after their condemnation, in maintaining both their place in the Church and their heretical opinions. The reappearance of the heresy was to be the occasion of a revolutionary change in this matter. The heretics would again be condemned, but they would now resist expulsion and backed by the Christian emperor, more concerned to avoid riots than to preserve the purity of faith, they would continue to maintain their places, and their offices, in the Church. They would even, for a moment, hold almost all the key positions, and a day would come of which St. Jerome could say: "The whole world groaned to find itself Arian."

The new heretic was a priest of Alexandria, Arius, a fashionable preacher, and a man of unusual culture. He was speedily denounced to his bishop, a council was summoned, and his theories were condemned. Arius, however, refused to submit and was consequently deprived of his church. The bishop of Alexandria circularised the other bishops, advertising the heresy and the sentence on the heretic. Arius was no less active and he speedily enlisted the sympathy of a friend of earlier days, Eusebius, his fellow-pupil at the theological school of Lucian of Antioch, where he had first imbibed the heresy. Eusebius was now a personage. He was bishop of the imperial capital, Nicomedia, and this position, added to his kinship with the emperor's family, made his adherence to Arius a matter of the greatest importance.

A war of pamphlets and hot controversy now began and the Christian east was everywhere the scene of conflict and disputes. Constantine, solicitous for the public order and scandalised at the display of feeling, cast about for a means to end the trouble. Who it was suggested the means actually chosen is not known, but, at the emperor's orders, all the bishops of the Roman world were summoned to Nicea, a town close by the capital, to take part in a great council which would judge the whole affair and restore peace.

The council met in June 325, and some three hundred bishops took part in it, under the presidency of the emperor and of Hosius, bishop of Cordova, his principal adviser in religious matters. The Roman Church was represented by two priests, who were given a place of honour and whose signatures head the long list of subscriptions to the council's decrees.

The active supporters of Arius were few in number. The council showed itself so hostile to his theories that his friends dared not even speak for him, but dissimulated and joined in the demand for his condemnation. Two bishops alone voted against it, and they, with their client, were forthwith banished.

This last point must be noticed. For the first time the State has intervened not merely to summon an ecclesiastical council, nor merely to give a certain "tone" to its acts, but to inflict a civil punishment on the recalcitrant heretic whom the Church has condemned.

From the moment of his condemnation Arius falls into the background and the leader of the movement, for the next decisive fifteen years, is Eusebius of Nicomedia. He was too shrewd to attempt any direct reversal of what had been decreed at Nicea. The new policy was to propose, in place of its rigid, unmistakable definition, new formulæ purposely vague and all-embracing, which Catholics could interpret in a traditional sense and the Arians in an Arian sense. So the Arians would be able to remain within the Church. There would be no tumults and an appearance of unity and good order.

It was to this policy, political, non-controversial, "practical," that Eusebius won over Constantine and, after his death (337), his second son Constantius II (337–361). It was the bishop of Nicomedia who organised the party and who, in constant movement, managed slowly to transform the Eastern episcopate, bringing about the deposition of the Catholic bishops, replacing them by Arians, and all this with the active support of the Court, the emperor lending police and troops to enforce the changes. The aftermath of Nicea was a half-century of ecclesiastical anarchy from which Eastern Catholicism never really recovered, and the establishment of imperial interference in ecclesiastical affairs as a permanent part of the Christian tradition.

The great champion of the Nicene doctrine during all these years was the bishop of Alexandria, St. Athanasius, the successor of the bishop who had condemned Arius, and the chief force at the great council. To displace this powerful and gifted leader was one of the chief objects of the Eusebian faction. Repeatedly he was accused to the emperor of serious crimes. One packed council after another declared him deposed. Twice the emperor provided him with an Arian successor. Five times he was exiled, and at one time, with a price on his head, he spent seven years lost from sight in the deserts to the south of Egypt.

By the time Constantius II had been ten years master of the east (347) the Church was split in two. Nowhere in the east was there left as bishop anyone who openly defended either the creed of Nicea or the innocence of its chief champion, St. Athanasius. The imperial power had effectively stifled the voice of the eastern episcopate. Only in the western half of the empire, where the emperor—Constans—was a Catholic, was Catholicism free.

In 350, however, Constans was murdered and the next few years saw his Arian brother and successor make a bold bid to subdue the west also to this new Court religion. The methods adopted were those that had been used in the east—no open denial, anywhere, of Nicea but the acceptance of new, compromising formulæ, packed councils where the emperor and his officials presided and where troops appeared to enforce their will, deposition and exile for the bishops who remained unconvinced, while Arians were installed in their place.

The peak of the imperial success was the joint council held in 359, at Rimini for the west and Seleucia for the east, where, under pressure, practically the whole episcopate consented to sign an ambiguous definition of the faith that could be interpreted in an heretical sense.

It was a barren victory, for a political revolution now took place and the emperor died. His successor was Julian the Apostate, and, after Julian's short reign, Catholic emperors once more ruled in the west, and, the Arian pressure removed, the episcopate returned spontaneously to the traditional orthodoxy. In the east the old troubles were renewed, for there an Arian ruled once more—Valens (364–378). His great opponent was the bishop of Cæsarea in Capadocia, St. Basil, and it was one of the tragedies of history that this great man died (379) just as the troubles neared their end.

For Valens was killed in battle in 378 and his successor was a Catholic, Theodosius the Great (379–395). The new emperor, by edict, decreed that all beliefs that differed from "the faith clearly taught by the pontiff Damasus and by Peter, bishop of Alexandria" were heresies and to be suppressed accordingly. This was the end of the State's patronage of Arianism. As a force in the life of the empire it was henceforth dead, though it survived, with very serious consequences, as the religion of the various barbarians converted from Paganism in the fourth century, e.g. the Goths in all their branches.

Theodosius did more than this, for he summoned a great council to meet at Constantinople in 381 which should reorganise the east after the long anarchy. The creed of Nicea and its famous term *homoösion*,[1] to describe the relation of God the Son to God the Father, the use of which marked off the Catholic from the Arian, were once again officially proclaimed. The bad new custom, that had only obtained since the days of Eusebius, of bishops interfering in the affairs of other sees was checked

---

[1] I.e. of one substance [with the Father].

by new legislation. The other mischievous innovation of the imperial interference in the election of bishops was left alone. And—a still more mischievous thing, as the event was to show—the council conferred on the bishop of Constantinople a splendid new prestige. Henceforward he was to rank before all the bishops of the world, the pope alone excepted. His jurisdiction was not increased, he still remained no more than the bishop of his own diocese. But the seeds of much new trouble were now sown. For how long would the second bishop of all the world be content with his tiny diocesan jurisdiction? How long would it be before this primacy of honour began to grow towards a primacy of fact under the influence of episcopal ambition and the interests of the emperor? Moreover, the principle on which the distinction was made was new and uncanonical: the bishop of Constantinople was declared to deserve his primacy because Constantinople was the empire's capital, was New Rome.

Meanwhile, however, the Church in the east was emancipated from the tyranny of the Arian minority, and for a few years there was peace. But not for long. For the bishops of Alexandria the council of 381 marked a diminution of prestige. And in the elections of a bishop of Constantinople in 381 and again in 397 the Alexandrian candidate was set aside. Theophilus, the powerful prelate of the Egyptian capital, who had become the embodiment of the local patriotism of that mysterious ancient land, bided his time. He was a capable politician, wealthy and unscrupulous, and in 404 he struck. The bishop of Constantinople was St. John Chrysostom, and Theophilus, on trumped-up charges, secured his deposition and exile. The emperor was a Catholic and so was Theophilus. There is here no question of heresy. But at the bidding of the emperor the canon law can be effectively ignored. In the east all depends on the court, and provided the court is Catholic no one refuses to make use of its extra-canonical suzerainty in ecclesiastical affairs.

Rome, only informed when all was over, protested and excommunicated the bishop of Alexandria and the successor intruded in the place of St. John. More than this it could not do. Twenty-five years later, however, a new flare-up found it better circumstanced. The new controversy centered, once again, round the bishop of Constantinople—since 427, Nestorius—and its high point was the General Council of Ephesus in 431. The point at issue this time was theological, a fundamental mystery in fact. How is Jesus Christ at once divine and human? Already in their effort to explain this, some thinkers had fallen into heresy, teaching that the sacred humanity was not a reality, but an appearance only. Then, in the third quarter of the fourth century Apollinaris of Laodicea had taught that although Our Lord had a real human body it was His divinity that in Him took the place of the soul. This too had been condemned. The solution of Nestorius amounted to this, that in Jesus Christ there is not one but two persons, so truly is He God, so truly is He man. This subtle discussion had gone on for years among the theologians, but in 428 it suddenly appeared in a form that troubled the whole Church when, at Constantinople, a preacher announced that it was wrong to give Mary the title of Mother of God. She was merely the mother of Him in whom God dwelt as in a temple. Immediately there were protestations, and, when Nestorius supported the preacher and punished his critics, still more violent scenes of demonstrations and riot.

Over the seas at Alexandria the news of all this stirred up a still greater personality than Nestorius. This was Cyril who, in 412, had succeeded Theophilus, his uncle, as bishop. St. Cyril was not only a theologian well versed in this particular controversy, but a thinker of singular power. Like his uncle he tended to rule matters with a high hand, and like him he was extremely suspicious of the Antiochene school of theologians—and Nestorius, like St. John Chrysostom, was an Antiochene.

He now sent to Nestorius a strong protest, denounced him to the emperor and also to the pope. With this intervention there begins one of the most complicated chapters of ecclesiastical history. We can but indicate its elements. They are: (1) Nestorius' errors; (2) the traditional faith upheld by Rome, by Alexandria, and by Antioch; (3) the rival theological explanations of Alexandria and Antioch, which did not so much differ in substance as in expression, the two theories approaching the problem from opposing points of view; (4) the triangular feud that for forty years now had antagonised the sees of Alexandria, Antioch, and Constantinople; (5) the imperial habit of managing these controversies and the habit of all concerned—except the popes—of appealing to the emperor for aid in these matters; (6) the personalities of Cyril—autocratic, Nestorius—fussy, vacillating, foolish, of Theodoret of Cyrrhus (the Antiochene leader), a more learned man than Cyril and an abler writer, convinced to the day of his death that Cyril was an Apollinarian; (7) the distance from Rome and Rome's dependence on Alexandria as its agent in the east.

The pope on receiving St. Cyril's appeal—Nestorius had already written to Rome—condemned Nestorius and commissioned St. Cyril to notify the sentence to him and to receive his submission. If this was refused Nestorius was to be deposed. St. Cyril now went a little further than the Roman instructions, and to prevent any evasion by Nestorius drew out the doctrine in twelve propositions which Nestorius must sign. But these propositions were Alexandrine in terminology. To anyone trained at Antioch they would sound Appollinarian. Nor had Rome authorised them as its own exposition of the faith.

Meanwhile Nestorius had appealed to the emperor for a council to judge the whole affair, and the pope had fallen in with the plan, naming three legates to take his place at it.

St. Cyril's commission might be considered terminated by the new arrangement. But the twelve propositions were public property, and their appearance had enlarged the whole field of discussion. All the bishops of Palestine and Syria, the Antiochenes, were up in arms against the attempt to impose Alexandrine views.

The council was to open on Whit-Sunday, 431. By that day Nestorius was there and St. Cyril with his Egyptian following. But the Antiochenes had not arrived, nor the Roman legates. There was a fortnight's delay to wait for the absentees and then, despite protests from 68 of the 159 bishops present, and from the imperial commissioners, St. Cyril brought about the opening of the council and himself presided.

Nestorius was summoned and refused to recognise the council. The whole matter of the orthodoxy of his teaching was examined and it was unanimously condemned, and then, on the strength of the pope's commission to St. Cyril, Nestorius was deposed. Four days later the Antiochenes arrived. They formed themselves into a council and, without more ado, excommunicated the other council and St. Cyril, its president, condemning his twelve propositions as heretical. Then arrived the legates from Rome.

They joined themselves to St. Cyril and in their presence the council held its second session. The pope's letter to the council was read. It contained a decision on the point of faith and, as the legates carefully explained, a demand that the council accept it. Next the legates confirmed all that had been done in the first session. Then, the Antiochenes, remaining absolutely aloof, were excommunicated too.

The bishop of Antioch appealed to the emperor. He it was who, in the emperor's plan, should have presided at the council, and on his appeal the emperor acted. To tell how the emperor confirmed the decrees of both councils, arrested both St. Cyril and Nestorius, how he was brought round to restore St. Cyril and to banish the bishop of Constantinople, would take too long. With his final decision, in September 431, the complicated business was at an end. One bitter legacy that it left was the abyss of misunderstanding between Alexandria and Antioch, a new serious division in the Catholic east. The pope refused to ratify the excommunication of the Antiochenes but ordered them to accept the decrees of Ephesus since they were the decisions of Rome. One thing alone stood in the way—the suspicions of the Antiochenes that St. Cyril was not orthodox. He must explain himself in language they could recognise as Catholic. In 433 this was done. He consented to sign a formula, drafted by Theodoret, that spoke of "the union of two natures" in Our Lord. Once more there was peace, after five stormy years, but, none the less, living memories of those years survived, and with them the seeds of further troubles.

Of the actors in the great events of 431 all but three were dead when, in 448, the controversies broke out again. These three were the emperor Theodosius II, Theodoret of Cyrrhus, and, in the place of his distant exile, Nestorius himself, writing those memories of the great crisis in his life which have been discovered only within the last few years.

The aggressor, this time, was Eutyches, the superior of one of the numerous monasteries of Constantinople, and the object of his attack was Theodoret.

The monk was ignorant but influential. The chief minister at the court was his godson and when Theodoret replied to the attacks made on him—he was accused of being Nestorian, his orthodoxy being judged by Eutyches' version of what St. Cyril had taught—the emperor ended the discussion by forbidding the bishop to proceed with the controversy and confining him to his frontier see.

Eutyches now sought to win the pope's approval of his theories, the chief being that there was but one nature, the Divine, in Our Lord,[2] but at this moment he was himself denounced as a heretic to his own bishop, Flavian of Constantinople. Whereupon a first-class crisis rose rapidly above the horizon.

Once more the rivalry of the great sees played its part. In all this campaign against Theodoret, the monk had had the support of the bishop of Alexandria, the successor of St. Cyril, Dioscoros. Flavian, another curious resemblance to the circumstances of 431, was an Antiochene. With his knowledge of Eutyches' power at court, of the influence wielded by Diosoros, and the record of the Alexandrian triumphs of 404 and 431, Flavian was not anxious to be the monk's judge. However, he had no choice but to act, nor any choice, once he acted, but to condemn Eutyches.

The monk appealed to Rome and to Alexandria. Dioscoros condemned the sentence given against him and demanded from the emperor a General Council to judge the matter.

Events now began to arrange themselves after the pattern of 431. The pope—St. Leo I—agreed to the council and named his legates. He wrote for the council, and entrusted to the legates, a decision on the point of faith—

---

[2] Whence the name *Monophysites* given alike to Eutyches and to the Catholics of Egypt who, after the definition of Chalcedon in 451, continued to cling to the Cyrillian terminology that spoke of "the one incarnate nature" of the Logos.

the so-called *Tome* of St. Leo. The council met at Ephesus, in the same basilica as the council of 431, on August 8, 449. The bishop of Alexandria, Dioscoros, presided.

What followed was a series of outrages. The president began by excluding all who had had any share in the sentence on Eutyches, and all whom he suspected of hostility towards the monk, enforcing his will on the council by threats of deposition, of exile, of death even, with a great parade of the soldiery and police placed at his disposal by the Government. Eutyches was restored, Flavian deposed—Theodoret too—and the twelve propositions of St. Cyril, taken in their Eutychian sense, were officially adopted as a definition of Faith. Flavian was imprisoned and so roughly handled that he died.

The Roman legates protested but were ignored, and it was only their flight that saved them from the fate of Flavian.

Once more, heresy had triumphed in the east and it had triumphed simply because the heretics had the emperor's support. Once more, also, Alexandria had triumphed over Antioch and had overthrown an Antiochene bishop of Constantinople—for the third time in fifty years. This last aspect of the proceedings must not be forgotten, for in the coming reversal of the proceedings of 449 the pride of Alexandrian local feeling was to suffer so acutely as to bring about a permanent breach of religious unity.

The twelve months which followed the triumph of Dioscoros were filled with unavailing protests by the pope to the emperor against what had been done. Not until April 450 did Theodosius II reply, and then in effect he proclaimed the right of the east to regulate its own affairs. But the pope refused to recognise the new bishop of Constantinople, Flavian's successor, so long as he did not accept the Roman definition of faith set forth in the *Tome* of 449.

How greatly the Church in the east depended on the court was shown dramatically when, July 29, 450, Theodosius II was killed, by a fall from his horse. His successors—his sister Pulcheria and Marcian, her husband—were Catholics. So the exiled bishops were recalled and the council for which St. Leo had been asking ever since the news of the assembly of 449 had reached him,[3] was summoned and the pope was asked to preside.

This was the General Council of Chalcedon and it met in October 451. Dioscoros, this time, was the accused. He was condemned, deposed, and sent into exile. Next the pope's definition of the faith was accepted, with great acclamations, the bishops crying out: "It is Peter who is speaking through the voice of Leo." Theodoret was restored and with him other victims of the Latrocinium.

Then the council turned to disciplinary matters. The bishops made a strong protest against the imperial interference in Church affairs and re-arranged the jurisdiction of the various great sees of the east. Jerusalem was given equal rank—i.e. as a patriarchal see—with Antioch and Alexandria, and a further new patriarchate was carved out for Constantinople, whose primacy of honour after Rome was reaffirmed. Also the see was made a court of appeal for all the east.

This reaffirmation of the primacy of honour the legates of the pope refused to confirm, and St. Leo supported them, declaring it to be null, as the canon of 381, on which it was based, was null. To this the bishop of Constantinople replied in a kind of disavowal of what had been done. It was all that the pope could hope to obtain, and in this unsatisfactory way, for the time being, the matter ended (453).

A more violent sequal to the great council was by this time absorbing the attention of the emperor, and indeed of the pope and the whole eastern episcopate—namely, a widespread revolt in Egypt and in Syria against the new definition of faith.

For Egyptian Christianity Chalcedon had been a terrible defeat. After three times triumphing in the struggle against Constantinople, Alexandria had been at last put down. After its long history as the champion of orthodoxy it now saw its theology condemned as heretical. Egypt was the first home of the new institution of monasticism, and the bishop of Alexandria had become a kind of patri-

---

[3] "Not a council," said the pope of this assembly, "but rather a den of thieves—*latrocinium*," and as the *Latrocinium* it has come down in history.

arch to all the monks of the world. St. Athanasius, Theophilus, St. Cyril, and Dioscoros had all been assisted in their various conflicts by armies of these grateful solitaries and cenobites. At the signs of coming crisis they swarmed by their thousands for the protection of their archbishop and for the propaganda of his ideas. And now once again they rallied throughout the east, this time to denounce the Council of Chalcedon and to rouse all the latent nationalism of Egypt and Syria against it as a piece of imperial Greek tyranny.

The bishops returned from the council to find their sees in the possession of Monophysites, and not until the Government sent troops to their aid were they able to recover their churches or to maintain possession.

For twenty-five years these disorders continued, with rival bishops—Catholic and Monophysite—claiming the great sees and only the armed forces of the Government saving the Catholics from massacre. The western empire had almost disappeared in the eighty years since the death of Theodosius the Great, and now the eastern empire was threatened with the loss of two-thirds of its territory because of this unlucky religious division. To heal the division, to reconcile the Monophysites, was henceforward a prime necessity of all imperial policy.

Twenty-five years of repression by physical force had achieved nothing at all to reduce the Monophysites when, in 477, a pro-Monophysite usurped the throne. He only lasted two years, but in that time he prepared an immensity of new trouble for Catholicism by the new policy of compromise he inagurated. To the Monophysites it was Chalcedon, and the Roman definition of faith there accepted, that was the stumbling-block. Whatever the shade of their own belief—and there were already sects among them—they all agreed in their condemnation of St. Leo's formula as heretical. Whoever accepted Chalcedon was, for them, necesssarily a Nestorian.

The usurper, Basiliscus, now published a declaration of faith that every bishop must sign. It repeated the condemnation made at Ephesus in 431 and it accepted the Latrocinium of 449. It condemned Eutyches too, but at the same time it condemned Chalcedon and St. Leo's formula.

This declaration—called the *Encyclion*—was the first of a series of such, put out successively by the emperors during the next hundred and fifty years, to bring Catholics and Monophysites together by making concessions to each. It was, however, the only one which contained an explicit repudiation of Chalcedon. Nevertheless it was a great success, and all the Catholic bishops of the eastern Church signed it, with one notable exception.

This exception was Acacius, the patriarch of Constantinople, and when the usurper was overthrown (477), Acacius became the chief adviser of the restored emperor Zeno. The *Encyclion* was withdrawn and the bishops obeyed, with equal unanimity and promptitude, the new imperial order to retract their signatures to it.

Acacius had been the one episcopal hero of the crisis of 477. He was now, by a strange mischance, to become the occasion of a schism which lasted for thirty-five years and which, teaching the east how to be Catholic without the pope, set the pattern for much of its later behaviour and, perhaps, for the great schism which still endures.

The patriarch's intentions were good enough—to reconcile the Monophysites, many of whom a mere difference of terminology was keeping out of the Church. The means he proposed was the acceptance, by Catholics and Monophysites alike, of a new formulary that should state the faith without any reference to the burning question of Chalcedon and St. Leo. This formulary was the *Henoticon*, published in 482, not by any council of the Church, nor by Acacius, but by the emperor. It was, once more, by imperial edict that ecclesiastical discipline was to be restored and the dispute about the faith brought to an end.

The *Henoticon* recited the definitions of the councils of Nicea, Constantinople, and Ephesus. As it condemned Nestorius to satisfy the Monophysites, so it condemned Eutyches to satisfy the Catholics. It included the famous twelve theses of St. Cyril, but not the *Tome* of St. Leo, and while it made no mention of the Latrocinium it was silent too about Chalcedon.

A more ingenious piece of theological trickiness it would have been hard to devise, so carefully did it steer betwixt Scylla and Charybdis. But, implicitly, it declared to be an open question, a thing of no importance, a matter that could be left to each bishop to settle for himself, the one point which divided Catholics and Monophysites, namely the orthodoxy of Chalcedon and St. Leo. And this in order to placate those whom refusal to accept Chalcedon necessarily stamped as heretics.

Like the *Encyclion* of 477 the new decree had a great and immediate success. The whole of the east went over to it, Acacius, who had drawn it up, leading the movement, Alexandria, Antioch, and Jerusalem following him.

The pope protested and summoned Acacius to take his trial. But at Constantinople the papal envoys, after imprisonment and even torture, were won over to the new policy. They too signed the *Henoticon*. Whereupon the pope excommunicated Acacius, and Acacius retorted by a like act against the pope. The east, save for a few individuals, was now entirely lost to the Church. Half of it was heretical—the Monophysites—and the Catholic half was in schism. This state of things lasted for thirty-five years, and during that time the Monophysites steadily gained ground.

Acacius died in 489, Zeno in 491. The new emperor—Anastasius I—was himself a Monophysite and his reign is noteworthy for his attempt to impose Monophysitism on the patriarchs of Constantinople who, although in schism, continued to hold firmly to the Roman Faith.

Religious affairs throughout the empire were once more in the wildest confusion. In Egypt the *Henoticon* regulated them, interpreted in a strong anti-Chalcedon spirit, as a preliminary to some future condemnation of Chalcedon. In Syria, too, the bishops accepted the *Henoticon*, but with a pro-Chalcedon interpretation, while the monks were divided. Constantinople—except the court—was Catholic but for one thing—the refusal to abandon the *Henoticon* and the memory of Acacius, its first promoter. The *Henoticon* policy could hardly be said to have ended the religious differences or restored the old political unity of the east, and after some thirty years of it, about the year 511, Anastasius planned a more definite anti-Chalcedon policy.

To assist him there now appeared in the capital the man

who was to be for thirty years the life and soul of the Monophysite party, the greatest theologian it produced and the real founder of Monophysitism as a separate Church—this was the Syrian monk Severus. Thanks to the support of his strong personality, and to his political talent which now for the first time made a force of what Monophysitism the capital possessed, the anti-Monophysite bishop of Constantinople was deposed and a heretic installed in his place. A similar change-over was brought about at Antioch, where Severus succeeded to the see, and the bishops of Syria now went over to the more radical, Monophysite interpretation of the *Henoticon*. At Jerusalem there was some resistance from the patriarch. He was deposed, by the emperor's orders, banished, and once again a Monophysite was installed. Nevertheless, for all that the activity of Severus had achieved—Monophysite in all the leading sees—there still remained enough of anti-Monophysite feeling (especially in the capital) and of dissident Monophysites in Syria to provoke the Government to further action. But at this moment—when affairs were slowly but steadily drifting from bad to worse—the aged emperor (he was eighty-six) died (July 9, 518). His successor, Justin I, was a Latin, and a Catholic.

The reaction was instantaneous. Mobs paraded the streets of Constantinople calling for acknowledgment of Chalcedon and St. Leo, and for the deposition of Severus. A council of bishops solemnly recognised Chalcedon, restored St. Leo's name to its place in the liturgy, deposed and excommunicated Severus—who had already taken flight. Everywhere, except in Egypt, the Catholics gained the upper hand, and within a month of his accession the new emperor had written to the pope, Hormisdas, and asked for the removal of the excommunication and for restoration to communion with him.

It was not until the following March (519) that the pope's legates reached Constantinople. They brought with them a document which all the bishops were to sign in testimony that they were Catholic, and as the condition of their reconciliation. This is the famous *Formula of Pope Hormisdas*. It acknowledges that the faith of the Roman Church has never failed, thanks to Our Lord's words to its first bishop: "Thou art Peter . . ." It condemns Eutyches as it condemns Nestorius (associating St. Cyril with the pope in this last condemnation). It explicitly acknowledges the decisions of Ephesus and Chalcedon alike. It condemns by name all the Monophysite leaders, Acacius also, and all those who have adhered to them. It explicitly accepts the *Tome* of St. Leo and, finally, it abandons all those "separated from the communion of the Catholic Church, that is, those who do not submit to the Apostolic See."

The emperor proposed a conference to discuss the *Formula*, but the legates were firm. They were come simply to gather signatures. The patriarch signed it, and so did all the other bishops present in the capital, and presently commissioners took the *Formula* to all the bishops throughout the east.

In the capital the task had been easy. Outside Constantinople things were very different. In many places—Ephesus, for example, and Thessalonica—there was opposition from those who, wholeheartedly Monophysite, were most unwilling to condemn with Acacius those successors of his who, during the schism, had suffered for their opposition to the Monophysite emperor, Anastasius. Most of the bishops of Severus' own patriarchate signed—forty, however, refused, and the monks everywhere resisted. They were only overcome by a general rounding-up. Their monasteries were dissolved and the hermits expelled from their solitudes—measures which greatly assisted the Monophysite cause by thus letting loose over Syria thousands of fierce apostles who preached wherever they went against the bishops and the Council of Chalcedon. Severus, from his hiding-place, directed the whole movement, and priests and deacons were ordained by the hundred to take the place of those who had "fallen" by submitting to Pope Hormisdas. As for Egypt, so certainly general would be the resistance to any attempt at a Catholic restoration, that the Government left things there untouched, and to Egypt there began to flow in all the persecuted and the dispossessed from the rest of the empire.

The Monophysite problem, then, remained a source of chronic political disorder for the empire, holding over the Church the menace that, whenever it might seem to further the promotion of good order or imperial defence, the emperor would not hesitate to compromise a defined and

fundamental article of the faith. With the advent of the
emperor Justinian (527–565) the menace once more descended, and the effect of his long reign upon the Church
in his dominions was to increase the power of the State
over it and to alienate it still further from the traditional
obedience to Rome and thereby from the belief in the
Roman primacy that is its basis.

Justinian, one of the greatest of all the emperors, who
has to his credit the reconquest of Italy and Africa, and
the great restoration of the Roman Law, was personally
orthodox in faith, and genuinely concerned that Catholicism should flourish. But like Charles V ten centuries later,
whom indeed he prefigures in more than one way, he so
read his rôle of religion's protector as to consider himself
the Church's chief executive, with the bishops—and even
the pope—as so many technical experts to advise him and
to carry out his decisions. In the great collections of
Roman Law that bear Justinian's name this mischievous
confusion of spiritual and temporal authority is carefully
set out as a normal settled part of the imperial policy.
"Nothing should escape the monarch to whom God has
committed the care of all mankind" is the principle on
which this new cesaropapism is based. Orthodoxy in belief
is secured by savage penalties against heresy. Missionary
activity inside and outside the empire is protected and
fostered. The bishops, who enjoy great prestige and play
an important rôle as judges, even in suits about temporal
matters and between laymen, are all, in practice, nominated by the emperor. The lives they should live, and the
lives of the clergy and monks, are all carefully regulated in
the new civil law. The pope has a place apart in the
system, but, in the mind of the emperor, he is in the system just the same. There is no attempt to deny the Roman
See's traditional supremacy. The pope is declared to be
"the chief of all the holy priests of God" and Rome "the
source of all priesthood." Also, alone among the sees of
the empire, Rome continues to enjoy the right freely to
elect its bishops, though the elect now asks confirmation
of his election from the emperor. But this papal supremacy
over the Church the emperor covets as an instrument of
government, and to bend it to be a servant of his policies
he will, at times, shrink from no violence.

The history of the fifth General Council and the relation to it of Justinian and Pope Vigilus are the most striking instance of this—though even here, it is to be noted, Justinian did not attempt to usurp any papal function for himself, nor to bring about an illegal change in the constitution of the Church. There is never any denial that the pope is pope, but there is evident a ruthless and un-Catholic determination to use the pope against the pope's will that, better than anything else, recalls Napoleon's treatment of Pius VII.

The complicated detail of this strangest of all the General Councils must be read elsewhere. It was the culmination of yet another imperial scheme to heal the breach wrought by the Monophysite heresy. The Monophysites declared that those who accepted Chalcedon were really Nestorians. To make clear beyond all doubt that the Chalcedonians—the Catholics—were as orthodox about Nestorius as the Monophysites themselves, it was now suggested that a solemn condemnation be made of three long-dead theologians who were friendly to Nestorius or to his doctrines. This done the Monophysites would have no case and, without a word being said for or against Chalcedon, the long division would be healed. The three items [4] of the coming condemnation were the person and writings of Theodore of Mopsuestia, the writings of Theodoret against St. Cyril at the time of the Council of Ephesus, and the letter in which Ibas, bishop of Edessa, relates to Maris, the bishop of Seleucia, the story of the Council of Ephesus. The first of these personages was the master of Nestorius, and one of the chief sources of his heresy. The second and third were close friends of Nestorius, and equally bitter enemies of St. Cyril.

The Roman objection to issuing the condemnation was that since Theodoret and Ibas had been solemnly reinstated at Chalcedon any attack on them must have a prima facie appearance of a move away from Chalcedon. And indeed this was the first and immediate reading in the west of the very qualified condemnation issued by the pope in

---

[4] *Capitula* in Latin, i.e. *Chapters* in English, whence the name of the *Three Chapters* given to this controversy.

548. There were passionate scenes everywhere, but in
Africa especially, where the pope was excommunicated.

The pope's position was all the more delicate—and his
acts open to misinterpretation—from the fact that he was
at this time Justinian's prisoner, having been kidnapped
in 545 and shipped to the capital when his first hesitancy
about complying with the imperial will had shown itself.

Between the condemnation of 548, which the pope withdrew, and the meeting of the council—May 553—there
were a succession of crises, and the council met with the
pope refusing to take any part in it. There were thus separate condemnations. One, by the pope, of the writings of
Theodore of Mopsuestia, the other, by the council, of the
Three Chapters—or rather an acceptance by the council of
Justinian's condemnation of them.

It remained to win the pope's assent, and after six
months more of bullying, of isolation and imprisonment,
Vigilius, an old man past eighty years of age, yielded. He
was then allowed to leave for Rome, whence he had been
absent nearly ten years.

Justinian's death was followed by a long, steady decline
in the prosperity of the empire. The Persians, who were to
the Roman Empire during these centuries something of
what the English were to France throughout the Middle
Ages, profited from the weakness of his successors, and the
provinces that fell to them, Syria and Egypt, fell the more
easily since affection for Monophysitism, and the sufferings endured for it, had so largely alienated the populace
from the emperor on the Bosphorus.

With Heraclius (emperor, 610–641) the tide turned.
Once more there was at the head of affairs a great character, a fine soldier, and an upright, capable administrator.
After nearly twenty years of reorganisation and of war the
lost lands were recovered, Jerusalem too and the True
Cross, and Heraclius could dictate a peace to the Persians
in their own capital.

His next task was to reorganise the recovered provinces
and, facing now the task of making Greek and Oriental
one in Egypt and Syria—an indispensable condition of any
future security—Heraclius found himself confronted with

the ancient problem of the Monophysites. The Monophysites themselves were not to trouble him much longer, for while he made his new plans a new power, Islam, was rising in Arabia that was swiftly to wrest Egypt and Syria from the empire and for ever—and this within fifteen years of the victory of 628.

But the new plan to reconcile the heretics survived the empire's loss of the lands where they lived, and it endured, to be for fifty years the cause of grave internal troubles among the Catholics themselves, an occasion of persecution and martyrdoms and of a new serious breach of relations with Rome.

The new plan had for its author the patriarch of Constantinople, Sergius. Once again there is in it no reference to Chalcedon or St. Leo, nor indeed any to St. Cyril. It is merely a statement that in Our Lord there is but one source of activity (one energy), seeing He is but one person. A more popular presentation of the theory spoke of Him as having but one will, and from this the heresy gained its name Monothelism. For heresy it was, the old Monophysitism latent in it, and apparent to anyone really versed in the controversy.

Heraclius was won over to accept it, and the Monophysites were favourable. But Sophronius, the patriarch of Jerusalem, saw the menace it presented for the faith and denounced it to Rome. Sergius had also written to the pope about the same time, and the slipshod action of the pope—Honorius I, 625–638—has made him one of the celebrated figures in the later controversy about papal infallibility. For Honorius, apparently, missed the point at issue, i.e. whether in Our Lord there is (1) a divine will and (2) a human will, and occupied himself with deciding another question altogether, namely, whether there could be any conflict in Our Lord between what He willed as God and what He willed as man. Since there is between these a most perfect harmony, we must, said Honorius, acknowledge in Him a Unity of Will. As to the discussion whether there are in Him one or two "energies," since either expression is bound to be misunderstood, it is better to avoid the discussion altogether.

This reply played into the hands of the Monothelite

leaders, for it gave a sanction to their phrase "unity of will" and it favoured the policy of "no-more-discussion-for-the-sake-of-peace."

Within eight years of this calamitous decision all the chief figures in the movement were dead, the heretics, the emperor, and the pope. And the Monophysite provinces were lost. But the new heresy was by now an official belief, and the State would continue to impose it. And Rome, once the real issue was clear, would equally be bound to fight the heresy and, if necessary, the emperors who patronised it.

The new development began in a series of Roman acts in which Honorius' successors explained what he had sanctioned and what he had condemned, and showed that he had by no means approved Monothelism. Also they condemned the new profession of faith, drawn up by the emperor, which contained the heresy, and ordered the patriarch of Constantinople to withdraw the adherence he had given it. On his refusal the pope excommunicated him. The emperor—Constans II (642–668)—replied by a new edict, the *Type*.

This decree simply imposed silence on all parties. Heresy was to be left in possession and Catholics must not urge the traditional faith. The first to break through the policy of the *Type* was the new pope—Martin I, elected 649—and he did it in the most public way possible. Before his election he had lived for years at Constantinople as the pope's ambassador at the court. He knew the whole controversy and the personalities concerned in it, and in October of 649, in a great synod held in the Lateran, he condemned the *Type* and its promoters, and defined as the Church's teaching that in Our Lord there are "two natural wills, the divine and the human." Furthermore, he directed that similar councils be held all over the west to spread the condemnation and the definition.

The emperor, in reply, began by attempting to win the pope over to his side. Next he planned to assassinate him and finally, after one abortive attempt, he had him arrested and brought to Constantinople. There every indignity was heaped upon him. He was tried (on a charge of treason) and condemned to death (654)—a sentence which was commuted to one of exile. Twelve months later, broken by his sufferings and still an exile, the pope died. Nor was he the only victim of the persecution.

So long as Constans II lived the policy remained the same. His son and successor, however, Constantine IV (668–685), did not share his father's enthusiasm for it. Although no formal reversion was made of what had been done, the *Type* ceased to be imposed as a profession of faith and ten years of more peaceful relations between emperor and pope prepared the way for the General Council of 680 at which the long deadlock was brought to an end. To this council the pope—Agatho—sent a letter setting out the traditional Catholic teaching on the dogmatic point at issue, viz. whether in Our Lord there were one or two wills, as St. Leo had sent the like kind of letter to Chalcedon. As at Chalcedon so now the 174 eastern bishops present received the pope's teaching with acclamations, crying out: "It is Peter who speaks through Agatho." The doctrine defined, the council turned to condemn the authors of the heresy, and with them it condemned Pope Honorius, not indeed as an author of the heresy but "because in his reply to Sergius he followed in all things that wicked man's opinion, and confirmed his impious teaching."

The date of the sixth General Council, November 680–September 681, is a reminder that in this rapid survey of the effect on Catholicism of the conversion of its chief in temporals, the Roman Emperor, we have long passed the conventional barrier that, for historians, divides the Roman Empire from the Byzantine. Nearly four hundred years have gone by since the conversion of Constantine, and in that time a new culture has come into being in the empire whose centre is now Constantinople, the city Constantine had created. The empire is now, in reality, a great Greek state, and the time is approaching when a Roman emperor will be able to speak of Latin as a barbarian tongue. It is high time to turn to consider how the Church has fared during these same four hundred years in those Western lands, Italy, Africa, Spain, Gaul, Britain, and Germany, where the emperor has, by 680, long since ceased to be ruler. But before we do so something needs to be said of a further great council, held at Constantinople in 692; for this council definitely marks the beginning of a new era in the relations between Rome and Greek-speaking Catholicism. Henceforth a new spirit is apparent, definitely and systematically anti-Roman, resentful of the Roman leadership and not a little contemptuous of the peculiarly Roman customs and of the barbarian West generally. The occasional insubordination of the emperor-aided, if not emperor-inspired, patriarchs of Constantinople begins now to take on the new note of a war of independence, and more, much more, than the schism of Acacius, the council of 692 is, in spirit, the prelude to Photius and to the schism of Cerularius which still endures.

The reason for the council was the desire to provide new canons of ecclesiastical discipline, a kind of supplement to the last two General Councils,[5] which had not dealt with discipline at all.

The council met in the domed hall of the imperial palace—whence its name of the Council *in Trullo*—and it claimed to legislate for the whole empire, and hence for Rome too. The new laws are for the most part a simple codifying of the old, but there are some new canons and these are undeniably anti-Roman. Thus the canon regulating clerical marriages goes out of its way to assert that the Roman custom is not according to the tradition of the apostles and, when legislating for fast-days, the canon notes the Roman custom of fasting on the Saturdays of Lent and proceeds to forbid the practice—even in Rome itself—under the penalty of excommunication. The sources, too, from which this new "code" is drawn include the canons of councils Rome had never acknowledged and of others which Rome had specifically rejected.

There was, of course, trouble as soon as the Roman assent to the new canons was asked. The pope—Sergius I—refused, and only a revolution at Constantinople (695) saved him from the fate of St. Martin I. When, ten years later, Justinian II was restored, he took the matter up once more with Sergius I's successor—John VII. This pope sent an ambiguous reply, neither confirming nor refusing to confirm the council. It did not suffice, and the pope was ordered to present himself at court. John VII was dead by

---

[5] I.e. of 553 and 680, the Fifth and Sixth, whence the name of *Quini-Sext*, sometimes given to the council of 692.

the time the order reached Rome, and it was Constantine who had to obey. In his suite was the deacon later to be pope as Gregory II, and, thanks to his skilful diplomacy, the matter was arranged without the pope's confirming the decrees.

The Catholicism of the centuries we have been dealing with has two great glories to its credit, the invention and first expansion of Christian monasticism and also the succession of those ecclesiastical writers of genius whom we call the Fathers of the Church.

The beginning of monasticism was the practice, as old as the Church itself, by which certain individuals, of both sexes, consecrated themselves to God through a vow of perfect chastity. These heroic souls—*continentes*—were to be found in every church, and the apologists make frequent reference to them as a proof of the sanctity to which the Faith leads men. As time went on, the ecclesiastical authorities began to lay down strict regulations for the protection of the virtue of these *continentes,* fixing the age at which the vow might be taken, determining a way of life for them, with special Church services and devotional exercises in common.

The next step was for these ascetics to live together entirely, and about 270 we find St. Antony of Egypt placing his sister in such a "convent."

Others of these *continentes* preferred to live a solitary existence far away from human beings, on the outskirts of the great towns first of all, and then in huts or caves in the desert. The earliest of these hermits was St. Paul of Thebes, whose disciple St. Antony was. Around such hermits, especially those who were saints, a crowd of disciples speedily gathered and by the time of the Council of Nicea (325) there were thousands of solitaries in the deserts to the south of Egypt. There was as yet no law or rule of spiritual exercises or penitential practice. Each did what seemed to him the best suited to his own needs. On Sundays they came together for Mass and to receive the Holy Eucharist and an instruction. They kept themselves by manual work.

The next stage in the development was to establish colonies with a common way of living, where all should live according to the same rule of prayer, austerities, and work, but under the direction of a superior, obedience to whose decisions should be the first duty of all. Here is the beginning of monasticism in the strict sense, and the first monastery was that founded at Tabennisi by St. Pachomius, about 320.

So far the movement had been confined to Egypt, but about this time a disciple of St. Antony introduced it into Palestine and in a new form, the *Laura*, which was a community subject to a common rule and a superior, but where each member lived solitary in his own hut. This form of monasticism spread rapidly through the Holy Land, many of these villages of monks counting their inhabitants by the hundred.

From Palestine monasticism spread through Syria to Asia Minor and here it met the great leader whose influence was to set its characteristics in a written rule that still endures and is observed by thousands of men and women. This leader was St. Basil (329–379), who, later, as archbishop of Cesarea in Cappadocia, was, as has been noticed, one of the greatest champions of the Faith against Arianism.

St. Basil, a man widely experienced, drew up a rule that was a real code of monastic life and not just a collection of wise general directions for holy living. Two things in particular mark out this rule. It provides for a novitiate—a period in which the aspirant makes trial of the monastic life, and is trained in its practice, particularly in the practice of obedience—and it also lays down that the monasteries shall not be over-large. There shall be no more than thirty or forty monks to each. Also St. Basil shows himself more paternal and kindly in all that relates to austerities and to penalties for breaches of the rules.

Within fifty years of the death of St. Basil, by the time of the Council of Ephesus (431), monasticism had so developed in the churches of the East that it might be said to be their most popular feature. Nor was it any longer a thing that needed deserts or waste places for its life, but, especially since the reforms of St. Basil, it was possible to have monasteries in the towns, and indeed the monks of such cities as Alexandria, Antioch, and Constantinople were numbered by the thousand, and often played a decisive part in the crises of ecclesiastical history.

The setting in which the genius of the greatest of the Greek Fathers was displayed was the long century and a half of theological controversy which has recently occupied us. Something has been said of that controversy as a thing that shook the very fabric of society and, at the same time that it produced the great definitions of faith, provided the State with an opportunity to enslave the Church.

There are other sides of the matter scarcely less important, and certainly more pleasant to consider, and among these is the astonishing development of Christian thought, of a correct systematic explanation of the mysteries of the Faith, in a scientific manner, that lessens for the future the chances of their being misunderstood, that assists the evangelist in his task of winning to Christ the sophisticated educated classes of the time, and that opens up to the believer ever newer depths of truth for his contemplation and for the consequent enrichment of his spiritual life. The great orators, the great writers, the stylists of Greek literature, in these last centuries of the empire, are not only Christians, but ecclesiastics, and their subject matter is the mysteries of the Christian Faith and the glory of serving Christ in the observance of His law.

As theologians—thinkers who face the task of explaining the traditional doctrine in a systematic manner, using natural knowledge and its laws to make the divinely revealed truth more intelligible—the Fathers are an immense advance on the Apologists. They have profited by the heavy labours of their predecessors and by the corrections and condemnations of all the councils of the last two centuries. The Faith is now better understood than then. There are the beginnings of a technical terminology in which to express its data. The new writers are ecclesiastics, if the word be allowed, by profession. They have, most of them, been Catholic from their cradles, and the education they have received in the various schools of the empire has been a better kind of thing than what was open to their predecessors. Hence, although there are still, here and there, certain stammerings and vague uncertainties in their language, one is immediately conscious, with all these writers, of a new maturity of expression as of thought. Their hold on doctrine and their handling of the twin techniques of language and philosophy is so complete that for originality and liveliness their work has never been surpassed, and these two centuries (328–461) remain unique in the history of culture as in that of the Church.

The first of these great writers was the chief defender of the Council of Nicea, St. Athanasius (293–373), bishop of Alexandria for nearly fifty years. Though in some respects a true descendant from the great Alexandrian tradition whose source is Origen, St. Athanasius is really a person apart, and if the necessities of his life made him largely a controversialist—in a very wide sense and on a scale that may be called gigantic—they only developed what was a natural genius for the choice of the word that means one thing alone, and the argument that proceeds by irrefutable logical sequence. Add to this, to complete the description of the manner, a flexibility of mind that left him ever ready to welcome new ways of expressing old truths and then, for the matter of his writing, the most fundamental of all the Christian dogmas, and the force incarnate in this mighty champion can be easily divined.

Closely related to St. Athanasius, not only by the fact of their common preoccupation with Arianism, but also by a certain community of spirit with Origen, are the three writers called the Cappadocians, from the province where they lived. These are St. Basil (329–379)—whose work as a reformer of monasticism has been mentioned—his brother Gregory, Bishop of Nyssa (335–395), and his intimate friend, Gregory of Nazianzen (330–390). All three have something of Origen's happy confidence as to the part reason can play in the interpretation of the mysteries of the Faith. All are, as we should say, humanists and, better than any so far, their minds are formed with all that Greek literature and philosophy had to offer. St. Gregory of Nazianzen is perhaps the greatest preacher of theology that has ever been known, an orator of such power and simplicity that the most intricate speculation is made understandable to the very simplest among his auditory. Of the three it is St. Basil's brother, Gregory of Nyssa, who is the most philosophical and the most evidently Origen's disciple.

These three writers are a kind of half-way house between the Alexandrian school of theology and the more geometrical, literalist, rationalist school of Antioch. One great difference between these schools must already have been noticed in the history of their conflict at the time of the Council of Ephesus (431).[6] In the consideration of the doctrine that Our Lord is both divine and human, the Alexandrian approach was from the consideration of the divine, and the school's great fear was of anything which should compromise the truth of His divinity. The school of Antioch began its exposition and defence of the doctrine by an insistence on the reality of Our Lord's humanity, and its writers were similarly suspicious of whatever seemed unduly enthusiastic about anything else. In their fashions of interpreting Sacred Scripture the two schools also differed characteristically. At Alexandria the allegorical method was popular. At Antioch it was the literal sense alone, almost, that was allowed.

The two great orthodox writers of this school are St. John Chrysostom (of whose career as archbishop of Constantinople something has been said)[7] and Theodoret, the friend of Nestorius and the opponent of Eutyches.[8] St. John owes his high place among the Fathers, not to his contributions to theology, but to an unrivalled mastery as an interpreter of Sacred Scripture, and particularly of the writings of St. Paul, where he is so powerful a guide that a modern scholar can say that all subsequent commentators have done little more than develop St. John Chrysostom. Again, in matters theological, this saint is rather a moralist than a speculative, and his work is directed more to the correction of the lives of Christians than to the advancement of their understanding of the mysteries of the Faith.

Theodoret, bishop of Cyrrhus, who died about 458, is almost the last of the Greek Fathers of this golden age, and he is perhaps best recalled in connection, and in contrast, with his great antagonist, St. Cyril of Alexandria (380–444). Here, in this conflict of two undoubtedly

---

[6] Cf. *supra*, p. 32.

[7] Cf. *supra*, p. 31.

[8] Cf. *supra*, p. 34.

Catholic bishops, is to be seen the conflict of the Alexandrine and Antiochene schools at its keenest. Of St. Cyril it has been stated, by one who is an expert in these matters,[9] that he is the most powerful theological thinker the Eastern Church ever possessed, and that, after St. Athanasius, none of the Greeks had so great an effect on the definition of Catholic Doctrine. Theodoret is the more accurate scholar of the two, and but for the fact that among his closest friends were to be found two of the greatest heretics of the day, Theodore of Mopsuestia, his master, and Nestorius, his fellow-student, he would no doubt have enjoyed the prestige certainly his due, a much higher place than has in fact been his lot.

Nothing was said, in the account of the Arian attack on the Church in the West (see above, page 42) about the "fall" of Pope Liberius (352–366), for the discussion about this episode is too complicated to suffer compression and remain intelligible. The view taken by Pierre Batiffol (*La paix constantinienne et le catholicisme,* ch. ix) seems to me the most likely. The point at issue between the pope and the emperor was the tacit disavowal of the Nicene formula, *homoöusion.* At the Councils of Arles (353) and Milan (355) the pope's legates gave way. Liberius remained firm, and, after stormy interview with the emperor, was banished (357). Next year, Basil of Ancyra, the leader of a group which, though Catholic, disliked the term *homoöusion,* because of its misuse in a third-century controversy, gained the emperor's favour. He then endeavoured to unite all the Catholics on the basis of a non-Nicene (but not anti-Nicene) formula. In the Catholic sense in which this was offered, and, with an explanation making clear what he was doing, Liberius, still a captive, signed this. The forgeries of Arian pamphleteers are probably the original cause of the confusion around which the discussion centres.

---

[9] Tixeront, *Histoire des Dogmes,* III, 2-3.

3

The Conversion of Western Europe, 313–755

BY THE West is to be understood the Western Empire as the final division made by Gratian left it in 378; that is to say, Italy, Roman Africa, Spain, Gaul, Britain, Greece, the Balkans, and Jugo-Slavia. Southern Italy and Africa apart, these regions were hardly Christian at all compared with the East, when, in 313, Constantine and Liberius ended the persecutions. The conversion of these provinces was still only in its first stages when the central government in the West collapsed and that chaotic state of affairs set in which it still remains convenient to call by the inaccurate name of the Barbarian Invasions. If we look for a picture of Western Catholicism under the Christian Roman emperors, it cannot be much more than the limited picture of the Church in Italy and Africa.

The most dramatic sequence of events took place in Africa, in the modern Tunis. Here the great persecution of 303–312 had for its sequel a terrible schism, whose basis was the refusal to recognise the archbishop of Carthage as the Catholic bishop, since he was alleged to have concealed his faith during the persecution. The accusation was false, and proved to be false by official investigations in which the police books and court records were examined. But Donatism—for so, from its chief, Donatus, the movement to replace the accused archbishop and all who stood by him, with other bishops of "surer" faith, was called—was by this time a vested interest, that had gathered to itself all the social, anti-Roman discontent of the turbulent province. Soon there were rival bishops in every city, and everywhere the Donatists showed themselves aggressively hostile. Constantine lost no time in his endeavour to heal the schism. His methods, and the spirit of his interventions, were those shown later in the Arian troubles by himself and by his successors. He first supported the Catholics—about whose case no man could have any doubts after the careful investigations—and then, when the Donatists showed that they were prepared to resist, and even to bring about a civil war, he adopted a policy of *laissez-faire*. In the end the schism dragged on for a century, until the Donatists had so consolidated their position that in many places the Catholics, cowed by their violence, against which the law no longer offered them any protection, made a show of becoming Donatists.

Finally the general situation became too bad for the most indifferent of Governments to tolerate and in the opening years of the fifth century, after a series of futile conferences, demanded by the Donatists and then rejected in advance just as soon as they saw the Government prepared to accord them, the emperior Honorius (395–423) re-enacted the decree for their suppression. Then came a civil war between the Romans themselves and, following on this, the invasion of the Vandals and the end of the Roman rule for a hundred and twenty years.

There is little of permanent interest in the history of Donatism, though the important theological principle that underlay its action should be noted, for it recurs again and again through the next thousand years, the theory, that is to say, that the validity of the sacraments depends on the state of the soul of the one who administers them. If a bishop, for example, apostatizes he loses all spiritual power and can no longer say Mass or absolve or baptize. Such a theory means spiritual anarchy, for no one can ever tell whether his neighbour is in a state of grace, and if the theory were true it would mean, not the end of certainty about salvation, but the establishment of an inevitable general doubt as to whether anyone, ever, received a sacrament.

More important than Donatism was the man who was,

in its last stages, its chief opponent. This was St. Augustine (354–430).

The story of St. Augustine's early life is one of the great stories that are part of all education. For he has recorded it himself in the book called his Confessions which, ever since it was written, has been one of the world's classic texts, a book in which every man may read something of his own life and character. The book establishes St. Augustine's claim to be regarded as the first modern man, the man passionately interested in his own mental and spiritual development and so artistically dispassionate as to be able to record it. It is the first appearance of personal literature.

St. Augustine is not important solely because he was a distinguished convert, nor because he was a bishop during forty critical years in one of the key provinces of the empire. He was an intellectual, trained to the last perfection in all the refinements of the ancient classical culture, a philosopher, an orator, a writer, a dramatist and a man of letters, a thinker of great power, a daring pioneer in speculation, a theological genius, and, rare combination with this last gift, he had all the sensibility and the communicative sympathy of the artist. The painters of the Middle Ages represented St. Augustine with a heart in flames, and the symbol, for once, really expresses the man's essential distinction.

It was his lot to pass through many great movements, and to play a leading part in all of them. Whence an immense output of literary work, philosophy, theology, history, letters, and in it all, visible and attainable, is the whole heritage of the culture of the old Pagan world now slowly disappearing. St. Augustine is the bridge over which what was best in that old world passed into the new. In him the Latin culture was baptised and, becoming a part of the Catholic tradition, passed into the foundations of the Middle Ages and thereby of all subsequent time.

Almost from the time they were written the different works of St. Augustine came to be, in the Latin west, a kind of universally accepted encyclopædia of the new Christianised culture. Scarcely a writer, a constructive statesman, or an ecclesiastical reformer who does not find in them his inspiration. For a good eight hundred years the saint, as thinker and teacher, ruled without a rival. It is not possible to exaggerate his influence on European life during this time.

In his own time that influence was principally felt in the two controversies of Donatism and Pelagianism. As bishop of Hippo in Roman Africa (396–430) St. Augustine brought the Catholic cause to victory—so far as argumentation could do this—and by his contribution to the argumentation he notably enriched the teaching of Catholic theology on the nature of the Church and of its sacraments.

Donatism—in so far as it involved an error about the faith—was a practical heresy, as has been noted already. The second heretical movement which St. Augustine met had also, for its subject, a truth of immediate practical consequence. Its author, Pelagius, was a British monk, an ascetic and a man of sympathetic temperament, a popular director of souls. His new theory dealt with the relation of the respective rôles of God and man in the affair of man's salvation, and amounted to an assertion that man is capable of attaining salvation by his own efforts, man being, by nature, wholly good. There is a denial here of the traditional doctrine of Original Sin and the consequences of the Fall, and there is also a denial of the reality of the effects of those divine aids given to man, technically called graces.

This second controversy drew from St. Augustine the works by which he is best known as a theologian, books in which he discusses, and with a power none has ever excelled, the nature of God's activity upon the soul of man, and the relation of this to man's free will.

But the book which, more than all, was to influence European life in the west during the thousand years that followed St. Augustine's death was the one *On the City of God.* It was provoked by the Pagan clamour against Christianity as the cause of the empire's decay. The saint spent twenty years on the work and produced the first of all philosophical histories, a vast repertoire of Pagan and Christian learning, a synthesis of original design and a storehouse of political and social ideals, as well as of religious apologetic, whose wealth, even yet, no later thinker has exhausted.

Arianism had scarcely touched the Roman west, apart from the imperial attempt to impose it as a kind of State religion (355–360), and the chief feature of religious interest in the fourth century was that gradual de-paganising of the State which has already been mentioned. The leading figure of the time, and this not in an ecclesiastical sense merely, was the bishop of Milan, St. Ambrose. In him it is not the Latin culture that is baptised so much as the Roman genius for government. Not that St. Ambrose lacked culture, and an appreciation for it. It was indeed in the distinction of his sermons that the rhetorician Augustine first understood that the religion of the Church and a cultivated mind were not incompatible. The many addresses and the treatises and the letters of St. Ambrose show him a master of Ciceronian style, and it was also through him that much of Origen's learning came to the Western Church. But the bishop of Milan was primarily the man of affairs who had made over to God's service his talent of rulership. In him we see fully developed the type of the medieval bishop at his best, the spiritual father of his people, their unfailing refuge and defence in even temporal necessities.

St. Ambrose is also entitled to a place apart as the first bishop to set out in theological statement the due place of the Catholic ruler within the Catholic Church. The pope Liberius (352–366) had already set a precedent, in the days of St. Ambrose's childhood, by his stern rebukes to Constantius II during the attempt to foist Arianism upon the west. But it was with emperors who were Catholics that the bishop of Milan had to deal, and at a time when Milan was the city of their residence. His firm insistence, despite violence, arrests, and threats of death itself, that "the emperor is within the Church, not over the Church," set a precedent for all future time in the west, and, humanly speaking, it is due to St. Ambrose above all others that the Church developed in the west more independently, in this respect, than it did in the east. Also, it is to be noticed, the saint had on his side throughout the struggle the strong, active support of his people. Here, too, we may see, before the Middle Ages had begun, that instinctive alliance of the people with ecclesiastical authority against the tyranny of the State.

A second contemporary of St. Augustine, destined like him to a never-ceasing influence on the Church and on Europe, was the monk St. Jerome (347–420). Of the three men we are considering he was the most learned, not indeed an original thinker at all, not a philosopher nor a theologian, but a man of immense erudition and a master of Greek and Hebrew as well as of his native Latin. As a young man he had gone to the east from northern Italy, where, most probably, he was born, to live the life of a solitary. He had returned to give Rome its first experience of monasticism, to be the adviser of Pope Damasus I (366–384), and to cause not a little heartburning among the worldly Roman clergy by his own ascetic life, by his successful direction of ladies of aristocratic rank, and by the biting phrases in which—a man no less impatient of shams than of fools—he defended their change of life and the monastic ideal against worldly traducers. After the death of Damasus he went back to the east and, established now at Bethlehem, gave himself to the work which has made him famous, the re-translation of the Bible into Latin, and the series of commentaries on the different books of the Sacred Text. If St. Augustine deserves to be called the father of Latin Theology, St. Jerome is no less truly the first begetter of the critical study of Holy Scripture, and, by his translations, he also exercised a lasting influence on the future history of the Latin language, not indeed as a rare antique or valued heirloom, but as a means through which men could continue, for yet another fifteen hundred years, to express their minds and communicate their ideas.

These three great saints are the human foundation of all that was Christian in the culture of the Middle Ages, and of much that was classical. But had it not been for the fact that they were churchmen and that the matter on which their minds were occupied was religious, it is not improbable that the immense legacy of ancient thought which they had to transmit would have perished. For they lived in the last generation that saw the Roman rule a reality through all the west. Within a few years of the death of St. Ambrose (397), and during the very lifetime of St. Jerome and St. Augustine, the catastrophe, so often threatened, came at last, and with the breakdown of the central government's hold on the provinces, with the invasion of such real barbarians as the Franks, the Vandals, and the Huns, the consequent pillage and senseless destruction, the day was to come when, of all the great institutions of the empire, the Church alone survived. In the midst of the chaos it remained, afloat, like the ark of Noe, battered, strained, and often enough drifting before the winds and the waves, but afloat none the less, secure, and within it many very precious things. Not least among these were the work and the tradition of Ambrose, Jerome, and Augustine.

The story of what it is still conventional to call the Barbarian Invasions belongs primarily to General History, but, thanks in no small part to the Barbarians, General History and Church History begin from this moment to be confounded, the Church being only civilisation regarded religiously, and civilisation being the Church, considered in the non-religious activity and life of its members. From the time these new social and racial troubles began their work of transforming western Europe in the fifth century, down to the time of the discovery of America in the fifteenth, Europe and the Catholic Church are two names for the one thing. This statement must not, of course, be taken too literally, but it is true enough for the practical purpose of guiding a beginner through the maze of the next thousand years, the period called the Middle Ages, and, for all its imperfections, the statement is the only key to the many apparent contradictions and riddles that the story of the Middle Ages presents to an observer who is himself a practising Catholic. More than this, the statement is so true that if one rejects it the attempt to explain the Reformation (whence dates the Modern Europe, no longer substantially one, but only accidentally so), and thereby our own time and its fundamental problem, must fail likewise.

The story of the Barbarian Invasions belongs then to Church History, too. The Barbarians were the peoples, of varying race, who lived beyond the frontiers of the empire, Germans, Goths, Huns, Vandals, and the rest. They all had this in common that they were pastoral peoples, masters of great herds of cattle, living a more or less nomad life, possessing no cities and not given to agriculture. The empire had always attracted them, for the easier, more secure thing that life within its frontier usually was. Families of Barbarians, tribes, and even nations sought admission and often it was allowed them. In one very vital business the Barbarians had been penetrating Roman life from about half-way through the second century, namely through being admitted as soldiers into the army. Gradually the Roman army itself, and not the auxiliary forces merely, became a Barbarian thing. Barbarians were next admitted to the command, and from the third century the novelty began to be seen of emperors who were Barbarian. In a State such as the Roman Empire, where the ruler was primarily ruler because commander-in-chief of the army, and where the succession depended on his personal military prestige and power, this development was bound, in the long run, to transform the State.

What happened in the fifth century was something like this. In the reign of an unusually weak emperor—Honorius (395–423)—an unusually strong attack was made on the frontier by Barbarians of a kind that, so far, had not had any semi-civilising relations with the empire. This horde, of Barbarians who were really barbarous, crossed the Rhine (406) and swept in a torrent on Gaul and Spain. Three years later Italy was the scene of invasion, and the invader here was Alaric, the chief of a nation in the service of the empire, the Visigoths. Alaric was discontented with the place allotted him in the imperial service, jealous of other Barbarians in the service, and it was to better his position in the empire that in 409 he crossed the Alps and swept into Italy. In the following year he took and sacked Rome itself. It is not necessary to say what a calamity this appeared to the generation that saw it. True enough the ancient city had no longer the political importance it had enjoyed in the time of Augustus or even of Marcus Aurelius. No emperor had lived there for a hundred and forty years. But it was still Rome, and in some indefinable way the prestige and the spirit of the imperial rule were incarnate in the city—and when it fell to the army of Alaric men felt the imperial idea as mortally stricken.

Alaric died a few months after his triumph, and the statecraft of the court—Ravenna was now the capital—set his successors to clear Spain and Gaul of the remnants of the invasion of 406–407. The final result of this was the establishment in southern Gaul of Visigothic chiefs as sovereigns, nominally the emperor's lieutenants, actually independent rulers.

In the same way that Gaul and Spain were thus silently slipping forever from the imperial control, Britain too disappeared. In 410 the needs of the continental crisis brought about a summons to the armies in Britain to cross the seas. They never returned, and the island entered upon the dark night of its history, a hundred and fifty years about which we have scarcely half a dozen established facts to record.

The establishment of the Visigoths in southern Gaul had not meant any serious dislocation of public life. This went on much as before, under the same laws and the same officials. But the Vandal invasion of Africa (425) a different kind of thing altogether, a real orgy of Barbarian destruction, of murder and pillage, and the establishment, finally, of a new Barbarian State, definitely hostile to the empire and to everything Roman.

This State had another peculiarity. It was militantly anti-Catholic, and the Vandal kings, from the moment they were supreme, persecuted the Church and enriched its history with a very full new martyrology. The Vandals were not heathens, but, like the Goths, they had received their Christianity with their first contact with the imperial court, and at the moment this was made the court was Arian. Thus it came about that fifty years after Arianism was dead in the east (for once the court ceased to be Arian the movement had collapsed utterly) it made its appearance in force in the west, and again, everywhere, as a court religion.

The divergence between the religion of the new rulers and that of their subjects and the trained officials whom they, necessarily, continued to employ, was from the first a serious weakness in all the new Barbarian kingdoms. It is not surprising that here and there (in Spain, for example, towards 485) there was persecution, but it was only in the Vandal kingdom that the persecution was systematic and continuous.

By the time St. Leo the Great was elected pope (440) and the events that centred round the Council of Chalcedon (451) were in progress, the effective jurisdiction of the emperor in the west was limited to Italy. After the death in 455 of the last descendant of Theodosius the Great, Valentinian III (425–455), the Barbarian Roman generals fought for the mastery, naming a succession of puppet emperors. The last of these was Romulus, whom, in a good-natured kind of contempt, men nicknamed Augustulus. The real ruler was the Herule, Odoacer, and he, tiring of the farce after some years, bade the emperor resign, and, packing up the insignia, sent them to the colleague of Romulus at Constantinople, Zeno, with the message that the west had no longer any need of a separate ruler. This was in 476. Thirteen years later a rival to Odoacer appeared, Theodoric the Ostrogoth, the chief of a race settled for half a century in the empire of the east and now despatched to Italy. There was a brief war, a compromise between the two Barbarians, and then, in 493, the murder of Odoacer by Theodoric simplified matters, and until 526 Theodoric ruled in peace. He too was an Arian, and of his reign more will be said later.

The Barbarian Invasions decentralised the political organisation of the west. They increased the importance of the locality, and made the men who were there socially important, important now juridically and politically. The Europe of the Middle Ages, with its myriad tiny principalities and jurisdictions, had begun. Increasingly the isolation of the locality set in. Communications became more and more difficult as the roads ceased to be maintained. Life was less urban, more rustic. Men were forced "back to the land" by the necessities of the case, and in these very centuries when the Church was ceasing to be an Asiatic and Oriental thing, it was ceasing also to be something that belonged to the cities. By its origins and its previous development it was an urban thing and now it had to face the problem of adapting itself to the new rustication of general life, and in doing so it suffered,

itself, inevitably from all the disadvantages that such rusti-
cisation brought with it.

Three saints sum up, in their lives, the movement of
the western Church to adapt itself to the new conditions.
In St. Martin, bishop of Tours (375–397), we see the
pioneer of the mission to convert the country folk; in St.
Benedict (480–547), the creator of a new monasticism that
is to show itself the mother of a thousand refuges for holiness of life in the midst of general moral disorder, refuges
which are to transform the country-sides, solving thus the
great problem of these centuries, and to be, incidentally,
the salvation of learning and literary culture in the darkest
hour the European intelligence has ever known. Finally
in St. Patrick (392–461) we see the first monk missioner
formed by this new rural Christianity, and he founds
not merely monasteries, but a whole people which, in
time to come, is to show itself a sanctuary for sanctity
and culture, and from Catholic Ireland, which is his creation, the light is one day to return to re-enlighten Europe
itself.

St. Martin was born in Pannonia, the Roman Hungary,
and, the son of a soldier, followed his father's profession.
His real vocation lay elsewhere, and it survived his military life. He wished to be a solitary, and it was a chance
meeting with St. Hilary, bishop of Poitiers, that led to his
establishment at Marmoutier on the Loire. Disciples
gathered round him and here, in the caves of the banks
of the river, the first monastic settlement of the western
Church developed (360–375). The life of these monks
was much the same as that of their eastern contemporaries.
The great difference was that in Gaul the surrounding
population was Pagan, and thence followed the first great
missionary effort to the peoples of the European country-
sides. In 375 St. Martin was elected bishop of Tours, and
from that date to his death he was the chief force in the
religious life of Gaul. He kept, as bishop, all the simplicity
of his primitive monastic life, the first of the bishop-
ascetics, and he also retained all his zeal for the evangelisation of the country districts. His monastery, too, continued to prosper, and his monks were sought as bishops
everywhere throughout Gaul. When St. Martin died his

tomb at Tours became, immediately, the scene of miracles and the goal of pilgrimages. He is the first non-martyr to whose memory we know liturgical honours were paid, the first confessor saint, to put the matter in modern technical terms.

In the generation that followed St. Martin's death the south of Gaul was the scene of a second great, monastic-inspired revival of religion. The centre here was the little island of Lérins, where a number of holy men lived a life much after the fashion of the Egyptian saints, half-hermit, half-cenobite, very austere and, the particular distinction of this foundation, marked by a great zeal for meditation on Holy Scripture. In the early years of the fifth century (426) the monks of Lérins began to be chosen as bishops, and one of these, St. Hilary of Arles, played the same part of bishop-apostle in the south of Gaul that St. Martin had played in the west.

Of St. Patrick's early life we know much and yet little. It is disputed where he was born, though it was in some part of the Roman province of Britain, and in one of the many raids from Ireland he was carried into captivity. After six years of slavery in northern Ireland, years in which he was converted from a somewhat careless boy and became a great pray-er, he made his escape, in obedience to a heavenly inspiration. He passed into Gaul and there became a monk. Lérins almost certainly knew him and Marmoutier too. Later he lived at Auxerre where he was ordained deacon by the great bishop, St. Germanus, whose expedition in 429 to reclaim the British from Pelagianism is one of the few authenticated facts of our own history at this time. Patrick was still at Auxerre when the great hour of his life came, and, consecrated bishop, he was charged with a mission to Ireland, some eighteen years after his escape.

For the next thirty years (432–461) the saint spent himself in an endless apostolate, preaching, baptising, ordaining, consecrating other bishops, everywhere establishing monasteries and a curious kind of ecclesiastical settlement, part monastery, part seminary, part centre of administration, which, in this country where cities were unknown, served as the bishop's see.

For a hundred years after St. Patrick's death (461) the

good work went on under the direction of his disciples, and, under the influence of those who were of British origin, the Irish Church became the most monastic of all so that the bishops are lost to sight behind the monastic community, of which they formed part, and its abbot.

In Ireland the western missionary had to meet a new difficulty. Here he was in a land that the Roman influence had never touched and where the Latin tongue had to be taught to what natives needed as priests and bishops, to sound the depths of their new belief. In this necessity is to be found, in part, the roots of that association between Catholicism and literary culture, particularly the culture of Latin letters, which was for centuries to mark the Irish Church. When it had all but perished elsewhere, and when even in Italy the ancient tongue had degenerated, the scientific knowledge of the Latin language survived in this one western land where the Romans had never set foot, and this knowledge, carried back by Irish monk missionaries, supplied the beginnings of the later European renaissance.

Irish monasticism was of the stern Egyptian type, so severe in its austerity and in the sanctions which guarded monastic discipline, that it was long styled "the white martyrdom." In the sixth century the Irish zeal to convert others was to send the Irish monks first to Scotland, with St. Columba, and then, with St. Columbanus, to continental Europe. Here in the seventh century Irish monasticism met another type of monk, the Benedictine.

St. Benedict, who was born at Norcia, seventy miles from Rome, in 480, had been a monk for perhaps thirty years when he wrote his famous rule. He had been a solitary, he had been a reformer, he had been a founder. His rule, which to-day is still the guide of the 25,000 religious who bear his name, had a fortune such as came to no other in the west. It became and remains *the* rule for monks. Its chief characteristics, the reasons for its success, were noted by the saint's first biographer, who was no less a personage than St. Gregory the Great. They are its practical moderation and its lucidity. Here we have a full code of monastic life, written for the average man who wills to give himself to God, "a school for beginners," says the rule, with monastic modesty, a school, however, where nothing less than perfection is aimed at and designed. The new rule is Roman in its impersonality. Not St. Benedict nor the personal prestige of any individual superior, but the rule, the "Holy Rule," the "Mistress Rule," is the final arbiter. It is objective, permanent, absolute—the abbot does but apply it, and first of all to himself.

The life it prescribes, though ascetic and severe, is never extravagantly so. Singularity is discouraged, and it is the common observance that is all important. There is no place here for the astounding feats of the earlier ascetics, and none for the eccentricity that was often their fruit.

The feature of the rule which was perhaps the most important of all, if the social effect of Benedictinism in the coming centuries be considered, was the monk's vow of stability. He became a monk pledged to live and die in the abbey to which his profession aggregated him. In a world where all was rapidly ceasing to be permanent, the stable Benedictine monk became universally the chief force staving off the final disruption.

Another feature of the rule must be noticed, for its immense effect on the spiritual life of the west, namely the devotion to the person of Our Lord which is evident in its every prescription. It is Christ whom the abbot must serve in his brethren, and the brethren obey in the abbot, and see in one another and in whoever they are called upon to help. The rule sets before the monk a daily "imitation of Christ" as his life's work, long before that famous phrase was coined, and wherever the rule went, there went as a first fundamental habit this fruitful devotion to Our Lord's humanity.

St. Benedict died about the year 550. Thirty years later the Lombards destroyed his foundation of Monte Cassino and the pope housed the refugee monks in the Lateran. The next pope—Gregory the Great (590–604)—was himself a monk, almost certainly a Benedictine monk, and he wrote the first life of the saint. They were Benedictine monks whom he sent to evangelise the English in 596, and in the next century the Holy Rule began to establish itself in Gaul. Slowly during the next hundred and fifty years, thanks in no small part to the willingness of the older monks to see its superiority as an instrument of perfection and as a code of practical life, the Benedictine rule replaced the rules of St. Cæsarius and St. Columbanus and the rest, and by the time of Charlemagne (768–814) it was in full activity as one of the main forces of social, as of spiritual, regeneration.

By the end of the fifth century the whole of the west was ruled by Barbarian kings, Arians all or Pagans. The emperor, too, at this moment, was the Monophysite Anastasius I (491–518). Nowhere, save in Ireland, did Catholics obey a Catholic sovereign. Then, in 496, Clovis, the king of the Franks, a Pagan, was baptised at Reims by the Catholic bishop St. Rémy. The importance of this conversion was immense. The Franks were perhaps the most brutal of all the barbarous Barbarians who had wrested kingdoms from the decaying empire. They were to show themselves the most capable, too, and they were the only Barbarians whom no difference of belief divided from the people they ruled. From the beginning the Frankish kingdom had the enthusiastic support of the Catholic bishops. Alone of all these races that then ruled the dismembered provinces the Franks survived, to be a permanent dominating influence in Europe.

The sixth century saw the Franks extend their power over the whole of France, subduing the Burgundians of the south and the east and the Visigoths of the south. Gaul was freed of its Arian kings. But the Frank, too often, did not lose his brutality at baptism, and the pages of the contemporary historian, St. Gregory of Tours, are filled with stories of treachery, rapine, and murder that have scarcely an equal in history. To the wars against the other Barbarians there succeeded civil wars between the descendants of Clovis, and in these the last material remnants of the Roman order were gradually broken and destroyed.

In this new anarchy the Church suffered heavily. It was a natural feature of the situation, under this first of the Barbarian races to be Catholicised, that the king's interest in Catholicism took the form of protection and patronage. It was unfortunate that the king managed from the first to gain a say in the nomination of the bishops. From the time of the Council of Orleans (511) no man could be consecrated without the king's leave, and there now began that close dependence of the Church on the State that has characterised Catholicism in France, and elsewhere, down to our own times.

The peculiar social development of which the anarchical sixth and seventh centuries were the scene, made the king's interest in the personalities of the bishops still more natural and more urgent, for as these centuries wore on, more and more did the process extend by which Gaul was governed by the local great man, layman or ecclesiastic, count or bishop or abbot, whose only tie with the king was that of personal loyalty. What came to matter most of the king was that the occupant of a see, the head of a monastery, was personally faithful to himself and capable of carrying the heavy burden of civil and military duties which accompanied the office and which, increasingly, overshadowed its religious implications. Already, and to some extent inevitably, by the force of circumstances no less than by the preference of individual wills, that mischievous institution the prince-bishop was beginning to show itself more or less everywhere. And in these two centuries when Gaul was slowly turning into France, the kings not only interfered with the nomination of the right kind of men to the episcopate, but very often thrust into it, for reasons of state, their own brutal warriors. Whence a whole train of eccesiastical scandals and a decay of religion in Gaul that, as the seventh century drew to its end, was well nigh universal.

Before that time, however, and before the great reforming effort of St. Boniface, there had been a notable reaction against this Paganising of Catholicism. It centred round the Irish missionary monk, St. Columbanus.

St. Columbanus, a native of Leinster, was formed in the great abbey of Bangor under its founder, Comgall. His letters and his poems show him to have been a master of all the culture of his time. Somewhere about his fortieth year, in 590, he won the reluctant consent of his abbot to a plan to go forth with twelve companions and, in a penitential exile, to settle abroad. The appearance at the court of the decadent kings of the Franks of these Irish monks, ascetics who were at the same time scholars and apostles, burning with zeal to instruct ignorance and

to reprove sin, was the sensation of the time. Their dis-
interestedness and sincerity, their utter fearlessness and
lack of human respect, their insistence on the need for penance and their new system of frequent private confession,
their whole manner of life, in fact, while it speedily
lost them the favour of the kings, brought armies of
disciples to their feet. Immediately monasteries of the Irish
type began to be founded in the wild country of the
Vosges—Annegray, Fontaines, and Luxeuil—and then, when
St. Columbanus had paid the inevitable penalty of his
candour about royal adulteries, further afield among the
Alemanni of the modern Alsace and in Switzerland and the
Lombard territories of northern Italy. Wherever the saint
passed monasteries sprang up, and at the most famous
of them all, Bobbio, in northern Italy, he died in 615.
His immense energy, his uncompromising devotion to
the double work of restoring Christian life and evangelis-
ing the heathen, he left as a legacy to all his many
foundations. And his great example was to be for generations yet to come a never-failing inspiration that drew
hundreds of other Irish monks to people these monasteries
and to found others and to become the first preachers
of the Gospel in southern Belgium, Luxembourg, Switzerland, Lorraine, and Bavaria. Among such Irish founders of
German sees are St. Corbinian of Freising, St. Virgil of
Salzburg, and the martyr, St. Killian of Würzburg.

And the great fervour of the new movement had its
effects, naturally, on the religious life of the Frankish
Church also. A host of new Frankish apostles went forth
from the new monasteries to reform the sees of Gaul,
St. Omer to Boulogne, for example, St. Amand to Flanders
to be bishop of Maastricht, St. Eloy to Noyon, St. Leger
to Autun, and many others.

While the Frankish kings were establishing themselves
as masters of France, the Visigoths and Suevi in Spain
were giving up their Arianism. The Suevi of Galicia and
Portugal were won over by the influence of St. Martin,
bishop of Braga, about the middle of the sixth century.
The conversion of the Visigoths, however, involved a great
family tragedy for the reigning house.

The king of the Visigoths, Leovigild, was a great law-
giver and reformer, a great soldier too. The first years of

his reign had seen Justinian's successful recovery of certain regions of the coast around Valencia, and the establishment in Spain of a regular Byzantine province. From that moment a natural suspicion of imperial schemes for such a complete reconquest in Spain as had just expelled the Ostrogoths from Italy took possession of the king's mind and, since the Byzantines were Catholics, there went with it a disposition to identify Catholicism with treasonable sympathies. Domestic religous dissensions brought the trouble to a head. By this time all the royal families of the West were Catholic, save the Visigoths. Wherever, in future, these Spanish kings married, they must marry Catholics if they married women of their own rank, and married to form alliances. So it happened that the wife of Leovigild's heir, Hermenegild, was a Catholic. To satisfy her Arian mother-in-law she was forcibly re-baptised. Her husband supported her protests and was thereupon sent in a kind of disgrace to Seville. There he became a Catholic under the influence of the bishop, St. Leander. The exact sequence of the events that followed is uncertain. There was a civil war. Hermenegild was defeated and imprisoned. His allies, the Suevi, fell with him and the Visigoths made themselves masters of the whole peninsula. Then Hermenegild was murdered.

The consequent repression of Catholicism lasted as long as Leovigild lived, but in 586 his second son, Reccared, who had succeeded him, recalling St. Leander, made him his chief minister and announced his own intention of embracing the faith of the dead Hermenegild. The Arian nobility were gradually won over and in a great council at Toledo, in 589, the great reconciliation was given due shape, the king, his nobles, and the eight Arian bishops making their renunciation and submission to Catholicism. It was just over two hundred years since the Council of Constantinople which marked the end of the heresy among the Romans themselves.

Spanish Catholicism had one great advantage unknown north of the Pyrenees, namely its organisation round the single primatial see of Toledo. It was also intensely national, the bishops being named by the kings, and the usual ills following in the train of this custom, whatever the benefits that came from it to the State. The isolation of Spain increased the evil. In the next hundred and twenty years no influence from the outside world seems ever to have disturbed the country's religious stagnation. Catholicism might have saved the national vitality, but Catholicism in Spain was, by the time of the Moorish conquest (711), very largely what the decadent monarchy and aristocracy had made it

There is, however, one great personage whose history relieves the dreary record of seventh-century Spain. This is St. Isidore of Seville, the one scholar the west produced at this time. For thirty-six years (600–636) he was bishop of Seville. A monk himself, he wrote a celebrated rule for monks, and in his works he provided his own age, and those that followed, with a very encyclopædia of religious learning, and thus he has the great importance, historically, that he is a link between the Fathers and the schoolmen of the later centuries.

The closing years of the troubled sixth century saw the election of the pope who is generally regarded as the greatest of all his line, St. Gregory the Great. His early life had been given to the service of the State and he had risen to be the chief magistrate of Rome, his native city. He had become a monk and then the pope sent him for some years to Constantinople, as his representative at the imperial court. He was fifty years of age when, in 590, he was elected pope.

St. Gregory has already been mentioned in connection with Benedictine monasticism, and the effect of his action here would alone entitle him to a great place in history. He has another claim in his vast array of writings on religious matters. It is no exaggeration to say that what St. Augustine was for the medieval scholar, St. Gregory was for the ordinary reader. For he is the great populariser of doctrine, one of the chief influences indeed on the popular faith and piety of the next thousand years, and his writings are the first great storehouse of stories about saints and their miracles. One of his books—the *Regula Pastoralis*—had a popularity, throughout the Middle Ages, equal to that of St. Augustine's *De Civitate Dei*. It is a practical treatise on the spirituality and the skill that should be found in bishops and in all who have the care of souls. For centuries it served to give the paro-

chial clergy their "professional" formation. St. Gregory
was one of those for whom solitude had always a strong
attraction. He was a chronic invalid and in the eternal
plague, famine and war that filled the life of his time,
he saw signs, not unwelcome, that the world was nearing
its end. His whole care was spiritual, to bring himself
and his flock to the approaching day of reckoning with
something like the required dispositions. And yet he was
the most capable, the most practical, and, in the ultimate effects of his action, one of the most successful of
all the popes.

Just midway between his birth and his election as
pope there had swept down upon Italy, barely recovered
from the thirty years' horror of the imperial reconquest,
the Lombards, the last wave of the Barbarian Invasion.
Justinian's achievement was in a few years all but destroyed. Everywhere, save in the great towns and their
hinterland, Italy fell to the invader, and for another hundred and sixty years the slow, steady Lombard attack
was to be pressed on the cities too. The empire was too
weak to conquer the Lombards, barely strong enough
to keep them in check, and too proud to negotiate with
them. St. Gregory was, nominally, merely a subject in the
empire, but it was to him that Rome turned at every
crisis where the Lombards were concerned. He begged
his people off and he bought them off. He ransomed the
captives and organised great relief services for widows
and orphans. Finally, in 598, he secured a thirty years'
truce. It was St. Gregory who, in these years, was the real
ruler of Rome and in a very real sense he is the founder
of the Papal Monarchy.

St. Gregory was a much-consulted pope and his letters
show him actively intervening in all parts of the Church.
A general reform of Rome and the sees of Italy began,
with such drastic remedies as the deposition of bishops
where this was necessary. In Gaul, too, he did his best
to promote the much-needed reforms, insisting that laymen should not be made bishops. But his appeals here
fell on deaf ears and he never saw assembled the national
council for which he so often appealed.

The greatest event, in the issue, of his great reign,
and one which gave the saint unalloyed consolation, was

the mission to convert the English. It was in 596 that the pope sent Benedictine monks, from the monastery he had himself founded in his own home on the Cœlian Hill, to the court of Ethelbert, king of Kent, whose wife was a Catholic, daughter of one of the Frankish kings.

It was not that there were none but Pagans in the island. The Church had been established there since the last years of the third century, for three British bishops sat in the Council of Arles in 314. But in this distant province the invasion of the Barbarians had been the most destructive of all. The new-comers in Britain were the closest to the savage of all the marauders of the times, except perhaps the Huns, and they showed a special hatred for all that was Christian. Between them and the older inhabitants, even a century after the worst of the fury was over, there was such a chasm of hate and mistrust that the British bishops flatly refused to do anything to Christianise them. The Roman mission to convert the English was to accomplish its work while they looked on. For a few years success came easily and sees were established at Canterbury, London, and Rochester. It is noteworthy that, in this church that was the direct creation of the papacy, no place whatever is given to the royal authority. Catholicism begins its life among the English in fullest independence of the State.

The next great development—after a Pagan reaction in Essex that lasted for several years—was the foundation in 625 of the see of York. Here, too, the king, Edwin, was presently converted and, gradually, his kingdom of Deira. But in 633 Edwin was killed in battle, fighting a strange alliance of Christian Britons and the Pagan Saxon king of Mercia. His successor, the head of a rival band of the royal family, was, however, a Catholic too and soon the work, so tragically interrupted, went forward once again. But it was not from Canterbury that Oswald had learnt his faith, nor from the Roman mission, but from the Irish monks established at Iona in Scotland.

This famous monastery had been founded in 563 by St. Columba, self-exiled in penance for his share in promoting a tribal war. It had been a centre for the conversion of the people of the Highlands, and now, with Oswald's succession as king of Northumbria, it was to provide for thirty years a succession of devoted monk-apostles who, tramping the fells and dales of northern England, first made it a stronghold of Catholicism. The first of these bishops from Iona was St. Aidan and he established his see at Lindisfarne.

Meanwhile the Roman mission in the south had continued to prosper. There was a second mission sent from Rome about 630, and by 644 the English had the first bishop of their own stock. And now, in Northumbria, the two branches of Catholicism met, one in faith, but with different calendars and different liturgical customs. A great conference at Whitby (664) settled that the Roman ways should prevail. Four years later there arrived from Rome the Greek monk, St. Theodore of Tarsus, as archbishop of Canterbury, and under his able practised rule the Church in England attained a real practical unity of life. He it was who finally arranged the different sees and introduced the Roman order throughout. He did more, for he was perhaps the most learned man of his time, and from Rome he brought the abbot Hadrian, the African, who founded a great school at Canterbury, and also Benet Biscop, a north-country nobleman turned monk, who was to establish two great monasteries at Jarrow and Wearmouth. From these foundations came all the early culture of medieval England, much of England herself, and the life which, along with what came from Ireland, was in the next century to revitalise the countries of the continent. The greatest glory of Benet Biscop's monasteries was St. Bede.

St. Bede (672–735) is the measure of the success and the importance of the Roman recapture of Britain. This Englishman, born within twenty years of the death of the last Pagan king, is not only the great scholar of his age, but one of the greatest of all time. Like St. Isidore of Seville he gathers up and transmits for the future of learning all he can salvage from the past. He comments on Holy Scripture, he writes on Astronomy and Mathematics, betraying everywhere what he was and what he gloried to be, the monk-schoolmaster. We have a number of his sermons, we have some of his letters, and we have his verses. But in St. Bede we have also something peculiar and personal, we have the first English historian. It is the

Ecclesiastical History of the English People that gives St.
Bede his great place, the place due to genius. The character of this work, its literary grace, the even fairness of
its treatment, make St. Bede the superior of any other
historian for centuries yet to come. It is the one production of his time that is as fresh and living to-day as when
it was written, twelve hundred years ago.

One of St. Bede's pupils, Egbert, was the founder of
the school of York, and from the school of York came
Alcuin, and at the end of this eighth century it was to
Alcuin, principally, that Charlemagne turned when he
sought a schoolmaster to revive the intellectual life of
Gaul and Italy.

A still more distinguished place in history must be
given to a contemporary of St. Bede, another English
Benedictine monk, Winfrid, or Boniface. His early formation, like that of St. Bede, was mixed, partly Irish, partly
Roman, and his great culture may stand as a symbol of
the Catholic achievement in the south of England—for
Boniface was born in Devon and formed in a Hampshire
monastery—just as St. Bede symbolises the peak of the
achievement in the north. Of St. Boniface it has been
well said that no other Englishman has ever had so great
an effect on European development. The justification for
this somewhat startling judgement is the work done by
the saint, not only in converting a large part of Germany,
and in reforming the church in Gaul, but also in giving
German Catholicism its definitive organisation and in doing this as the accredited mandatory of the Roman See.

The saint, under Roman directions, first served a missionary apprenticeship of three years with St. Willibrord,
the English missionary who had founded the see of Utrecht and is the pioneer of Dutch Catholicism. Then, in
722, the pope, Gregory II (715–731), recalled him and
consecrated him as chief of an independent mission to
Germany. The status as agent of the Apostolic See and the
protection of the king of the Franks, Charles Martel,
were to be the saint's chief support in the next thirty
years. In that time, with the help of a host of English
Benedictines, men and women, St. Boniface evangelised
Hesse and Thuringia, founding monasteries, reviving ancient sees, and establishing new ones. The next pope,

Gregory III, gave him the pallium of an archbishop, and soon there were eight of these new churches—Salzburg, Freising, Ratisbon, Passau, Duraburg, Erfurt, Würzburg, and Eichstätt—founded now in a stable, permanent fashion, with a bishop resident as in the Roman tradition, and the one weakness of the Irish mission thereby well guarded against, namely the lack of local stability in the missioner or bishop.

As reformer in Gaul St. Boniface had before him a more difficult task than that which he faced in Germany as reformer. The Frankish kings, who were willing enough to protect the mission that worked on the frontier of their power and beyond it, looked askance at a movement of reform and reorganisation that must, necessarily, weaken their hold on the Frankish episcopate. The saint managed, indeed, to convoke the national council that the popes had desiderated for a century. Many vacant sees were filled and new sees founded. The discipline of clerical life was restored, at any rate as an ideal towards which all ought to work. But to the new device of subjecting the bishops to the archbishops, for the preservation of the newly restored order, the kings were steadily and successfully hostile. Not until the time of Charlemagne, sixty years later, did this essential feature of the reform find royal support.

St. Boniface's first missionary inspiration had been to evangelise the hardy, savage Pagans of the coast of Frisia. Thither, in the last years of his life, he returned, and there, at the great age of seventy-five, the welcome grace of martyrdom crowned his long life for Christ (755). The abbey church of Fulda, which he had founded, and where he lies buried, is to this day the centre of German Catholicism, a monument at once to Benedictine monachism, to English missionary zeal, and to the Apostolic See's use of both in the service of the gospel.

4

The Assault on Christendom
and the Recovery, 74–1123

ABOUT THE time when St. Gregory the
Great was beginning his career as papal ambassador at
Constantinople (580), a boy was born in Arabia whose
life was to cause a revolution in the east that still endures
and to affect the Church and all Europe very intimately.
This was Mahomet, and the means of his influence was
the new religion he created, Islam. It was a simple creed,
simply organised, with elements copied from Judaism
and, to a less extent, from the heresies of the Monophysite
Christians of Arabia. There is one only God. Mahomet is
his prophet and on God's revelations to the prophet all
was founded. The morality was not exacting, the ideals
proposed were extremely materialist, a simple code of
external ritual justified the believer and maintained him
in holiness. And upon the believer there lay the sacred obligation to propagate his creed, to destroy the unbeliever,
and to wage the holy war for this end.

Islam's first achievement was to unite the wandering
Arabs of the desert. In Omar, Mahomet's first successor,
they found a military leader of genius and within ten
years of the founder's death the Mahometans had not only
overrun the whole Arabian peninsula, but were masters
of the Persian Empire, of Egypt, of Palestine, and of
Syria. Fifty years later the advance was renewed. It was
now Roman Africa which fell to them (695), and in 711
they crossed the straits of Gibraltar and conquered Spain.

Nor did they halt, but passed the Pyrenees and overran all the south of France. All the great islands of the Mediterranean—save Corsica—were Mahometan too, and in 717 they laid siege to Constantinople and came within an ace of capturing it. The hero of the siege, and of the Mahometan repulse in the east, was the emperor Leo III (717-741). In the west it was the Frank, Charles Martel, who stemmed the advance, defeating them with great slaughter in 732 at the battle of Poitiers. But the whole Mediterranean, from the Rhone westward to Gibraltar and thence east to Alexandria and north again to Antioch, continued to be in their power. The siege of Christendom had begun, and in every generation, for another nine hundred years, there was made upon it, from some quarter of the Mahometan world, a violent assault.

It was now to be one of the greater misfortunes of Christendom that, in the first centuries of this new religious menace, the long-latent antagonism between Latin-speaking and Greek-speaking Catholics grew steadily more acute, and the obedience of the east to the Roman Primacy was, first of all, seriously weakened and then disappeared altogether.

The occasion of the first trial which, during this period, afflicted the much-tried churches of the east was the series of religious reforms introduced from about 725 by the emperor Leo III. Leo's immense services to the empire and to Christendom as the common defender against Islam have been referred to. He has also a great place in Byzantine history for his scientific reorganisation of the State. His religious policy, a practical demonstration that the emperor was supreme in ecclesiastical affairs no less than in matters of state, was not unnatural, given his character and upbringing. The point at which it came into most serious conflict with traditional practices was the imperial prohibition to give any religious reverence to the images of the saints, and the order to remove these from the churches. Everywhere there were riots and presently, for the recalcitrant clergy, deposition, imprisonment, and even sentences of death. The popes intervened with protestations, and even with the bold reply, to the emperor's threat of an invasion of Italy, that they would summon the Barbarian princes to defend them. And it was only the lucky accident of a tempest destroying the imperial fleet sent to arrest him which saved the hardy pope.

The emperor clung tenaciously to his policy, and his successor, Constantine V (741–775), showed himself yet more bitter. In this reign, indeed, the State went still further. Not only was the practice of honouring images forbidden, but the principle of so doing was attacked as sinful, and at the Council of Hieria the emperor found 338 bishops willing to proclaim this as Catholic teaching (753). This decree was the signal for a real crusade of Iconoclasm. Most of the clergy yielded, like their bishops. But the monks held firm everywhere, and presently they began to be put to death and tortured throughout the empire.

When Constantine V died the persecution slackened, and after the coming to power in 780 of the empress Irene (regent for her baby son, Constantine VI) the first moves were made towards a Catholic restoration. This was formally accomplished at a General Council [1] in 787. The pope—Adrian I (772–795)—sent legates to preside at it, who were bearers of a letter setting forth the traditional Catholic teaching on the lawfulness of reverencing images. The Roman directions were accepted and the decree of 753 condemned.

But its sixty years of vigorous triumph had made Iconoclasm a vested interest in the Byzantine state. The army, in particular, was attached to the heresy, and a military revolution in 813 gave it twenty years more of life. It was the work of the empress Theodora (regent from 842 for the child, Michael III) and of St. Methodius of Constantinople finally to re-establish Catholic practices and to bring about the general acceptance of Catholic teaching. But for the best part of a century there had been a most serious division between the eastern bishops and Rome, and the nascent, anti-Roman spirit had been greatly strengthened by it. If ever the occasion should have come when, in just such another schism, Rome did not have to her advantage that the point of division was a traditional Catholic practice as dear to the Byzantine people as to herself, if ever that time should come, the

---

[1] Reckoned as the Second Council of Nicea.

link between the churches would be seriously and permanently menaced.

Charles Martel, whose victory at Poitiers in 732 saved France and northern Europe from Mahometanism as Leo III's defence of Constantinople saved the east of Europe, was not the titular king of the Franks. His power came from his being the chief of a family which, for some generations now, had really ruled, the kingship of the decadent half-imbecile descendants of Clovis being hardly even nominal. He was the greatest soldier the west had seen for centuries, and in the nearly thirty years of his power (714–741) he gave France such a unity as it had not known since it was the Roman province of Gaul. His son and successor, Pepin, continued the great work, with less ferocity and a new finesse, and in 752 managed to bring about the explicit transfer of the royal authority to his own family. The pope's sanction was asked, and obtained, for the *coup d'etat*, and the new king was solemnly consecrated to his office by St. Boniface. Three years later the ceremony was repeated, the pope himself now anointing Pepin and with him his two sons also, Carloman and the future Charlemagne, and declaring: "It is the Lord who through our lowliness consecrates you as king." In that act there was inaugurated an alliance between the Papacy and the French people that was destined to be the cornerstone of the building up of medieval Europe, an alliance which is by no means yet at an end, an association that would seem to have about it something that is perpetual. Certainly nothing, ever since, has been able to affect one of these powers that has not simultaneously affected the other.

This papal ratification in act, of the decision previously given, was associated with another set of happenings destined also to furnish the Middle Ages and all later history with one of the most striking figures in its complex design, namely the establishment of the popes as temporal rulers in Italy.

Like many another great change this was not the outcome of any cleverly thought-out plan so much as what was found to have resulted once a problem had been faced and a practical solution attempted. Ever since the time of St. Gregory's youth Italy had been the scene of a

long war of raids and sieges between Lombards and
Byzantines. With every generation the Byzantines grew
more feeble, and the new anxiety caused by the establishment of the strong Mahometan states left them less energy
than ever to defend what little territory remained to them
in Italy—Venice, Naples, Ravenna, Rome, and the country-
sides about these cities.

The pope was torn between the two forces. The Lombards were, by now, converted and showed themselves
pious Catholics, more than once being persuaded for love
of St. Peter to abandon their conquests and to raise the
siege of Rome. The loyalty of the popes to the decayed
and perishing Byzantine regime was its one last security.
This the folly of Leo III seriously undermined when, in
pursuit of his policy to reform popular religion,[2] he
planned to kidnap Pope Gregory II (715–731) as Constans II had kidnapped St. Martin.[3] At Rome everyone
rallied to defend the pope and a Lombard army too
marched to his aid. The emperor had to be content with
confiscating the vast papal estates in Sicily, from which,
very largely, the poor of Rome had been maintained for
centuries.

All was ready for a breach between the emperor and
this last loyal subject—subject in name merely, and really
an independent prince whose prestige the emperor could
not afford to lose. The advent of a new Lombard king—
Aistulf—in 749, who was not to be bought off by hints
about St. Peter, brought matters to a crisis. There was a
new invasion. The emperor could do nothing and would
do nothing, except order the pope to order Aistulf to
retire, and in despair the pope—Stephen III—went for
aid to the king of the Franks. It was while on this momentous errand that he re-consecrated him as king.

Pepin and his people rallied to the cause of St. Peter.
The Franks invaded Italy and drove out the Lombards
from the menaced territory, and then settled a great deal
of the course of future history by handing it in sovereignty
to the pope.

For fifty years the popes had enjoyed a *de facto* in-

---

[2] Cf. *supra*, p. 78.
[3] Cf. *supra*, p. 52.

dependence of any political power. Now they were to be, *de iure* too, the subjects of no earthly ruler. If only the new State could maintain itself, a chronic anxiety was solved—if only the popes could secure that the new sovereignty never became, what every other sovereignty has become sooner or later, the object of human ambition, human lust for money and for power.

Alas, the first years of its history showed that along with their new security the popes had acquired a new source of anxiety of the gravest description. It was a rough and barbarous age, when treachery and cruelty stalked undisguised and were the ordinary accompaniment of what, for want of a better word, we must call political life. These dark forces were now to play about the new papal throne too and, inevitably, to affect the papacy with it.

The ruler of the new State was a priest and the most important personages in it were clerics. A clerical aristocracy was inevitable. But the older military aristocracy made a strong bid for supremacy. It was natural, and inevitable, that the easiest way to secure this was to secure the papacy for some baron. So far it had never been worth any layman's while to make himself pope, but now whoever was pope was king, and for generations henceforward the baronage lost no opportunity to install its own candidate as against the candidate of the electors, the clergy of Rome.

The first attempts at violence were made on the death of Pope Paul (767) when the military succeeded in installing their candidate, a layman, Constantine. He managed to keep his hold for the best part of a year, and then the clerical party, with the aid of the Lombards, overthrew him and, with cruelties equal to those he had himself used, Constantine and his successors were thrust out.

Pepin died in 768 and by 771 his younger son, called Charlemagne, was master in his place. His advent coincided with the election of the long-lived Adrian I (772–795).

The first great event to mark the period of the peaceful co-operation of Adrian and Charles in the general superintendence of the well-being of Christendom—for this and nothing less was what Charlemagne's regime entailed—

was the Frankish conquest of the Lombards (773-774). The king of the Lombards henceforth was the king of the Franks—whence the first appearance, for the ruler of the papal State, of the menace whose possibility was always, hereafter, to haunt his dreams, a menace to be conjured away by all the means he could dispose of; to wit, the strong protector who was also his next-door neighbour. Charlemagne, king of the Franks, ready from the other side of the Alps to descend and protect the popes when need called for it, was one thing. Charlemagne as the most powerful ruler in Italy was another, and soon the inevitable had happened. The new ruler of the Lombards could not but be the most interested person in Italy in all that regarded the fortunes of the papal State, and his honorary title, "Patrician of Rome," afforded him a means of establishing himself at the heart of the State's administration, so that, gradually, imperceptibly, the State began to be considered as in some way within the empire Charlemagne was building up. The change was very definitely marked when Pope Adrian died (795), for his successor, Leo III, notifying Charles of his election, begged a deputation from him to receive the Romans' oaths of fidelity. Charles is now, in some way, joint sovereign with the pope, and in his reply he admonishes the pope to show himself a good and wise ruler. As he had already done in the east, Cæsar was now obtaining a kind of suzerainty over the Church in the west.

It was Charlemagne's achievement to build up a great State that stretched from the Ebro to the Elbe and from the North Sea to beyond the Tiber. It was a real State, not a mere collection of territories and jurisdictions, and its basis was a serious attempt to bring about the City of God upon earth. Charlemagne is the Christian prince in a far truer sense than could ever be asserted of Constantine or Justinian. It was through the common faith of his peoples that he ruled, and upon that faith that he built, and it was to promote the well-being of that faith, and the exension of its empire, that he toiled for forty years. He was its champion against Islam in the south and against the heathen tribes of Germany—the Saxons in the north.

It took thirty years of war before he had these last finally tamed and Christianised by force—an unfortunate introduction to the Church which may have affected all subsequent German Catholicism. In this new Christian province eight new sees were established. It was a kind of completion of the labours of St. Boniface, and it is worthy of note that it was the fellow-countryman of St. Boniface, Alcuin, who led the protest of the Church against Charlemagne's forcible conversion of the vanquished enemy.

The long years of Charlemagne's reign (768–814) were filled with the work of restoration. Schools were founded everywhere, ecclesiastical life was reformed and reorganised, every aspect of religious life became a main interest for the State's protecting care. Church and State seemed at last fused into one thing, bishops and popes were the Frankish king's enthusiastic assistants. When, on Christmas Day, 800, Leo III solemnly crowned Charles as emperor, restoring the empire of the West in his person, the gesture seemed to seal divinely the great successes of his life.

There is, however, another side of this picture. In this the new State is seen as something that threatens to swamp the Church. The emperor's will is everything. If he is friendly the Church will advance. Where he bids her halt, halt she must. Charlemagne was, for example, no lover of monasticism. Learning and ability to rule were what he sought in ecclesiastics. He continued to use the great abbeys to reward the faithful service of his great men, and if, very often, the high officers of State were clerics they were by no means always models of clerical life. It was the emperor who named the bishops, and as innovation, from the time of Charlemagne's son, Louis the Pious, he began to name the pope too.

How the Church would have freed herself from a patronage that, in the end, must stifle all her liberty of action it is difficult to say. The titanic struggle that must have ensued never took place, for in the half-century after the great emperor's death his empire fell to pieces, and nowhere had the Church a second Charlemagne to contend with. The one great problem, for the rival kings, no less than for the popes and the bishops, during the next hundred years (814-936) was to survive the social effects of the political chaos and the chronic civil war.

To add to the horror the Mahometans renewed their aggression, taking now to the seas, so that the western Mediterranean was closed to Christian shipping, raiding the coasts of France and Italy and, in 844, sacking Rome and the tombs of the Apostles. And from the north another enemy descended, the pirate tribes of Denmark, hordes of savages, ferociously anti-Christian. It was in the last years of Charlemagne's reign that they had first appeared in force. They sacked Lindisfarne in 793 and made their first raids on Ireland—where they finally established a kingdom—in 795. So began a new hundred years' scourge. Soon no river city was safe from their attacks and England especially lay at their mercy. Murder and pillage, the destruction of abbeys and shrines, everywhere marked their coming, and, their raids giving rise to settlements, for another hundred years and more they hung over northern Christendom, a menace that nothing could shake off. Alfred, in England, only saved half his kingdom at the cost of recognising their sovereignty in the Danelaw (878), but this partial arrest of their progress was followed by their complete failure in the famous siege of Paris (888) and their defeat in the great battle of Louvain (891). The survival of Christendom was secured. But these pirates had effected the most serious setback the Church had known since the Roman persecutions ceased, four hundred years before. By the end of the ninth century western Europe presented a scene of indescribable chaos, an immense waste, with only a few islets of security and ordered life scattered about it here and there. And for another generation what was left of Christendom had barely strength to breathe.

In these years of endless disorder, these centuries of continuous invasion, war, rapine, and destruction, the nascent ecclesiastical system collapsed along with the rest. Learning disappeared and the clergy, too often, hardly knew more than the bare rudiments of Christian Doctrine and the forms of sacramental practice. Clerical discipline there was little or none. The correction of disorders and ill-living became difficult to the point of impossibility, even where bishops were to be found zealous for the old traditions of holiness of life. Such bishops were rare. The unfortunate fusion of civil, military, and religious offices in the person of the bishop, his duties as a temporal ruler, bore, in the circumstances of this time, all the fulness of their evil fruit. And there came to its terrible maturity the practice of lay usurpation in the matter of episcopal and abbatial nominations. Never has the Church known, before or since, such bishops as those who, all too frequently, in these terrible centuries, preyed on the sees of western Europe. They were in ways of life exactly like the brutal, illiterate, and licentious baronage from whom they sprang. Often, in defiance of all law and tradition, they married and then made it the main object of their life to transmit the see, like some piece of personal property, to one of their sons. Often, again, they had bought their nomination to the see, and their reign was a long financial torture for the unfortunate subjects, while the prelate endeavoured to recoup his initial expenses.

A study of the scandals which, almost without a break, disgraced the first of all the sees for a hundred years and more, reveals the extent to which the bankruptcy of elementary order and security had damaged the Church. The situation at Rome was complicated by the magnitude of the prize which the see offered to wickedness, by the new tradition of lay domination in the—nominal—election of the pope, and by the permanent place in the papal State of a barbarous and unruly baronage. Between the murder of Pope John VIII (882) and the Council of Sutri (1046), which marks the definite end of these horrors, there were in a hundred and sixty years, thirty-seven popes. By no means all of these were bad men. The majority were good, and among them were many energetic reformers. But far too many of these good popes died violent deaths at the hands of their opponents. The climax came when the Roman family called the House of Theophylact laid hands on the see, and for nearly seventy years its chiefs appointed as pope whom they willed—the real "bad popes" who are the stock figures of religious controversy.

Nevertheless, a ninth-century pope—St. Nicholas I—is

one of the three to whom alone, out of the 260,[4] posterity
has given the name of "the Great." He played a masterly
part in the affair of the schism of Photius,[5] and showed
the fulness of the traditional Roman concern for principle
in his refusal, despite threats and an invasion of his States,
to acknowledge the divorce of Lothair, King of Lorraine
(863).

Whenever the masters of the Roman see were the military aristocracy, it might almost be taken for granted that
a bad election would be made, and once the empire of
Charlemagne had really disappeared, the only competition was between the rival Roman families.

Half-way through the tenth century, however, Germany
produced a great king, Otto I (936–973), and in him the
empire was restored, Rome given a new nominal master,
and the much-tried papacy a faint hope of better days.
In 963 Otto deposed (quite unlawfully, but none the less
effectively) the thoroughly unworthy pope John XII (955–
964), and for the rest of his reign kept as strict a control
over Rome and the papal elections as circumstances allowed. His son—Otto II (973–983)—and his grandson—
Otto III (983–1002)—followed the same policy, and
hence, during the last half of the tenth century, thanks to
the imperial intervention and the emperor's support of the
reform element, good popes were at times enabled to
stem the evil tide. But, once again, for all that the system
was now bringing good results, it was the same bad old
system of dependence on the State. Reform, the permanent good living of Christians, was at the mercy of a
chance, the chance that the emperor was himself a good
man and interested in reform. What would happen should
an emperor succeed who was no better than the baronage
he had supplanted? The next century was to see two
such emperors, Conrad II (1024–1039) and his grandson,
Henry IV (1056–1106) and in the reign of this last
prince the great war for the independence of religion
began in earnest.

These emperors of the new German tradition were not,

---

[4] The other two are St. Leo I (440-461) and St. Gregory I
(590-604).

[5] Cf. *infra*, p. 96 seq.

however, the only forces working for reform, nor yet the first in the field. To say nothing of the different popes who only failed because the material circumstances of their reign made success impossible, but who, none the less, by their efforts kept alive the memory of ideals, there was the great movement associated with Cluny, and the successful local efforts of such prelates as St. Dunstan, Archbishop of Canterbury (?907–908).

The Benedictine monastery of Cluny in Burgundy was founded in 910. From the beginning its aim was a complete restoration of the life according to the Holy Rule strictly interpreted, and the centre of that life was the sacred liturgy carried out with all the perfection possible. The monks of Cluny never left their cloister. Their apostolate consisted in attracting men to the cloister by the holiness of their own lives and the fact, evident above all else, that the life was a complete and entire service of God. Cluny was exceptional in its status, among the abbeys of the time, for its only earthly superior was the pope himself. This was a revolutionary change in the canon law, which for five hundred years nearly had placed every monastery under the jurisdiction of the local bishop. The episcopate was now so generally corrupted by the spirit of the world that to be subject to it was often a direct menace to spiritual and temporal well-being. Cluny was exempt and independent of the bishop.

The second new feature about the Cluniac life was that when the abbey, little by little, found itself called in to reform other monasteries and to found other monasteries, it brought about an affilation between these and itself. Soon there was in existence something the Church had never before seen, a great congregation or order of monks, living in hundreds of priories, and all subject to a single common superior, the abbot of Cluny. Such a strict union and dependence of the lesser houses upon Cluny was a safeguard for their spiritual future—for they all enjoyed the Cluniac exemption—and a source of immense strength to the movement for reform. Another source of the prosperity of the movement was the rare good fortune that the first five abbots of Cluny were not only men of exceptional personality and holiness of life, but also men with the art of being long-lived. In two hundred and fifty years there were but six changes of ruler,[6] and from within a century of the foundation, the abbot of Cluny was, after the pope, the most important personage in the Church, a kind of universal counsellor of popes and kings in all their difficulties.

Besides Cluny and the new form of Benedictine life it developed, the older tradition also at this time saw great reforms continually sweeping away the abuses that were inevitable in centuries of such disorder. St. Gerard of Brogne, about the time Cluny was founded, inaugurated a Benedictine revival that spread all over Flanders; other saints did the same for the country between the Moselle and the Vosges. The local princes aided in all these foundations, and so too did the bishops of the sees concerned, Cambrai, Liège, Metz, Toul, Verdun, Cologne, Mainz, Augsburg, Constance, and Ratisbon.

Germany had its own Cluny in Hirschau, and a similar movement to unite the abbeys to a single common centre met with equal success in Italy, both in Piedmont and in the south where the ancient abbey of Cava had presently four hundred other houses dependent on it.

Italy, from the end of this tenth century, was the scene of a still more striking monastic revival, the foundation by St. Romuald, in 982 of the order of Camaldoli. These new monks were hermits, and their whole way of living, the perpetual fast on bread and water, with vegetables as a feast-day luxury, and the terrible bodily penances, recalls the greatest days of the Fathers in the desert.

A second Italian foundation of this same time was that of the monks of Vallombrosa, made by St. John Gualbert. Here the life was Benedictine, but the spirit in which the Holy Rule was read was more that of St. Romuald.

All these new foundations, made in a time of such general laxity, were encouraged and blessed and supported even by the least likely of the popes of the time, John XI and John XII (for example) being among the strongest supporters of Cluny.

But it was Cluny that was the most flourishing of all the new ventures, and it stood in relation to them pretty much as the Jesuits, six hundred years later, were to

---

[6] A period in which there were forty-eight popes.

stand to the host of similar orders founded at the same time.

The successor to the emperor Otto III was St. Henry II (1002–1024). He showed himself a model sovereign and an energetic reformer of ecclesiastical life. In this he had the constant support of the pope Benedict VIII (1012–1024). In 1024 both the good pope and the saintly emperor died, and to each there succeeded a man thoroughly bad, the emperor Conrad II and Pope John XIX, Benedict VIII's unworthy brother. When John XIX died, eight years later, his nephew succeeded as Benedict IX and the worst scandals of the preceding century were speedily renewed. The crisis came in 1046. Benedict had abdicated and Gregory VI had been chosen—by simony it is usually said—in his place. Benedict had then returned and endeavoured to reinstate himself. Meanwhile there was a third claimant to the papacy, Silvester III, the product of a "deposition" of Benedict IX in 1044. The new emperor, Henry III (1039–1056), was the patron of Benedict's party among the baronage and in 1046 he marched on Rome with an army to put an end to the scandals and protect his own interests. At the Council of Sutri he deposed all three claimants, and nominated as pope a good German prelate, the bishop of Bamberg, who took the name of Clement II. The emperor had no sooner gone back to Germany than Benedict IX reappeared and, aided by his faction, re-established himself, while Clement died, apparently of poison. It was a year before the emperor was free to intervene, and he then (1048) named a second German pope, Damasus II, who reigned only three weeks. Again there was a long vacancy—during which Benedict IX finally disappeared—and then in 1049 the emperor named his third pope, the bishop of Toul, who took the name of Leo IX. With this appointment a new age in the history of the Church and of Europe definitely begins.

St. Leo IX brought with him to Rome in 1049 a whole *cortège* of able reformers, eager to assist in the great work now about to begin against simony and clerical ill-living, and the lay usurpation of the right to appoint to ecclesiastical offices. The reformers were not, however, by any means agreed as to the best means of the restoration, nor of the same mind as to its fundamental causes. Their divergences caused more than one halt in the next ten years, and they can be traced in the curious variations of policy shown in the four short pontificates of St. Leo IX (1049–1054), Victor II (1054–1057), Stephen X (1057–1058), and Nicholas II (1059–1061).

The main point about which the differences of the reformers centred was the attitude they should adopt towards the Catholic princes, and in the first place towards the emperor. One party, grateful to the emperor for all that he had done in the cause of reform, would willingly have seen the old tradition of Charlemagne's time strengthened and continued, and was quite willing that the emperor should name popes and bishops, provided he named good men and did not sell the appointments. St. Leo IX was, at first, of this way of thinking, and so, too, was the great Italian cardinal, St. Peter Damian. Another school of thought saw in this royal and imperial interference in ecclesiastical nominations the ultimate source of all the evils of the time. They wished, therefore, to see it utterly extirpated as a vicious innovation, and to restore everywhere the old tradition of the free elections of bishops by their clergy and of abbots by their monks. The first great leader of this party was Humbert, abbot of Moyenmoutier, whom Leo IX brought to Rome and, creating him cardinal, employed as his legate on important missions throughout his reign.

The new age began when St. Leo IX left Rome and began to tour Europe, holding councils everywhere in Italy and in France, where he preached the reform, and deposed unworthy bishops, punishing simony and clerical incontinence with the old penalties. From Reims and Mainz and Pressburg down through Italy to the south, the pope toiled unwearyingly in one council after another. Where he was unable to go he sent the new cardinals as his legates, and gradually the whole of the western Church came to understand, by personal contact with the pope, that the Roman See was giving itself wholeheartedly to a general restoration of Christian life in the Church and to the suppression of the shameful abuses that had, almost everywhere, become second nature.

St. Leo had begun his life as a soldier, and it was in a war for the defence of the people of southern Italy against the brutalities of their Norman invaders that his life came to an end (1054). To succeed him the emperor named the bishop of Eichstadt, who took the name of Victor II. He was the fourth, and the last, pope ever to be pope by the mere nomination of the emperor. For Henry III predeceased Victor, and the fact that the new emperor—Henry IV (1056-1106)—was a child of six gave the reformers in Rome their chance. Without awaiting any intimation of the imperial wishes, within a few hours, indeed, of the arrival of the news that Victor was dead, they elected one of St. Leo's cardinals, the abbot of Monte Cassino, Frederick of Lorraine. Stephen X—for so he called himself—was the first pope for centuries to be freely elected by the Roman clergy. All the pacts made in the last dark centuries giving the emperor rights in the matter were, this time, ignored. In this great gesture the will of Rome to emancipate the Church was manifest beyond all doubt.

Pope Stephen died, however, in less than a year. The Roman nobility, returning to the bad old days, forced the installation of a candidate of their own—Benedict X. But the clergy refused him recognition, and so, too, did the imperial court. In place of Stephen X the bishop of Florence was elected—Nicholas II—a disciple of Cardinal Humbert, the most radical of all the reformers and a Burgundian. The short two years of his reign saw two innovations of immense significance. A law was made, at the Roman Council of 1059, that henceforth the pope was to be elected by the cardinals alone, and an alliance was made between the papacy and the Normans. The emperor was thus shut out from all future interference in papal elections, and the popes had a protector should he attempt, by force of arms, to assert his claims.

By the time Nicholas II died (1061) the reform movement, it may be easily imagined, had made many enemies. There were the deposed bishops, and their families, and the families and friends of bishops not as yet deposed but likely to meet that fate if the reform was not checked. There were the various claims of the Roman baronage, foiled now for nearly thirty years, and since the recent new law about elections, there was the imperial court. The result of this was seen at once, in 1061. The cardinals elected the bishop of Lucca, a tried and experienced reformer, who had served preceding popes as legate. He took the name of Alexander II. The court, four weeks later, chose the bishop of Parma, the candidate of the Roman baronage, and sent an army into Italy to support him.

It was three years before the schism ended, and it did not end until Alexander had consented to lay his case before an imperially summoned council (1064). For the remaining nine years of his reign the pope was free to continue the great work of reforming the sees and abbeys through his legates and the councils they summoned. When he died (1073) the reform was solidly established, though by no means perfected, in almost every part of Christendom. Even the prince-bishops of Germany had had to bow to the inevitable and come to Rome to stand their trial for simony.

Then, with the death of Alexander II, there appeared at last in the supreme place the reformer who, despite his subordinate position, had towered above all the rest for nearly thirty years. This was the Cardinal Hildebrand, now elected pope as Gregory VII. His career had begun in 1045 as a secretary to Gregory VI. St. Leo IX had brought him back to Rome, made him a cardinal, and sent him as a legate to direct the reform in France. He had enjoyed the full confidence of Victor II and still more of Stephen X, whose dying instructions were that not until Hildebrand returned was the new pope to be elected. He had thus been instrumental in the election of Nicholas II and, two years later, it was his influence that brought about the election of Alexander II, too.

St. Gregory was a monk, and though not himself a Cluniac, in closest relation with Cluny and an enthusiastic patron of the great abbey whose abbot, St. Hugh, was one of his closest friends, and whose prior, Odo, he took away to become as cardinal-bishop of Ostia the chief of his legates and later Pope Urban II.

Hildebrand stands head and shoulders above all his contemporaries, and this not merely by strength of character or clearness of purpose, but by a realisation that the issues about which the battle was now joining were truly fundamental. He saw that the Papacy alone could save the Church, and that it was by a restoration of the tradition that salvation must come, and he saw, too, that a kind of campaign of scholarship must re-educate the Church with regard to such matters as the primatial action of the Holy See, the freedom of episcopal elections, the heinousness of simony and of breaches of the old tradition of clerical celibacy. He was the first to see the necessity of such propaganda, and from the moment of his return to Rome—twenty-three years before he was elected pope—he set himself to organise the necessary researches. The result was the gradual appearance of canon law books of a new type from which there came forth ultimately the great work of Gratian and the scientific Canon Law that has been the Church's most powerful instrument for the maintenance of good order.

St. Gregory VII was essentially a man of peace and, in all the long years he served the Holy See as cardinal, he is never found among the extremists. It is always his desire, saving the independence of the Holy See, to work with the emperor's co-operation. It is only by force of circumstances, faced with the fact that if the Church cannot dominate the emperor it must submit to be his servant, and that the emperor designs to make it his servant in perpetuity, that he is pushed into a war to the death and a policy that goes contrary to all his natural desires. The twelve years of his pontificate (1073–1085) were years of scarcely interrupted storm. The lay appointing to ecclesiastical offices (lay investiture) was forbidden now in stronger terms than ever and excommunication was threatened against those who disobeyed. The emperor Henry IV was notorious for his cynical traffic in bishoprics and abbeys, and when he openly flouted the decree, the pope picked up the challenge. He excommunicated Henry IV and, a new, unprecedented act, he deposed him and absolved all his vassals from their oaths of allegiance. This was revolutionary.

The emperor was at the moment in an apparently strong position, for he had just broken a great revolt of the vassal princes. But the papal sentence gave the rebellion new life, even Henry's bishops deserted him, and a national assembly (October, 1076) ratified the act of deposition. The emperor was lost, and took the only means open to him, that of personally making his submission to the pope, who was already *en route* for the great German council that was to choose and install his successor. Pope and emperor met at the castle of Canossa, January 28, 1077, in one of the most famous scenes of medieval history, and St. Gregory, hardly convinced of Henry's sincerity, and against his judgment as a statesman, was yet not able, as a priest, to refuse to absolve the imperial penitent.

The war in Germany continued, the vassals electing a new emperor and the pope declaring himself neutral. When Henry returned to his old practice of nominating to sees and to abbeys, the pope, stressing his bad faith, renewed the excommunication and acknowledged his competitor Rudolf of Swabia. This time, however, the German bishops stood by Henry, and, denouncing all manner of calumnies against the pope, declared him deposed and elected in his place (June, 1080) the archbishop of Ravenna, who, for ten years, had led the opposition to the popes in Italy. Next Rudolf was slain in battle and the emperor marched into Italy to carry out the deposition of St. Gregory VII and instal "Clement III" as his father in 1046 had deposed Gregory VI and installed Clement II.

One town after another opened its gates to him, all the local discontent, whether with the Reform or against the pope's ally, the great Countess of Tuscany, Matilda, rallying to him. In 1082 he laid siege to Rome. The next year he took St. Peter's while Gregory sought refuge in the fortress of St. Angelo. In March, 1084, the city, weary of the siege, surrendered—a surrender in which treachery, the treachery even of cardinals, played its part —and "Clement III" was solemnly installed in the Lateran.

It was St. Gregory's Norman allies who saved him. The emperor fled as they approached. They sacked the city, none the less, and when they retired they took the pope with them. He had only a few months to live, and on May 28, 1085, still the semi-prisoner of his allies, he died at Salerno. The anti-pope was once more reigning at Rome, the loyal cardinals were scattered, and for the moment it seemed that the cause of reform was lost.

For nearly three years the Holy See remained vacant, the emphemeral Victor III reigning for a matter of weeks only in the summer of 1087. His election was a last flicker of life from the party of St. Peter Damian, that disapproved of the new policy and looked for salvation to co-operation with the emperor. Then on March 12, 1088, the long night ended with the choice of Odo of Cluny, Urban II. In him Rome received the true heir to St. Gregory VII, and in the eleven years he reigned he made good the losses suffered since 1080, and kept out of Rome for years by the imperial armies, he renewed the practice of St. Leo IX, summoning local councils throughout Italy and France and personally presiding at them. The greatest of these councils was that of Clermont (November, 1095) where the Crusade was first proclaimed, and to which there came an immense crowd of a hundred thousand visitors and pilgrims.

This popularity of the popes and of the whole reform movement is one of the striking features of the time. The average man understood very well that the popes were concerned to break, once and for all, a wealthy aristocratic clique that had monopolised the offices of the Church for generations and had used its wealth for the enrichment of their families. In more than one place the laity had banded together, with what clergy they could get to support them, to expel the simony-tainted bishops and the married priests. Milan, in particular, had been the scene for years of a miniature civil war on this account. This popularity was to endure all through the coming, twelfth, century and to be one of the foundations of the papal success in the next great contest for the liberty of the Church in the time of the emperor Frederick Barbarossa and Pope Alexander III.

Urban II, despite his conciliatory gifts, was not destined to see the end of the investiture contest. This was left for the next French pope, Calixtus II (1119–1124), and meanwhile, under Pascal II (1099–1118), a combination of weakness and lack of political gifts nearly wrecked the cause altogether. At one moment the pope offered to surrender to the emperor all the church properties and temporal jurisdictions and rights. At another he surrendered the right of investiture itself.

It was as a leader of the opposition to Pascal II that

Calixtus II—then archbishop of Vienne—first came into history. The settlement he made with the emperor, called the Concordat of Worms (1122), secured that henceforth all elections of bishops and abbots should be freely made by the proper ecclesiastical electors. The prince's anxiety as to the loyalty of the prelates, in so far as they were also his barons and vassals, was set at rest by the provision that they were to make him the due oath of homage for the temporalities they held of him, and to be invested with these by a touch of the royal sceptre. But investiture with the crozier and the ring, by which the king gave the see or abbey and so made the man bishop or abbot, he now abandoned.

The opening of this period of "Assault and Recovery" was marked in the east as we have seen by a new exhibition of the State's eagerness to control the Church, namely the long persecution of the Iconoclastic emperors. This was scarcely ended (842), through the good offices of the empress Theodora, when new troubles arose, less important in themselves—since the issues were personal, and involved no doctrine—but destined to re-echo through all the subsequent centuries, and to supply to the disputants on both sides in the ensuing schism the watchwords, the charges, and the party cries that still have life and power.

When Methodius died, in 847, he was succeeded as patriarch of Constantinople by a son of the emperor Michael I, Ignatius. The new patriarch, a man of holy life, was somewhat lacking in political ability. He was a zealous supporter of the empress-regent and an opponent of the young emperor's other guardian the Cæsar Bardas. The long conflict between Ignatius and Bardas grew in intensity after the retirement of the empress and reached its climax when the patriarch publicly refused Holy Communion to Bardas as a notorious evil liver. The crisis was resolved, as so often in Byzantine history, by the resignation of the patriarch. In his place, as a kind of compromise between the ruling factions, the council of bishops elected Photius, a layman. He was the head of the civil service, a man who was not only the greatest scholar of his century, one of the most learned men indeed who have ever lived, but a man of irreproachable life and character. The compromise was not too successful. Soon there was talk of electing a new patriarch. The partisans of Ignatius began to revoke the assent they had given to the election of Photius, and finally Rome intervened in the person of the reigning pope Nicholas I (858–867). To the coming council at Constantinople (861) he sent two legates. They took the part of Photius and the Government and assented to the solemn condemnation of Ignatius which the council pronounced. But the pope—manœuvred, it is suggested, by the partisans of Ignatius—disavowed his legates and, indeed, cashiered them. More, he definitely declared for Ignatius.

Here it has to be stated that there entered into the debate two other elements, sources of long-standing differences between Rome and the east. There was, first of all, the question of the restoration to the pope's jurisdiction, as patriarch of the west, of the churches of Illyricum, over which, since the time of Leo III, the patriarch of Constantinople had exercised a usurped jurisdiction. Secondly, there was the thorny question whether Bulgaria was to be evangelised by Latin missionaries from Rome or by Greek missionaries from Constantinople. Nicholas I in supporting Ignatius had had not a little hope of his protégé's giving satisfaction on both these points.

But the effect of the council of 861, in despite of the papal refusal to ratify it, was that Ignatius was held a prisoner, while Photius wrote his polemical anti-Roman works which have been the main quarry from which Orthodox, anti-Roman controversialists have ever since dug their most serious arguments.

In 1867 the emperor who had patronised Photius was murdered. The assassin succeeded him as Basil I and, in the general reaction against Michael III, Photius was forced to abdicate and Ignatius was restored. Nicholas I died this same year (867), and it was to his successor, Adrian II (867–872), that the invitation came to send legates to a great council which should undo the mischief caused by the "usurpation" by Photius, and restore the fulness of communion between Rome and the east.

The council—reckoned as the eighth of the General Councils—met in 869. It solemnly anathematised Photius and it confirmed the restoration of Ignatius. For the moment all was well, and Photius and Ignatius contrived to live together amicably for the few years of life that remained to Ignatius.

The relations of the restored patriarch with Rome were less happy. He did not make the expected restoration in Illyricum, and he showed himself vigorously anti-Latin in Bulgaria. The pope with whom he had to deal, John VIII (872–882), retaliated with vigour, and it was only the patriarch's opportune death that saved him from excommunication.

Photius once again took Ignatius' place. He demanded, and was granted, a council to enquire into the whole matter of the legality of his first appointment and consecration in 858 and of the action of the council of 869. To the new council—held in 879–880—John VIII sent legates. When it reversed all the proceedings of the council of 869 they assented, and John VIII ratified their assent.

So ended the curious and involved history of Photius. For the rest of his life, save for some critical months when the deacon Marinus, who had been one of the legates to the council of 869, ruled as pope, his relations with Rome were peaceable, and he died at a great age still in communion with Rome, though not in possession of his see, for in 886 the emperor Leo VI again deposed him to make room for a young scion of the imperial house.

The unique importance of the schism of Photius is that never before had the differences between Rome and Constantinople been so related to principle by the rebels. Now for the first time it is made a charge against Rome that by tolerating the addition of the word *Filioque* to the creed—teaching that the Holy Spirit proceeds from the Father and the Son—she has corrupted the Faith. Henceforth all the differences of ritual and of ecclesiastical discipline between the two halves of Christendom will be related to and argued about in the light of a theological theory wholly unconnected with any one of them. And these petty differences will come to matter as though they were themselves fundamental doctrines.

It was some hundred and fifty years after the death of Photius when the trouble revived once more. This time the main cause was the personal ambition of the patriarch, Michael Cerularius, to which must be added the mishandling of the situation at Constantinople by the ludicrously ill-informed Roman legates. Cerularius had suddenly begun an active anti-Latin campaign in his patriarchate (1053). He had, to justify his violent closing of the Latin churches in Constantinople, revived all the accusations of the time of the Photian schism. The legates were too ignorant to be able to argue. Actually, incredible as it may sound, they replied to the charge about the *Filioque* by accusing the Greeks of having cut the word out from the original text. Then, on a day full of fate, July 16, 1054, they solemnly excommunicated the patriarch.

The tragedy is that the pope in whose name they were acting, St. Leo IX, was dead, and at the moment they acted the Holy See was vacant. Nor was any other than Cerularius excommunicated. And as late as twenty years after this, Cerularius being long in his grave, Rome was still in communion with Antioch, which in turn was in communion with Rome. But whatever the niceties of the canon law which interprets, if it does not regulate, such a situation, from the time of the excommunication of Cerularius the two sees, and the sees depending on them patriarchally, drifted apart. By the time the Crusades were a part of Christian life there was the definite rupture of schism. And the contact made through the Crusades, the mutual hostility of Latins despising the Greek treachery and of Greeks despising the Latin barbarism and the fighting Latin bishops, continually widened the breach. Then came the fanatical sack of Constantinople by the Crusaders in 1204, the establishment of a Latin emperor and of a Latin bishop in the see of St. John Chrysostom. From this moment to be anti-Latin was a fundamental element of eastern patriotism.

Reunion projects would henceforth never be more than political scheming on the part of the Greeks, the device of expediency at its wit's end where to get help against the Turk. The reunions achieved at the General Councils of Lyons, in 1274, and of Florence, in 1438, were short-lived in the extreme. And the schism still endures, though the presence in the Church to-day of some 8,000,000 Catholics of Oriental rite gives an assurance that what once was may yet be once again.

5

Christendom Triumphant in the West, 1123–1270

THE CONCORDAT OF WORMS was a compromise, but the main principle for which the popes had fought for now two generations was victorious, namely that kings should not control the Church through their right to appoint its bishops. It was just over six hundred years since, with Clovis, this bad custom had first taken root in the new Christendom of the west. To root it out had entailed a struggle that had shaken German Catholicism to its foundations, but a struggle which, curiously enough, had released other spiritual energies too, so that the two centuries that include and follow the Hildebrandine restoration are probably unique in history for the scale of the immense revival of human life and culture in all its forms that fills them.

The end of the struggle saw established the new habit of papal initiative in all the affairs of every part of the Church. By the nature of the events there had developed a new centralisation of ecclesiastical authority. The papacy had been the instrument of the reforms, the support of good bishops everywhere, and more and more from every part of the Church the bishops turned spontaneously to Rome for aid against tyrants and for the solutions of their many daily problems. To assist the working of this new centralisation the popes had two new instruments of the greatest value, the permanent *corps* of legates working upon the local hierarchies in the great provincial and national councils now held continuously throughout the West, and the newly organised Canon Law. Seventeen years or so after the Concordat of Worms there appeared the most famous of all Canon Law texts, the so-called *Decretum* of Gratian, a professor of Canon Law in the nascent university of Bologna. This was not merely a collection of decrees, old and new, classified according to subject-matter, but a work of jurisprudence and legal science that discussed the means whereby apparently contradictory laws should be reconciled in practice by the lawyer, and thus offered the beginnings of a real legal science of church law.

About the same time there appeared also the manual which had the same immense effect as Gratian's work, but in the field of theology. This was the *Liber Sententiarum* of Peter the Lombard, a master in the schools of Paris. For nearly the next four hundred years it was to be the classic text upon which all who taught theology anywhere in western Europe were to base their lectures. The appearance of these two great books can be taken to symbolise the rapid progress of that revival of learning of which the last half of the eleventh and the whole of the twelfth centuries were witness.

Another aspect of this, whose fruit was not, however, to ripen for yet another half-century and more, was the revival of interest in philosophical studies, a revival stimulated and transformed by the appearance of the first Latin translations of the writings of Aristotle. These translations were largely the work of clerics in Spain, who owed their interest in philosophical and scientific questions to their contact with the Moors, amongst whom, for centuries now, there had been a real cult of Aristotle and of the Neoplatonic philosophers. At the same time that Aristotle's *Logic* and *Physics* began thus to be made known to the Catholic west, these Spaniards began to publish translations of his Moorish and Arabic commentators, of Avicenna (980–1037) first of all and later of Averroës (1126–1198), the greatest of them all.

Two names stand out among the pioneers of this great revival of thought—St. Anselm, the Benedictine abbot of Bec who (1093) became archbishop of Canterbury and a great champion of Hildebrandine ideals against the two

English kings, William II and Henry I, and Peter Abelard, one of the most brilliant teachers in all history and, by his use of the new logic in the study of the traditional doctrine, one of the creators of scientific theology.

Another effect of the general revival is the multiplication everywhere of new parishes, the building of churches, of abbeys and the new cathedrals which still remain to challenge human endeavour. Preaching revives and more than ever it begins to be allowed as a part of the work of the priest—where it had been an exclusive duty of the bishop—and the new theologians draw up new schemes of doctrine for the instruction of the laity. The practice of religion by the individual Catholic finds a powerful aid in the new tendency to meditate on the human life of Our Lord and of His Mother. St. Anselm is, here too, a pioneer, though the most famous exponent of the movement is St. Bernard, one of the greatest preachers of all time. It is now that the *Salve Regina* and the *Hail Mary* make their first appearance and the feast of the Immaculate Conception is first celebrated—again by St. Anselm. One effect of this preaching is a new devotion to the Passion of Our Lord. The crucifix begins to be popularised and the devotion to the Five Wounds. The *Jesu Dulcis Memoria* is written.

But the most striking signs of all that a new age has dawned are the many religious orders, especially the new monks of the Order of Cîteaux and the new Canons Regulars of *Prémontré*. Cluny was, for the moment, in a state of eclipse. Too great prosperity and an unworthy abbot had brought about a temporary decline after nearly two centuries of high spiritual service. Then, after the foundation of the two semi-hermit orders of Grandmont and Chartreux, came the reformed Benedictinism of the abbey of Cîteaux founded in 1098. The real founder of the order, by his authorship of the *Carta Caritatis* which organised it, was the third abbot of Cîteaux, the Englishman, St. Stephen Harding (1134). But the best known of all its monks was the abbot of Clairvaux, St. Bernard (1101–1153). The rule was that of St. Benedict, but the end the Cistercian monk had in view was penance in expiation of sin, of his own sins and those of his brethren in the world. The life was one of harsh ascetic practice; the abbeys were built in the wilds, and the order owned no property except what provided the manual work by which the monks lived and which served as their daily occupation. In the marshes, the wild forests and heath lands of northern Europe, the Cistercians, for the next hundred years, laboured unceasingly, and they must be set down as the pioneers of agriculture whose labours transformed many a desert into valuable farming land. They did not propose to undertake the care of souls and in their churches and their liturgy a stern, severe simplicity marked them off sharply from the older monks. The buildings were bare, devoid of ornament. The crosses and furnishings were of wood and iron. But the greatest innovation of Cîteaux, and one destined to influence all the subsequent history of religious orders, was its system of government. Over and above the autonomy of the abbey was the authority, not of the abbot of Cîteaux, but of the general chapter of all the abbots that met annually to discuss the state of the order. Here was an instrument that might be held to be the best security yet devised against relaxation, and not an order since has been founded that has not, in some fashion, copied Cîteaux here.

The speed with which the new order grew is beyond anything modern times have to show for any religious movement. There were 19 abbeys in 1122, 70 in 1134, 350 in 1153, 530 by the end of the century.

The Order of Prémontré was also a reform movement, but of clerics not monks, and of clerics who lived a common life while they served a church with cure of souls, members of a chapter, canons. This common life had been prescribed for such clergy by Nicholas II in 1059 and there had been several efforts since then to organise this common life on the basis of the rule of St. Augustine and the three vows of poverty, chastity, and obedience. The order founded at Prémontré in 1120 by St. Norbert (1080–1134) was the most famous and most successful of them all. The spirit of the rule was as austere as that of Cîteaux, but, for the first time in the history of the Church, intellectual discipline, study, and classes formed part of the spiritual rule—naturally and inevitably in view of the apostolate of preaching and service of souls to which the Premonstratensian was vowed. As with the Cistercians the success of the new order was something unprecedented. In the life of its second general, Blessed Hugh of Fosses, more than two hundred new abbeys were founded —the first seminaries the Catholic Church ever knew.

Everywhere, too, hospitals, orphanages, homes for the aged, and for penitents, were building, leper-houses, too, and everywhere brotherhoods of laity were founded to support them and religious congregations to serve them. This movement to provide a kind of collective security for the piety of the layman also found expression in the system by which he could now affiliate himself to the abbeys of the new religious orders, and in the *fratres ad succurendum* of the Premonstratensians may be seen the beginnings of the "third order" movement that was, in the thirteenth century, to work so great a change in the social life of the time.

Two aspects of ordinary human life were especially affected by the religious revival and the revival of law which it bred. The old reverence for marriage, for its indissolubility and its sanctity, that had so suffered in the centuries of anarchy was gradually restored, and along with this campaign for morals, in the strict sense, there was waged an equally vigorous war on usury and on the brutality to which such institutions as the tournament and the ordeal equally bore witness. Again it is the Church that institutes and propagates the practice called the Truce of God, in an endeavour to save civilians and non-combatants from the violence of the continuous private wars and vendettas. By this, and by the consecration of knighthood as a religious service, the soldier pledges himself not to molest women nor traders nor peasants, not to lay waste the crops or destroy orchards, and not to fight during certain holy seasons, nor, for reverence of the holy days, from Thursday night to Tuesday morning. And at the same time the movement continues that aims at the extirpation of slavery and the slave trade and that will slowly transform the serf into a free peasant.

The principal theatre of missionary activity and expansion during these years of general restoration continued to be Scandinavia, the lands between the Elbe and the Vistula, Bohemia and Poland. The chief agents of the work in these Slavonic countries were the new orders of Cîteaux and Prémontré. The great obstacle to the spread of the Faith was the fact that the missionaries were mostly German and, in their methods, Germanisers. Bohemia especially suffered from this, as German Catholicism had once suffered from the fact that the first apostles it knew were Franks. The see of Prague, for example, was a dependency of Mainz and of its first seventeen bishops seven were German. The Hildebrandine reform was a century late in reaching the Czechs.

There was the same obstacle to the spread of Catholicism in Poland, but the Poles made closer and more systematic contact with the Holy See and so protected themselves against Germanisation. Between 1050 and 1150 many new sees were founded in Poland, and Polish missionaries began to convert Pomerania and Prussia.

The thirty years that followed the Concordat of Worms and the First General Council of the Lateran (1123–1153), the years that saw the flowering of most of the development the last few pages have chronicled, were years of peace between pope and emperor. Before we come to the story of the new war between them it remains to complete the picture of the age of Hildebrand by a reference to the new Christian offensive against Islam. When Gregory VII was elected pope, Christendom was still in an inferior position to Islam in every material way. The Mediterranean was still a Mahometan sea, the culture and prosperity of Mahometan Spain rivalled anything the Catholic west had to show, and a new race of Mahometans —the Seljukian Turks—were making a fresh bid for Constantinople and had overrun the still Christian lands of Asia Minor, defeating the Byzantine emperor, with great loss, at Manzikert in 1071.

In Spain the eleventh century had seen the beginning of a most successful anti-Mahometan offensive. The new Catholic kingdoms of Aragon and Castile had gradually extended their territory at the expense of the Islamic south, and the exploits of the great hero we know as the Cid, and the capture of Toledo (1085) make the century glorious in the history of Catholic Spain. Had there been less rivalry between the different nascent Catholic States the offensive might have been more successful still. As it was it went no farther in the east for yet another century, but a western crusade delivered Portugal and in 1147 captured Lisbon.

The Islamic victories in the east had moved St. Gregory VII deeply and he had planned a general European movement to recover the lost lands. It was not to be in his time, and it was left to his chosen disciple Urban II to launch the new offensive at the Council of Clermont in 1095. To all who pledged themselves to fight for the deliverance of the Holy Places from the Turks the pope granted a plenary indulgence, and in huge armies and enormous hordes the knights and soldiers and peasants of the west set out to free Jerusalem and save their souls. Never before had Europe known such a vast and successful propaganda as the preaching of this first crusade, and its success is a most eloquent proof of the reality of the new reform papacy's hold on the average man and of its popularity with him.

At the same time it must not be supposed that the immense movement was miraculously delivered from the pests that always thrive when humanity *en masse* is in motion. Tricksters, swindlers, adventurers, criminals of all kinds, false prophets, and religious quacks and fanatics found here their own inglorious hour, and hung on to the skirts of the great spiritual adventure. Nor, of course, did every rude soldier cease to need the virtues of Justice and Temperance once Faith had consecrated his Fortitude in the service of God.

The great armies moved slowly to the East through 1097 and 1098. They took the Turkish strongholds in Asia Minor, and in June 1098 Antioch fell to them after a long siege. On July 14, 1099, they captured Jerusalem—the goal of their dreams—and set up the several Latin States of the east, around whose fortunes an immense amount of the history of the next two hundred years was to turn.

These States were never in a really strong position. It is doubtful if they could ever have been established had it not been that Islam was rent by internal schisms at the moment of the crusaders' attack. Once these dissensions ceased, whenever Islam recovered its unity and a new leader appeared, they would immediately be in very grave danger. To defend the Catholic hold on the Holy Places there now sprang up the most striking of all the institutions of medieval Catholicism, the religious orders whose members were not priests but soldiers, vowed to poverty, chastity, and obedience and also to defend with the sword the Holy Places. The most famous of these military monks were the Knights Hospitallers and the Knights of the Temple.

But apart from what dangers the Mahometans offered, the Catholics of Syria had a second perpetual foe in the Byzantine emperors, who, only too willing to call in the west against Islam, had not been prepared to see their champions install themselves as rulers of the lands they liberated. From the first contact of Crusaders and Byzantines there was trouble of the most serious kind, treachery on the one side, violence on the other, and a feud that weakened the whole movement and that culminated in the Latin conquest and sack of Constantinople in 1204 and the establishment of a Latin as Byzantine emperor.

It was as a kind of sequel to a war between the Byzantine and the Latin States that the Mahometan offensive made its first gains, capturing Edessa in 1144. The disaster was the signal for a renewal of religious fervour in the west. It was St. Bernard, who dominated every aspect of his age as it has been given to few to do, that preached the crusade, and soon new armies had been organised and the emperor and the King of France had both taken the cross. But a series of disasters thinned the armies long before they reached Jerusalem (1148). They could not recover Edessa and they failed to take Damascus. It was a wretched ending to what had promised well, and the very idea of the crusade suffered a blow from which it never really recovered.

The fiasco of the second crusade may be taken as a mark that the spiritual energy that had produced the Hildebrandine restoration was spent. Another witness to the same fact was a new attack on the Church's freedom in which the aggressor found allies among the bishops and even the cardinals.

A struggle was about to begin which would involve nearly a hundred years of strain and fighting, in which the newly accomplished reformation of morals and the restoration of Christian ideals would be gravely compromised. The same century would see also the rise of a double menace, not only to the Church as the dominating feature of Christian life, but to its very existence, in the rapid revival and spread of Manicheeism and the diffusion of a material and atheistic philosophy in the nascent universities. The Church was, however, to retain its vitality. Though sorely stricken by the long fight with the secular princes, it yet managed to overcome the other dangers, it founded the universities and a new Christian philosophy, and it produced the two new religious orders of the Preachers and the Friars Minor.

The new struggle with Cæsar did not begin as a fight to wrest from the emperor rights he had usurped over the Church's life, but as a defence of the newly-won freedom from an attempt to impose by force something of the régime under which the Church had wilted in the east. The emperor Frederick I (1152–1190), called Barbarossa, explicitly declared himself to be the successor of Constantine and Justinian no less than of Charlemagne, and claimed the same authority over Christendom that they had exercised over the empire in their own day. To support his claims and to give them an appearance and form of legality, he invoked the newly rediscovered Roman Law, with its concept of the absolute state and its vast repository of principles and enactments that applied this doctrine. "The law is whatever the emperor wills," his chancellor declared at the Diet of Roncaglia (1158) to the papal legates. The danger from such a development was all the greater because Frederick did not propose to confine the reality of his rule to Germany, but seriously planned to make himself the active ruler of Italy, too, and of Rome. "If I, Emperor of the Romans, have no rights in Rome," he declared, "I have no rights anywhere." After several years of skirmishing with the pope—Adrian IV (1154–1159) [1]—in which the issues were made clear and the papacy brought itself to face the fact that, unless it was prepared to fight, it would soon see Frederick the real ruler of Rome and the Church's master, the war began in April, 1159, with the third of the emperor's many

---

[1] The one Englishman to reach the papal throne.

invasions of Italy. Five months later the pope suddenly died and the emperor's partisans elected a pope of their own in opposition to the pope chosen by the majority of the cardinals, Roland Bandinelli, who called himself Alexander III.

The new pope was one of Gratian's most distinguished pupils, and the first of the great canonists to sit in the chair of St. Peter. It was the Church's good fortune that he reigned for twenty-two years (1159–1181), and the immense mass of decisions given by his trained mind, and set out in scientific legal terminology, decisions in reply to appeals from all over Europe (and from nowhere so much as from England) was to be the principal element in the first official compilation of Canon Law made in 1234 under his successor Gregory IX. In this day-to-day activity of the Roman Curia, caring now for all the churches of the world, we begin to see the fruits of the new centralisation, the new way of exercising its primacy, that, since the restoration under the popes of the Hildebrandine age, had become a second nature to the papacy. Alexander III as a constructive statesman and legist must be ranked among the very greatest of the popes, one of the first ten in the long line of 260. His activity in this respect, the activity of a constructive reformer, reached its climax in the legislation of the General Council he summoned in 1179.[2]

Like all the medieval popes, Alexander III's great anxiety is Christian good living, and his most serious problem is how to get his decrees obeyed. Communications were difficult to an extent now almost impossible to realise, the medieval pope was never so free in the choice of his subordinates as the modern popes generally are, and even when he could choose his bishops, the circumstances of the time locked up so much of the bishop's activity with civil and political and military employments, that the pastoral office was always obscured and only too often altogether forgotten. The best of laws have always languished when there is no means to compel obedience to them, and laws that are constructive—not punitive merely—must work otherwise than by fear of sanctions if they are to bear the

---

[2] Reckoned as the Third Council of the Lateran.

intended fruit. "It is the spirit that giveth life" here as elsewhere, and though the spirit never ceased to struggle throughout the Middle Ages, the world was, very often indeed, too much for it in the development of the ecclesiastical bureaucracy and the whole business of Church government. The splendid programme of Alexander III was never really carried out, and forty years later, at the next General Council,[3] his great successor, Innocent III, publishing a still more wonderful body of salutary laws, several times declares explicitly that he does but re-enact the canons of 1179 which nowhere have been obeyed.

With regard to Frederick Barbarossa, with whom while yet a papal legate he had already personally crossed swords, Alexander III took from the first a firm stand. He refused to submit to any arbitration in the case between himself and the emperor's anti-pope, and though speedily driven from Rome by the imperial army, he managed to keep the schism from spreading to France and to England. His political genius also rallied to the cause of the Church the great cities of northern Italy, whose independence, too, was threatened by the new spirit in Germany. Frederick replied by measures which anticipated those of Henry VIII of England against a later pope. All bishops, abbots, priests, and monks were ordered to take an oath abjuring Alexander and acknowledging the anti-pope. The penalty for refusal was deposition, loss of goods, mutilation, and exile. An intensive propaganda forced the acceptance of the oath throughout Germany. Thus for the second time in a hundred years Germany was forced into a kind of anti-papal Catholicism. This situation was to recur time and again during the next two hundred years, and the recurrence should be remembered as explaining a great deal of the success which the greatest of all movements against Rome was to enjoy in the Germany of the sixteenth century.

The war dragged on with varying success for seventeen years until at the great battle of Legnano (March 29, 1176) the army of the Italian cities utterly routed the emperor. By the Peace of Venice (1177) he acknowledged Alexander as pope, sought absolution, and promised to

---

[3] Reckoned as the Fourth Council of the Lateran, 1215.

come to an understanding about the restoration to the
pope of the lands rightly his in Tuscany.

Four years later Alexander died. He had reigned for
twenty-two years, and it was now the Church's misfortune
to have no fewer than five popes in the seventeen years
that followed, old men all of them, very old men, the
last of them close on ninety when he was elected. In these
years much of the good work done by Alexander was
undermined and, in a fatal moment, one pope, Lucius III
(1181–1185), consented to a marriage between Barbarossa's heir—Henry—and the heiress to the throne of
Sicily. If Henry ever succeeded as emperor—the dignity
was elective, and only the pope could consecrate and
crown the emperor-elect—the papacy would be in an even
worse position than in the time of Alexander, for the kingdom of Sicily included all southern Italy, and if its ruler
were also emperor and strong and unscrupulous, the papal
state and the pope's independence would be at his mercy.

Barbarossa died in 1190, *en route* for the Holy Land
to take part in the Third Crusade. Henry, already ruler
of Sicily since the death of his father-in-law in 1189, was
elected emperor, and to face this formidable personage
the cardinals elected as pope an old man of eighty-five,
Celestine III (1191–1198). For the next seven years Henry
VI marched from success to success. He crushed his various rivals and rebellious vassals, he made himself really
master of Germany and of southern and central Italy, occu-
pying much of the Papal States themselves. He planned to
make the empire hereditary in his family, which, had he
succeeded, would have meant the end of the papal independence, and he dreamed of a new crusade that should
establish him as emperor in the east as well as in the west.

What delivered the Church was Henry's sudden death
(September, 1197). A few months later the aged Celestine
III died too. Henry had left a baby of three to succeed
him in Sicily. The cardinals elected a young man of thirty-
seven, Lothario of Segni—Innocent III. He was to reign for
eighteen years (1198–1216), and his pontificate is usually considered the high-water mark of the papal control
of Europe.

There is good reason to regard the seventeen years
(1181–1198) that separate Innocent III from Alexander

III as the most critical period of the Middle Ages, and if this is true, Innocent, because of the successful solutions he adopted to meet the crisis, is the saviour of medieval, and therefore of later, civilisation. Of all the dangers that threatened, the greatest of all was the revival of Manicheeism which, beginning a hundred years before this, had by now made its own all the south of France (Provence) and much of northern Italy. The situation was more serious in France because the reigning family, the counts of Provence, patronised the movement. It reappeared with all the familiar trappings. There was the old, apparently obvious solution of the problem that has always tried thinking man, viz.: What is evil, how does it originate, how can we escape it? Evil, for the Manichee, was matter, and matter was evil. Along with this there went the belief in two gods—a good and a bad god [4]—and the practical doctrine of abstinence, abstinence from food and from marriage and especially from conception. Starvation, suicide, and abortion were good acts. "Free love" and unnatural vice, though wrong, were, nevertheless, less serious than the fruitful intercourse of marriage. There were the two divisions, of the Perfect (who practised the ascetic teaching in its full rigidity) and the Believers, who did no more than pledge themselves to future enrolment among the Perfect. To this day they were admitted by the rite called *Consolamentum*, and so long as this was received on their death-bed, salvation was assured to them. The sect had a cult that included explanations of the Bible, and it had a hierarchy of officials. It was well organised and it speedily gathered recruits from the cultured nobility of this land of troubadours and also from the wealthy merchant class. Everywhere the sect, called "Albigenses," after the city of Albi, Provence, built schools and opened workshops to provide a living for its adepts.

The south of France had been a curiously orientalised province since the days of the Mahometan invasion five hundred years before this, and from the number of Jews who flourished there it had long been called the second Judea. By the end of the twelfth century the signs were

---

[4] This is an extremely crude, but not substantially untrue, way of expressing it.

that between the papacy and its two great supporters, the Churches of France and England, there was to intervene a new anti-Christian culture, actively and militantly hostile.

Innocent III treated the affair as its gravity and urgency required. He tried persuasion and he tried preaching. When the missionaries failed—it was naturally to the Cistercians he turned for auxiliaries in this Cistercian century, as later popes turned to Jesuits—and when his legates were murdered and when the treachery and anti-Catholic intentions of the reigning prince, Raymond VI, were manifest beyond all doubt, he launched a crusade against Provence. For twenty dreadful years the struggle continued, the popes not always succeeding in keeping the crusaders within the bounds which the morality of war requires, and faced from the beginning with the inevitable difficulty that, allied with zeal for the Faith, there often went greed for the heretics' goods and territories. The political result of the war was that the king of France became master in the south as in the north.

Two other products of this defence of religion and civilisation from the gravest danger that had yet menaced it, were to have a great future: the Inquisition; and a new religious society, the Order of Preachers, founded by a Spanish Canon-Regular, Dominic of Osma.

The Inquisition was a new tribunal, set up by the papacy and responsible to the popes, whose business it was to discover and to punish Catholics who adopted heresy. Long before the Church decreed any particular punishment against the heretic, public opinion throughout Europe had shown itself savagely hostile to heretics, and many of them had met their death in acts of lynching. The princes, too, had shown no disposition to be less cruel, and it was, in a measure, under pressure from them that the popes, from the end of the twelfth century, had begun to decree other punishments for heresy besides excommunication. The final steps were the decree of the Lateran Council of 1215, enacting confiscation of goods and banishment for all heretics, and the establishment by Gregory IX (1227–1241) in 1233 of the special tribunal to deal with the matter. The Inquisitors travelled round much in the way the new assize justices travelled in England, and about the institution a new body of law and criminal practice gradually gathered. In two important respects this was influenced by the contemporary revival of Roman Law, in the introduction of death as the penalty for a convicted heretic, that is to say, and in the use of torture in the examination of those accused.

St. Dominic was a Spanish canon-regular whom the accident of a diplomatic journey brought into contact with the Cistercian mission to the Albigenses, about the year 1205. He realised that the official pomp of the legates and their aids was a great hindrance to the work, and furthermore that the Catholics who were wavering could only be held to the Faith by clergy who know it well enough to defend it as well as to hold it, and who were in the manner of their life as detached from wealth and from material comforts as the ascetics of the sect. In the life of the body of preachers he gathered round him, all these ideals found a place, and from this chance companionage there grew a religious order of a new kind altogether, the first religious order properly so called. Hitherto there had been canons-regular and monks, and in some cases the various monasteries had been linked by a common superior, the abbot of Cluny, or the General Chapter of Cîteaux. But it was to the particular monastery that the monk was bound, and each monastery, in both these systems, had a very real autonomy of life. The Friars Preachers were not a collection of houses, they were an army of priests, organised under a Master-General in provinces, and ready to go wherever they were needed, without any obligations of stability to this house or that, owing their stability, not to any particular house, but to the order and the will of their superior. This was a surprising and most fruitful innovation, and every order since has adopted it.

The brethren of St. Dominic did not give themselves to the cure of souls generally, as the canons-regular of Prémontré had already done, but to the specific work of preaching. This entailed for the members of the new institute a special obligation to study, as a part of their religious life and discipline, such as no order before had known. Here again was change of a very far-reaching kind, and before the century was out, the order had already attained that character of a society of professional theologians which it still keeps. The Constitutions were an interesting combination of Cîteaux and Prémontré with a new flexibility to meet the new needs. It is not surprising that the expansion was rapid and that all Europe soon came to know the new institute.

But for all its rapidity the expansion was not nearly so rapid as that of another contemporary new order, that of the Friars Minor. If the rise of the Preachers, whom Innocent III did not indeed live to see organised,[5] bore witness to a need of re-instruction in the Faith, that of the Friars Minor was testimony to the growing worldliness of Catholics whose faith remained orthodox, and to a certain dissatisfaction among the pious laity with the low standards of spirituality among the clergy in general.

The long struggle of pope and emperor had provided endless opportunities for evidence to appear that the morals of Christendom were still far from being established in perfection. The ancient greed and rapacity, the disregard of marriage laws, carelessness of human life and the eternal preoccupation of prelates with the affairs of this world, their neglect of their elementary duties of preacher and teacher and spiritual father, gave rise, throughout the revival of the twelfth century, to a host of movements more or less anti-clerical, whose common aim was a return to an imagined perfect age of Christianity, when, if there were any priests, they were always all that they should be, and when hierarchical distinctions mattered little, if at all. Often these movements were heretical as well as anti-clerical. That preached by Peter of Bruys, for example, called for the abolition of all organised religion and denounced the Mass as a vain show. The most famous of all these twelfth-century groups was that called the Waldenses, after its founder, Peter Waldo, a converted merchant of Lyons. The Waldenses were, to begin with, orthodox in faith and their special devotion was to a life where no one was an owner. Property was to be sold and the proceeds given in charity. They set themselves to practise poverty and to preach it. As they were laymen they soon found themselves forbidden to preach in many places. Whereupon many of the Waldenses turned rebel-

---

[5] It was his successor, Honorius III, who, in 1216, called them into being.

lious and began to denounce ecclesiastical authority and soon the whole movement fell under the suspicion of heresy.

Lay movements to live a life of consecrated poverty and to preach that life to others were, then, no novelty when, one day in 1208, a young citizen of Assisi, John Bernadoni, commonly called Francis, or the Frenchman, because of his early affectation of French fashions and a French way of life, appeared before Innocent III and sought the pope's blessing on this way of life This new recruit to the apostolic life was the son of a wealthy merchant, and his generosity, his wit, his poetical and musical gifts, his miraculous natural gaiety and high spirits had long made him a leader of the youth of Assisi. Then he had turned to God and he had given himself unreservedly. With his handful of friends, living in huts built of twigs and clay, he preached penance for sin and the happiness of a literal following of Our Lord, and for a living he depended on what the charity of the town gave him.

The movement was, however, absolutely orthodox. There was a remarkable devotion to the Church, to its officers, and to its sacraments. Here was all the austerity of the Waldensians and the poetry of the troubadours allied to the most conservative Catholicism. The pope blessed the work, and all the band were ordained, Francis to the diaconate, the rest to the minor orders. They dispersed to preach throughout all the villages and towns of central Italy.

This was not a learned apostolate designed to regain those who had gone over to heresy, or to strengthen Catholics who were wavering in their faith. It was a mission to Catholics whose lives were disordered morally, in whom worldliness and material good fortune had dried up the springs of charity. What St. Bernard had done for the monk and the cleric in his Latin sermons, this new order of the Lesser Brethren (Friars Minor) did for the ordinary man through sermons in the vernacular. They set before him, with all the Gospel simplicity and pathos, the events in the human life of Our Lord, invited him to look in the Gospel as in a mirror, and to make the necessary amendment.

The Friars Minor had the most extraordinary success any order has ever known. Where the Dominican friars founded their tens of convents these founded their hundreds. Within ten years from the approbation given by Innocent III there were five thousand Franciscans, and to their general chapter in 1221 there came five hundred new recruits seeking admission. Something more than the personal contact with St. Francis and the evangelical generalities of the first rule were needed, if a movement that was growing so rapidly was to keep its true direction. A new, more detailed rule was therefore drawn up, under the inspiration largely of the cardinal Ugolino who was later Pope Gregory IX (1227–1241). The great speciality of this order was its extraordinary devotion to poverty—and in this, before the death of St. Dominic, the Friars Preachers speedily imitated it. A personal poverty had, of course, marked the earlier monasticism also. Where these new orders innovated was that not only could the friar not own, but the very order as such refused to hold property, launched itself into the world dependent utterly on what God's providence would send it. In this matter it was the Preachers who had been the borrowers. In their turn they lent to St. Francis when the Friars Minor took to the study of theology, as their work developed and as priests joined them. Very soon the two orders, though each retained its own very distinctive aim, spirit, and system of government, were occupied everywhere with much the same kind of work. Side by side with the Dominicans the Franciscans taught theology and philosophy in the universities, and in most towns where the one order had a convent and a church, the other would also be found. Henceforth, so long as they flourished and wherever they flourished, the Church had what had hitherto been lacking, an active corps of professional preachers and trained confessors. The importance of these two orders to the general well-being of Catholicism in the later Middle Ages is something not easy to overrate.

One very special means of their success was the establishment of the Third Order—a real religious order open to lay folk, by means of which men and women, married as well as single, who continued to live in the world, following their professions, rearing their families, lived under the direction of the Friars, according to a modified version of the Friars' own rule, lived in the spirit of the order, sharing in all the spiritual advantages of such close associations with it, and helped in their life by a constant endeavour to introduce into it something of the order's own ideals.

The Preachers and the Friars Minor were the principal, but by no means the only, orders of Friars. To complete the picture of the wonderful influence of the movement mention would have to be made of the Carmelites too, of the Servites and the Augustinian Hermits, and of the bodies of lay folk associated with them. And at least a mention should be made of two most devoted societies who laboured for the redemption of those taken captive by the Moors, the Friars of the Trinity, and of the Order of Our Lady of Ransom.

Such was the background of general willingness to serve God and be united with Him through His Church, against which the more spectacular fight for the Church's independence of lay control, for its supremacy in all that related to men's souls—and therefore in all its own affairs and in many of the affairs of the Christian nations—continued to go forward with unabated violence.

Innocent III is the pope in whose time the Papal Monarchy, that is to say the effective sovereignty of the pope over the whole public life of Christendom, is usually considered to have reached its zenith. The Church was now, at last, a world State, not so much international as supra-national, organised as a State with its judiciary and its law, its centralised bureaucracy, its financial system and its armies, prepared to coerce by force of arms, by the threat and the reality of a holy war, any rebellion against the standard doctrines of belief and conduct or against the papal policies.

It was, however, the good fortune of this great lawyer-pope that he never had to face the major ordeal of an opponent such as Barbarossa had been in the preceding generation, or as Barbarossa's grandson, Frederick II, was to be in the years to come. Frederick, in Innocent's time,

was the child king of Sicily,[6] the pope's vassal, and his
faithfully protected ward, while in Germany rival princes
strove for the empire in a civil war, giving the pope the
best of opportunities for the proclamation of his doctrine
that the emperor is emperor by the grace of the pope, and
the empire exists to serve the Church. Here is a striking
reversal of what had obtained, four hundred years earlier,
under the first of these medieval emperors, Charlemagne.
Then the emperor had practically governed the Church.
Now the pope, God's vicar, proposed to govern the State
and this everywhere. Half of Europe was already feudally
engaged to the papacy as to its suzerain and the reign
of Innocent saw England, too, subject itself in like fashion. In France a marriage dispute between the king
and the pope had brought down the threat of deposition,
and the king of Leon was excommunicated for a similar
reason. Wherever this pope struck he was, seemingly, victorious. Even the great tragedy of the reign, the wicked
subversion of the Fourth Crusade in the interests of
Venice, and the sack of Constantinople which ensued,
he seemed to be able to turn to good once the Latin empire of the East was installed.

The pontificate closed with the pope everywhere supreme, and in the Fourth General Council of the Lateran
(1215) he presented Christendom with the most extensive
examination of its spiritual and temporal state it had ever
known and with an elaborate, detailed programme of
further constructive reforms.

How far these would be put into execution depended
ultimately on the interest and good will of the bishops
throughout the world, and on the papacy's being free
enough from other cares to supervise the bishops. The
next forty years, however, were to find the popes busier
than ever in the fight for existence against yet another
imperial rival. Also, it must be borne in mind, the spirit
of the papal leadership was changing rapidly. The Benedictine popes of the age of Hildebrand had not only been
apostles of reform, but had fought with spiritual weapons

---

[6] The heir to the emperor, Henry VI, who died in 1197. Cf.
supra, p. 120.

i

in the main, and their priestly, pastoral intention had never been obscured. But now it was the canonist, the church lawyer, the ecclesiastical statesman that was beginning to be uppermost in the successive popes, and there is not henceforth so evident in their personality that happy combination of ruler, reformer, and spiritual guide which had marked the struggle of the earlier century. It is not without its significance that while two of the earlier group of eleven popes have been canonised and two others beatified, of the fifteen popes who fought the menace of the Hohenstaufen none has so far been even mentioned for such recognition of sanctity. These later popes, none of them bad men, turned to the weapons of this world. They used them well and were victorious. But they were victorious at a terrible cost, the cost of the prestige of their administration, if not, as yet, of the prestige of their see.

The new enemy was the young king of Sicily, Frederick, elected emperor in 1213 by the will of Innocent III. It had been a condition of this election that Frederick would never unite his two dignities, but in 1220 he had the son to whom, on his election, he had made over Sicily, elected King of the Romans, emperor-to-be. And meanwhile he built up scientifically in Sicily the most elaborate despotic State western Europe had seen since the old Roman Empire. Frederick had eleven years in which uninterruptedly to lay the foundation of his attempt to master the papacy, the eleven years in which his old guardian ruled as Pope Honorius III (1216–1227). But the successor to Honorius, Gregory IX, the friend and patron of St. Francis, was cast in another mould. He was a relative of Innocent III,[7] a scholar, a canonist, and a practical diplomatist. He acted immediately and by a peremptory summons to Frederick ended the eleven years' farce of the emperor's annual vow to go on the Crusade and his annual contemptuous neglect of it. The emperor, in reply, denounced the pope and was excommunicated. Thereupon he left for the East with an army and, coming to terms with the Sultan, crowned

---

[7] As Innocent had been a relative of Clement III and as Gregory himself was of Alexander IV, and as Alexander IV was of Boniface VIII; the new growing nepotism should be noticed.

himself king of Jerusalem in the church of the Holy Sepulchre. The pope had taken the opportunity to invade his vassal kingdom of Sicily, of which Frederick had been solemnly deprived. The emperor returned to find the papal troops in possession. A short war drove them out and then Sicily was given over to Frederick's vengeance. Gregory re-excommunicated him and endeavoured to rouse Christendom against him, but in vain, and then, by the peace of San Germano (1230), the emperor suddenly yielded on all points, was absolved, and reinstated.

Ten uneasy years went by, in which Frederick consolidated his power in his own kingdom and, buying peace in Germany by liberal concession to the princes, made himself master of northern Italy as of Sicily. Gregory IX could do little but negotiate and plead, and then, in 1239, he renewed the excommunication. For two years the duel continued, the emperor's counter-denunciations replying to the papal thunders, and writers on both sides appealing in violent pamphlets for the sympathy of Christendom. Then Gregory died, with Frederick's advancing armies only nine miles from Rome (August 21, 1241).

For the next two years the Church was without a pope,[8] Frederick holding prisoner two of the eleven cardinals while the rest scattered, in fear of their lives. Then the king of France, Louis IX, intervened and, the emperor releasing his prisoners, an election took place. The new pope was yet another canonist, after Alexander III the greatest of them all, Sinibaldo Fieschi, who took the name of Innocent IV (1243–1254).

Frederick's acts and his manifestos left no doubt of his intentions. He would be master in the Church as in the realm of Sicily. The perhaps not unnatural anti-clericalism of a ruler faced with the contemporary clerical claims was now allied to the old Pagan doctrine of the omnipotent State, and the emperor invited all the princes of Christendom to join him in a crusade to destroy the Church as a society independent of the State.

Innocent's intentions were no less clearly set forth. He aimed at the destruction of Frederick and all that he stood

---

[8] Save for the seventeen days' reign of Celestine IV in the summer of 1241.

for. In 1245 he convoked a General Council at Lyons and Frederick's case was tried and he was condemned. As Innocent III had dealt with the counts of Toulouse, so Innocent IV would deal with Frederick II. A great crusade was preached and an attempt made to rouse all Germany against him, while the pope looked for allies in Italy, raising armies and lavishing subsidies.

The war went on with varying successes and then, after a series of defeats, while meditating new schemes and a renewal of the war, Frederick died (December 13, 1250). Four years later his eldest son, Conrad, died, leaving only a baby to succeed him, and naming the pope as his guardian. But the war was not yet ended. Another of Frederick's sons, Manfred, still held out and towards the end of the same year (1254) inflicted a heavy defeat on the papal army.

Five days later Innocent IV died. His successor, Alexander IV (1254–1261), was weak and vacillating and during the seven years of his reign Manfred marched from victory to victory. By 1261 the papacy's influence was as low as in the days that preceded the election of Innocent III, seventy years earlier. The cause was saved by the successive elections of two able French popes, Urban IV (1261–1265) and Clement IV (1265–1268), both of them practised administrators. They reorganised the *curia* and, not their least important achievement, they reorganised the papal finances. They negotiated new alliances and at last secured the active, if indirect, co-operation of the king of France, Louis IX, who had hitherto studiously remained aloof from the titanic struggle. He now allowed his brother, Charles of Anjou, to accept the pope's offer of the throne of Sicily, and in 1265 Charles arrived in Italy and proceeded to dispossess Manfred.

On January 20, 1266, Manfred was defeated with great slaughter, and himself slain, at Benevento, and Charles was king of Sicily in fact as well as in name. He began his rule with such despotic severity that his patron the pope was moved to strong protests. His oppressed subjects cast about for a leader and recalled from Germany the young duke of Swabia, Conradin, the son of Conrad IV [9]

---

[9] Cf. *supra*, p. 120.

and the grandson of Frederick II. He set out in September, 1267, and, as he marched south, one Italian city after another gave him a welcome. Rome went over to him and Charles failed to recapture it. But on August 23, 1268, the fiercely fought battle of Tagliacozzo ended the long struggle. Conradin was defeated, and, after a kind of trial, Charles had him publicly beheaded at Naples.

It was the end of the Hohenstaufen, but not, of course, the end of the papacy's troubles. It had rid itself of the German foe by calling in the Frenchman. Now it remained to be seen how far the Frenchman would show himself ready to continue to be the pope's subordinate and obedient vassal. Already in the first year of the new alliance there had been signs of coming trouble. And now there fell upon the Church the great disaster that after the death of Clement IV (1268) the Holy See remained vacant for three years, the second long vacancy in thirty years.

During these years of the struggle against the Hohenstaufen emperors, there had been in progress another contest no less vital to the fortunes of Catholicism. This was a great philosophico-theological controversy and the issue was nothing less than whether the Faith was or was not to be transformed, by the use of new methods of explaining and defending it. It was the old difficulty of the days of the Apologists and the Gnostics all over again. The cause of this resurrection was the gradual discovery, by the Catholics of western Europe, of the whole body of Aristotle's teaching, a discovery that was more or less complete by the end of the first quarter of the thirteenth century.

We can hardly realise the effect, on the two generations that now first saw it, of the gradual unfolding of all that the genius of Aristotle had accomplished. Here was an encyclopædia of human knowledge, wide and detailed observation of life in all its forms, description, analysis, and coordination. The physical universe, man, man's life of thought, the nature of things, the causes of things, the first cause of all, man's end and the ideals of human conduct, all this was systematically set out in Aristotle. It seemed as complete a guide to life as Christianity claimed to be and it was purely rational. How did all this new knowledge square with the traditional faith? Were Catholics to ignore it? Could they ignore it? And if not, could they continue to be Catholics and to hold to it?

From about the time of the foundation of the University of Paris in 1205—the first and most famous of all universities, and for long, as an institution of European importance, on a par with the empire and the papal monarchy—these questions began to be debated passionately everywhere, theologians and philosophers fighting each other with great fury.

What complicated the matter was that hardly any of the disputants possessed either the actual text of Aristotle, or sufficient knowledge of Greek to suspect the accuracy of the translations they had to use. From about 1220 translations made directly from the Greek did indeed begin to appear, but until then the Latin text was often only a translation of an Arab translation of a Syriac translation of the original. Also, much passed for Aristotle that Aristotle had never written, neo-Platonic works of one kind and another. These neo-Platonic works had, in general, a prima facie appearance of being most sympathetic to Catholic teaching and practice. They laid great stress on such doctrines as the immortality of the soul and the reality of Providence, and furthermore the systems offered themselves as a practical road by which the soul could unite itself in ecstasy to God. What was mischievous—and not by any means so obvious—was that the systems were often, at basis, really Pantheist, as Aristotle was—in appearance at any rate—materialist, fatalist, and atheistic.

It was a further and final complication that this Aristotelian corpus of learning, of science, logic, and philosophy, came to the West introduced by Arabs, Moors, and Jews. It was in the different parts of the Mahometan world—in that much more cultured world that all but surrounded the Christian West for all these centuries, and which had come within measurable distance of destroying Christendom and swamping its cultural life altogether—it was here that, for five hundred years now, the cult of Aristotle had developed, and here that the great commentators had arisen through whose learning the West first came to know and to interpret Aristotle himself. The names of at least two of these must be mentioned—Avicenna (980–1037) and Averroës (1126–1198). The conflict in the thirteenth-century universities may indeed be summed up as a duel between Averroism and Catholicism.

Authority's first device was to forbid the study of Aristotle—except his works on logic: not by any means an unnatural device, nor illogical, given the confusion general in men's minds. The first of these prohibitions was in 1210. Twenty years later Gregory IX renewed it, but with modifications. Study was gradually making clear what was valuable in the new learning and where exactly the danger of abuses lay. Aristotle, where forbidden, was now only forbidden "until corrected." The movement to "correct" the texts and to distinguish the doctrines continued to go forward until, finally, the position was reached that the popes were making the study of Aristotle's Physics and Metaphysics obligatory for all candidates for a degree. Aristotelianism had become, what it still remains, the most precious of all the Catholic Church's human aids in the explanation and rational defence of Revelation.

The names of three great saints are associated with this revolution and with the Catholic fight against the threat to "averroise" Christendom: St. Albert the Great (1193–1280), St. Bonaventure (1221–1274) and St. Thomas Aquinas (1225–1274). The first and last were Dominicans, the second a Friar Minor.

It is St. Bonaventure's merit that he it was who first attacked Averroism as philosophically false and fought it with the weapon of natural dialectic. His work he never really completed for, at the age of thirty-six, he was taken away from the life of the universities to become, as its general during seventeen years, the second founder of his order (1257).

St. Albert was an intellectual of another order altogether, a kind of Catholic Aristotle, the complete scientist as well as the complete theologian, who, in Aristotle's spirit, set himself to acquire and to make accessible to others all that could be known of the created universe and its relation to its Creator. He was not a polemist, and though the Averroist problem naturally occupied much of his thought, and is the subject of one of his most famous

works, his influence was the indirect one of seeking another, and Aristotelian, solution for it. It was St. Albert
who trained the greatest of all Catholic thinkers, St.
Thomas Aquinas. In him, at last, Aristotle met the Catholic perfectly equipped to understand him, to distinguish
him from the commentators, to understand where his
thought was incomplete, and to develop it in the Aristotelian spirit, and show it to be in harmony with Catholic
doctrine. To the future history of all European thought
he contributed very largely indeed by the use he made
of St. Albert's scientifically drawn distinction between
philosophy and theology, and his insistence on the rights
of philosophy as an independent science. Reason and Faith
are distinct, and reason, too, has its rights. Reason is supreme in its own domain, and because that domain is
limited there are things that reason cannot discover, and
truths which, when known otherwise than through reason, reason cannot domonstrate to be true.

To his contemporaries the synthesis of St. Thomas—contained notably in his *Summa Theologica*—was a revolutionary thing. In many of his leading theses he fell foul of
the traditional methods of apologetic and came into direct
conflict with that other school of anti-Averroism which
St. Bonaventure had founded and which, in a way, he
still continued to lead. Pioneers of thought rarely live to
see their new ideas triumph. St. Thomas was no exception to this rule, and for long after his death his
disciples had to keep up a double fight, against the
Averroists and against the other Catholics who opposed
these. Though Rome never condemned St. Thomas, the
theologians of Paris did so more than once, and so, too,
did prelates of his own order. Not for fifty years after his
death was his position absolutely established as entirely
orthodox. It is not too much to say that this slow recognition of the genius sent by God to deliver Catholicism
from the most subtle trap ever laid before it, and to construct the most valuable of all syntheses of faith and
reason, this slowness to realise what St. Thomas was and
what he had accomplished, is one of the major tragedies
of medieval Catholicism. Tragedy truly, for it arose from
no man's ill will, nor from stupidity.

6

The Decline, 1270–1517

ST. THOMAS AQUINAS died in 1274 on his way to the fourteenth General Council [1] to which Blessed Gregory X (1271–1276) had summoned him. Two hundred and forty-three years later, only a matter of weeks after the solemn close of the eighteenth General Council,[2] a German friar, Martin Luther, began that attack on the government of Pope Leo X, which was to be the occasion of the ending of the world St. Thomas had known, and that his life's work should have perfected into a kind of eternity. The period between St. Thomas and Luther stands in the greatest contrast to the previous two hundred years or so that separate St. Thomas from St. Leo IX. Then all was constructive in the general effort of Catholic activity, every generation saw some new attack on an old abuse, wholeheartedly launched, popularly supported, and Catholic welfare was the leading interest in life for every member of the whole Church. The abuses were, it is true, never wholly reformed, and some of the necessary construction was never more than begun, but the main trend of the time was continuously in this direction.

The last hundred years of the great period—from the beginning of the struggle with the Hohenstaufen in 1155—

---

[1] The Second Council of Lyons.
[2] The Fifth Council of the Lateran.

saw new abuses grow, partly out of that struggle and inseparably from it, partly from the new perfection to which the ecclesiastical bureaucracy and its instrument the canon law were reaching, and partly, too, because human nature is always human nature, and the Church's battle against this, because it is never ended, must always have about it an air of defeat. The concubinary priest never by any means wholly disappeared, nor the professional monk, nor the political bishop. The problem of the training and the professional education of the parish clergy was hardly considered. Against these evils and shortcomings the fourteenth-century pope who took his office as seriously as it deserved had to fight as continuously as his twelfth-century predecessor. But he had to fight, also, against new evils and under new handicaps.

There is the new evil that the elective system as a means of appointing bishops and abbots—the system which the Hildebrandine popes had laboured to restore as a means to rid the Church of lay control and to make secure the selection of the best man for the post—had broken down badly. Elections had meant competition and, only too often, cliques, permanent rivalries, feuds, riots, rival bishops, and—sought on all sides—the intervention of the lay power. Partly to counter this, partly in natural sympathy with the general tendency to centralise, the popes, since Clement IV (1268), tend to substitute for absolutely free election (and for nomination to the lesser benefices) a kind of indirect nomination from Rome. They "provide" the new bishops, abbots, canons, and so forth. Inevitably Rome—or rather the papal court, which, only too rarely resident at Rome during the thirteenth century, is permanently absent during three-quarters of the fourteenth, established, with the popes, at Avignon in France—the Curia becomes a centre to which those in search of Church appointments, whether for good reasons or for bad, flock in their tens of thousands. The vast administration is expensive and there are fees to be paid at every turn. And there are those other financial corollaries, inevitable then as now in every court, and in all bureaucracies governed by autocrats who have too much to do to be able really to control their subordinates, and too many expenses to see that they are all fairly paid. The benefice system as it developed and was administered through the fourteenth and fifteenth and early sixteenth centuries, and increasingly as the years went by, offers in many respects one of the major scandals of the history of the Church.

Another scandal of the same financial order was the papal taxation, levied on the property of the Church—ecclesiastical revenues, salaries, pensions, and so forth—throughout the universal Church. Registers were drawn up to assess the value of these, and in every country there gradually appeared a new hierarchy of tax-collectors, intermediaries between the pope and the monies due to him from the local clergy.

This money was all of it badly needed, and especially needed once the papacy was permanently established in France, cut off, and seemingly forever, from its own States and what revenue they might ever have brought, and once the vassal kingdoms ceased to be so except in name. This money maintained the papal court. It was needed to finance the so-called crusades, that is to say, the papal wars against the emperor, or the wars of Catholic princes against heretics when the pope decided to subsidise these, and it was needed for the rival popes to fight each other once Christendom had reached that unhappy period of forty years (1378–1417) in which a pope at Rome and a pope at Avignon divided its allegiance. And, it must be stated, not a little of this money frequently found its way into the pockets of the popes' relations. When Clement V died in 1314 there were over a million gold florins in the treasury, but only 70,000 of them reached his successor. Legacies accounted for the rest. So it was to be time and again, and since the funds must be found for the eternal wars in Italy against the plunderers of the papal State, the papacy had not only to levy what taxes it could, but to go to the bankers and borrow extensively, and at heavy interest.

All these financial operations made the centralised papacy the object of resentful criticism throughout the Church. Since the time of St. Gregory VII the popes had a new responsibility to the Church in general. They had centralised their power. They had monopolised the initiative very largely. If they were good men and wise rulers the whole Church might profit and all men would bless them, for all men now knew their acts. If they were foolish, or weak, or—as was next to be the case—bad and vicious, the papacy, for the same reason that it now tended to be omnipresent, would suffer loss of prestige as never before.

Another new papal habit, bred of the conception of the Church as a state, albeit a supra-national state, was that of playing off one foe against another. So the early popes allied themselves with the Lombard League of cities against Frederick Barbarossa, and in the next century Innocent IV, Alexander IV, and Urban IV strove to win help against his descendants by offering the crown he had forfeited to Richard of Cornwall, Edmund of Lancaster, Alfonso of Castile, and Charles of Valois in turn. Based though this action might be on the essential unity of a Europe where, all men being equally Catholic, all were equally at home in every part of Europe, such a practice tended ultimately to help to break that unity. National hates were already active in the thirteenth century, as the Sicilian rising of 1282 against the French king, Charles of Valois, whom the pope installed, had shown, and the enthusiastic massacres of the French that accompanied it. This feeling of nationality was to grow steadily, thenceforward, everywhere. The papacy was to be suspect in fourteenth-century England because the popes were Frenchmen and living in France, with which country England was waging the Hundred Years War. Later still the popes, when pressed by need, were to form alliances with what powers seemed friendly against the power that menaced them, and a whole succession of Holy Leagues and Alliances was to result. All this may have been inevitable, but the proceeding was never miraculously saved from the bad effects which usually accompany it, and in addition to being hated for its financial exactions, the papacy came to be despised and feared for its political rôle. And then the last stage of degradation was reached, and for fifty years a succession of popes strove to use what advantage their position gave them to establish their kinsmen as reigning princes in Italy, and to marry them into the royal houses of Europe.

The period 1270–1517 is, then, one of steady decline,

but in every generation there appear reformers, to fight against the tendency of the age, to recall the old ideals, and to denounce in the most outspoken language the abuses around them and their causes. Nor are popes by any means lacking among these reformers. But vested interests are, only too often, more than a match for the best of reforming popes, and the chief obstacle to reform, time and again, is the Roman Curia, and at its head the College of Cardinals.

The first unmistakable sign that a new age had begun for Catholicism was the breach between the papacy and its traditional support, the French monarchy, in the closing years of the thirteenth century. It ended in a crushing defeat for the papacy.

The French king, Philip IV (1285–1314), called the Fair, in the process of extending and centralising the royal power, and especially in the matter of taxation, found the rights of the Church an important obstacle to his schemes. Without consulting the pope he levied taxes on the clergy and terrorised most of them into paying. They appealed to Rome, and the pope, Boniface VIII, in a famous bull, *Clericis Laicos*, repeated the traditional theory that the lay power must not tax the Church without the Church's consent (1296). The bull forbade the payment of the taxes and excommunicated all who paid and all who received the money. The king replied by a vigorous defiance. The State is supreme in its own domain, and in temporal matters the king has no superior in this world. A royal decree forbidding the exportation of gold and silver held up the papal taxes due from France. The pope gradually drew back from his position, and for four years (1297–1301) there was an uneasy peace. The occasion of the renewal of the fight was the French king's arrest of the Bishop of Pamiers. When the king refused satisfaction to the papal protests, Boniface withdrew the concessions made in 1297, and in the bull, *Ausculta Fili* (1302), lecturing Philip on his various public crimes and the tyranny of his absolutist regime, threatened him with deposition. Furthermore, he summoned all the French bishops to Rome to discuss with himself the best measures for the protection of religion in France. The king replied by a counter-assembly of prelates and nobles to protest against the pope's usurpation of jurisdiction. Then for a moment the crushing defeat of the French army at Courtrai (July 11, 1302) halted the king. To gain time he feinted submission while Boniface in the bull *Unam Sanctam*, solemnly repeated the doctrine that the salvation of every human creature turns on his obedience to the pope.

The quarrel had thus brought about a discussion of fundamental principles. On both sides writers were active and a busy propaganda went on, theologians on the pope's side and lawyers—not canonists, but scholars trained in the newly revived law of the old Roman Empire—equally active for the king.

After the final declaration of *Unam Sanctam* (November, 1302) the king determined to strike a new blow. He despatched an expeditionary force into Italy to arrest the pope and bring him captive into France. On September 7, 1303, the French broke into the papal palace at Anagni and, in an awful moment for Europe, the weakness of the papacy, the eternal weakness of right before might, was revealed. Boniface stood firm against the threats, and refused to repeal his decrees. The French commissioner hesitated. To kill the pope would be foolish, and yet to conduct him through Italy, a prisoner of the foreigner, of the detested French, hardly possible. While he debated, the people of Anagni rose, the invaders were driven out, and the pope was saved. But the shock of the outrage was too much for him, and a month later he died (October 11, 1303).

It is not to be denied that a certain rough violence and a haughty nature in the pope did much to aggravate the quarrel, nor can it be denied that in Philip the Fair he had to meet an adversary more dangerous and better armed than was ever Frederick II or Henry VI. But the importance of the event transcends these details of personality. The whole question of the Church's power over the kings had been brought into question. A king had defied the pope openly, and at Anagni "the unthinkable had been put into action." And the papacy had to accept the situation. One immense shock had brought down its prestige forever, not indeed in every respect, but brought it down from that region of things accepted universally as essential to life.

The new pope, Benedict XI, in his short nine months' reign, though he excommunicated the actual leader of the French army, did not venture to condemn the king. Then for a year there was a vacancy in the Apostolic See, and when, finally, this was filled by the election of Clement V, a Frenchman, it was only to usher in a reign that marked the very nadir of the papal claim to political independence.

The king of France did not cease to pursue his enemy Pope Boniface. The great decrees against the royal tyranny still stood, and nothing but the condemnation of Boniface as a heretic and a false pope, which he had striven to obtain while the pope lived, and which was still possible now he was dead, could sterilise the importance of his acts and the principles they embodied. From the beginning of the reign of the unhappy Clement V (1305–1314)—an invalid racked with all the horrors of a painful cancer—the French king insisted that this trial of Boniface should take place. The pope, though he revoked the bulls *Clericis Laicos* and *Unam Sanctam* "in so far as they were an injury to the king," refused the proposed trial, and successfully. But at a heavy cost, the cost of being the king's accomplice in the suppression and destruction of the great religious order of the Templars, one of the greatest crimes of all history, a horror of treachery and cruelty.

Clement V died, as he had lived, in France. He had not ever the design of permanently establishing the papacy away from Rome, but the state of his own health, the reports he received of the troubled conditions, the anarchic conditions of life in Italy and Rome, and the immediate urgency of affairs of the utmost importance to be negotiated with the French king, continued to keep him in his native land. In 1309 he took up his residence at Avignon, in the priory of the Friars Preachers. It was a much more significant thing that, out of the twenty-four cardinals he created, twenty-three were French.

The first of these French popes had lowered his flag to France. It was the misfortune of his immediate successor—John XXII (1316–1334)—to fight a losing battle with the emperor, a battle in which, alas, no great principle was involved, and which tact and political good sense on the part of the fiery-tempered old pope might soon have ended and, possibly, have averted altogether.

John XXII was elected after the Holy See had been vacant almost two years. One of the last acts of his predecessor, on the death of the emperor Henry VII (1314), had been to declare that in virtue of that prince's oaths of fidelity and the powers committed to St. Peter by Our Lord, the empire as a state was subject to the pope to rule it during the vacancy. The prince-electors had been unable to agree on an emperor, and John XXII found Germany divided between the rivals, Lewis of Bavaria and Frederick of Austria. He forbade either to consider himself as emperor and announced his intention of judging the matter himself. Meanwhile he, the pope, would administer the empire, and he appointed a vicar for the imperial rights in Italy. The war went on, despite the pope, and in 1322 Lewis definitely overcame his rival. The pope refused, however to recognize him and presently the two powers were at war in Italy, and all the discontented forces in the Church were rallying to Lewis.

Among these, one very important party was that of the Franciscan extremists called the Spirituals. These were the Friars who wished that the absolute poverty practised by St. Francis and his first companions should be imposed as the rule for all the order. They would hear of no mitigation in practice, and from denouncing the popes whose practical sense allowed such mitigations, the Spirituals came to the heretical position that these mitigations were themselves heretical. For this they had already suffered at the hands of John XXII, and the emperor found them useful auxiliaries.

Another source of aid in his fight was that of the three great thinkers of the age, William of Occam, Marsilio of Padua, and John of Jandun.

The pope summoned Lewis to cease his exercise of the imperial rights and, when he refused, excommunicated him (March 23, 1324). The emperor retaliated in a manifesto denouncing the pope as a heretic, and Marsilio pub-

lished his epoch-making work the *Defensor Pacis*. Here
there was set out a complete theory of European politics in which all was subordinated to the emperor as the
representative of the people. The papacy was explained as
a human institution, subordinate to the General Council,
and the General Council it was the emperor's right to
summon.

Lewis next invaded Italy and in solemn assembly at
Rome was accepted as emperor by popular acclamation
(January 11, 1328). Six days later he was consecrated
and crowned, and then, in April, having been a third or
fourth time excommunicated, at a further popular assembly he pronounced the pope's deposition for heresy
and treachery. To complete the full Marsilian programme
it only remained to give John XXII a "successor," and
Lewis found one in a Franciscan, whom he publicly appointed, giving him the name of Nicholas V, and personally investing him with the Fisherman's ring.

The quarrel dragged on for years yet to come. John
XXII died, and his more conciliatory successor Benedict
XII (1334–1342) also, without seeing its end. Meanwhile German Catholicism was a prey to all kinds of
disorder, one party in every see, and in all the religious orders, supporting the pope and another the emperor. The popes proceeded by the usual method of
finding allies among the German princes, but here, too,
their rights suffered a serious reverse when at Rense (July
16, 1338) the princes who had the office of electors made
a declaration that the dignity of emperor came directly
from God and that it fell to whoever had the majority of
their votes. The emperor once elected had no need of
any papal confirmation to enter lawfully on his functions.

Two years later Lewis was forced to abdicate, and the
pope—Clement VI (1342–1352)—had the satisfaction of
bringing about the election of Charles of Bohemia, who
had given satisfactory guarantees in the matter of his
subordination to the papacy.

But the papal triumph was a mere show. Once really
emperor, and disembarrassed of his rivals, Charles showed
himself as independent of the pope as his predecessor—
though more honest and more respectful. in 1356 he renewed the declaration made at Rense, eighteen years

earlier, in the most striking fashion, publishing the so-called Golden Bull, which determined the conditions under which all subsequent emperors were elected. The Golden Bull named the seven princes who had the rights of electors, and it laid down who should administer the imperial power during a vacancy. Of the Church, the pope, and the rights claimed for so long, and exercised so often, by the Roman See there is not a word. The empire is a secular thing and in it the papacy has no rôle at all. The empire is altogether independent of the papacy, the temporal of the spiritual. Nor did the pope—Innocent VI (1352–1362)—protest. He even—under pressure from this prince so favourable to the Church that he was mocked as "the priests' emperor"—watered down the declaration of Clement V,[3] as Clement had watered down those of Boniface VIII under pressure from Philip the Fair.

The popes have already begun to travel along that road of concession to Catholic princes, sometimes made under pressure, sometimes proffered as a bribe, which will lead them, ultimately, to surrender wholesale the rights and exercise of jurisdiction for which St. Gregory VII and his age had fought so splendidly and so successfully. And upon these concessions and surrenders there will follow, in all the different countries of Europe, a renewal of all the disorders from which the Hildebrandine restoration had for a time saved the Church.

Midway through this lamentable century came the immense catastrophe of the Black Death. This was a kind of bubo-plague, brought from China and India along the trade routes. It was extremely contagious. Those whom it attacked died within a matter of hours and there was no known remedy for it. Also it was the young and healthy that chiefly fell victims to it. Italy was the first country of the west where it showed itself—early in 1348. It spread rapidly. Spain, southern France, and then Bavaria and the Rhineland were infected, and by the summer of the same year it had reached England. Not a country of Europe escaped and it spread even to Iceland and to

[3] Cf. *supra*, p. 144.

Greenland. The mortality was incredible. At Avignon, for example, the pope, in addition to other charities organised on the most lavish scale, made over lands for a special cemetery, and in six weeks eleven thousand corpses had been buried in it. In England half the population perished in twelve months. No class suffered more than the clergy, and while this stands as testimony to their fidelity to duty, it was an inevitable accidental consequence that not only afterwards was there a shortage of priests, but that the depleted ranks were very often filled with untrained and unsuitable subjects.

The total effect of this sudden sweeping pestilence, that in a matter of less than two years destroyed some forty million people in western Europe, can hardly be exaggerated. How it disorganised the economic life of the century is a matter for the secular historian. A student of Church History will notice how, in many ways, it broke the spirit of the generation upon which it fell. The temptation to despair of the spiritual and to live only for what the day brings took hold, very generally, of the survivors. Henceforth a new spirit of carelessness and of reckless defiance of divine truth and divine sanctions alike is very evident. The spring was gone out of the year. Something had disappeared from the life of Europe that had animated it since the great victory over the chaos of the tenth century. Henceforth there is abroad, very generally, the sense that anything may happen, and a general indifference to what it may be and when it may come.

These long duels with France and the Empire were the major actions in a fight between the Church and her children which went on, more or less continuously, all over Europe during this unhappy fourteenth century. No country enjoyed peace. England was engaged on one of the greater wickednesses of its long history in that succession of pillaging raids on France that goes by the name of the Hundred Years War, and the losses to Catholicism that ensued from this Catholic power's plundering of a neighbouring Catholic country were such that, in the end, Providence intervened directly and, to rid the country of the scourge, sent the inspired generalship of the Lorraine peasant girl, St. Joan of Arc (1428).

One notable feature of fourteenth-century life is the social and political discontent bred of a rapid increase of wealth and of the increase of individual greed that accompanied it. Everywhere the wealthy *bourgeoisie* grew wealthier. It fought the nobles for the control of the towns and it began to establish itself as a closed oligarchy in the trade guilds, devising means of locking the workers into a caste from which they could never rise. And both parties, nobles and *bourgeoisie* alike, found a common victim to assault in the ecclesiastical lords. All over France and Germany and Italy the tiny ecclesiastical principalities where bishop or abbot was lord were gradually falling before the violence of their lay subjects.

Everywhere, throughout the century, there are signs that the growing individualism and particularism resents the subjection to a system of moral laws imposed from outside, and to the clerics who are the officers of the system that embodies the authority and administers such laws. The vassal States gradually throw off their subjection to St. Peter. England repeatedly refuses to pay its arrears of tribute and, in 1364, king and Parliament flatly repudiate their papal suzerain and declare that, in making over his kingdom to Innocent III, John was acting *ultra vires,* for he did it without the consent of the nation. It is in England, too, that the statute of Provisors (1351) becomes law, to prevent clerics provided by the pope with English benefices from prejudicing the rights of English patrons, and the statutes of Præmunire (1353, 1393), to punish with loss of all goods and life imprisonment whoever attempts to retaliate by appeal to Rome, on those making use of the earlier statute.

The chief mischief the French popes of the fourteenth century wrought, after their imprudent over-development of the financial system, came from excessive affection for their own countrymen. They so packed the college of cardinals with Frenchmen [4] that the danger appeared of an official world to which a non-French pope seemed an abnormality, and to which any measures seemed lawful which would secure the French succession. This mentality

---

[4] Of the 134 cardinals created by the seven French popes between 1305 and 1378, 113 were French.

played no small part in the schism with which the century closed.

The first attempt to bring back the papacy to Rome was made by the Benedictine pope Blessed Urban V (1362–1370). He had never been a cardinal, and he owed his election to a deadlock between contending factions in the conclave that followed the death of Innocent VI. As pope he continued to lead the holy life of prayer and penance which he followed as a monk. It was in 1366 that his thoughts first turned to the idea of returning to Rome. The king of France, the cardinals, and all the papal court put every possible obstacle in the way. Urban remained inflexible, and on October 16, 1367, he entered the city which had not seen its bishop for more than sixty years.

But, in little more than two years, revolts, in which the Romans had as auxiliaries the bands of brigands led by the English *condottiere*, John Hawkwood, made Rome unsafe. Nor did any of the Christian kings to whom the pope made appeal come to his aid. He determined to return to Avignon, and despite the entreaties, and the prophecies, of St. Bridget of Sweden, he held firm to his plan. On September 27, 1370, he re-entered the great palace on the Rhône, and in December, as St. Bridget had foretold, he was dead.

Eleven days later, after a short conclave of a few hours, the cardinals unanimously elected pope the youngest among them, Roger de Beaufort, forty-two years of age. He took the name of Gregory XI. His first thought was to carry out the enterprise his predecessor had had to abandon. One obstacle after another, of a political kind, presented itself. The date of departure was often fixed, and as often revoked. Finally there came from Italy, to strengthen the pope's will, and force the last hindrances aside, the voice of the one really great personage this wretched century produced, St. Catherine of Siena. On September 13, 1376, the pope left Avignon, and on January 17 of the next year he made his entry into Rome.

Gregory XI survived his return to Rome a bare fourteen months and then, on April 8, 1378, with all the mob of the city howling around the Vatican, "Elect an Italian or you die," the sixteen terrified cardinals chose as his successor the archbishop of Bari, the first Italian pope for seventy-four years. He took the name of Urban VI.

Was Urban VI (1378–1389) validly elected? Almost universally scholars to-day assert it. But there was, in the circumstances of the election, enough of a case to be exploited against its validity should it be to anyone's interest to do so. And soon it was very much to the interest of many people to be rid of Pope Urban, and by any possible means.

As Bartolomeo Pregnani, archbishop of Bari, Urban had been a model official in his high place of vice-chancellor at the Avignon court. His life had been austere and he was known as a strong supporter of reform. Now, upon his election, his whole manner changed, or his great zeal for reform swamped his practical judgment. Later his actions were such that there is something to be said for the theory that his reason had suffered, and it may be that this trouble began at his election. Certain it is that his tactless, tyrannous manner speedily alienated the cardinals who elected him, and who, in order to elect him, had gone outside the Sacred College. One of his most loyal supporters was St. Catherine of Siena, and we find her writing to him: "For the love of Jesus crucified, Holy Father, soften a little the sudden movements of your temper."

Slowly the opposition grew, and the cardinals—all but five of the sixteen in Rome were French—began to escape from the city. In June Urban tried to win them back, but the only result was to provoke a declaration that they doubted if the election made had been valid—and this after three months in which they had all repeatedly recognized him, sought and accepted favours from him as pope and proclaimed him as pope in a joint letter to the Christian world.

In August they announced that he was no pope. They had elected him simply to escape the death that otherwise awaited them. Meanwhile, they had managed to sow doubts in the minds of others, and notably in the mind of the king of France, Charles V (1364–1380). When the thirteen cardinals came together at Fondi a letter from the French king ended their last hesitation. They proceeded to a new election and—the three Italians not voting—unanimously chose the cardinal Robert of Geneva, who had been for some years, as legate in Italy, the successful commander-in-chief of the papal armies, and inevitably something rather more than less of a *condottiere,* He called himself Clement VII.

All the cardinals—with one exception—recognized Clement as pope. What was Christendom to do? How was it to decide between the conflicting accounts of the rivals? And how was it to judge on which occasion this same body of cardinals had really, by its unanimous vote, elected a pope, in April or in September? Christendom speedily divided, along lines more or less political, according as its sympathies were French or anti-French. And both camps were equally representative of the Church, holy people, since canonised, being found among the supporters of the Avignon pope as well as among those of his Roman antagonist. Was the Church divided? On one point only, the point of fact, was Urban truly pope or was Clement? On all points of doctrine, on the point of papal powers and the obedience due to the pope, all were in agreement. There was nowhere any rebellion against an admittedly lawful pope. The division was not a schism in any real sense of the word. But it was a very real division, and it lasted for just short of forty years.

Urban VI died, and his cardinals—the new Sacred College he created after the election of September, 1378, and his excommunication of all who took part in it—elected Boniface IX (1389). Then Clement VII died (1394), and his cardinals, refusing to end the division by themselves electing Boniface, elected Peter de Luna, who took the name of Benedict XIII. When Boniface IX died (1404) the Roman cardinals replaced him first by Innocent VII and then by Gregory XII (1406). The miserable truth has to be faced that no pope, on either side, was at all worthy of his office. They were, all of them, little better than partisan leaders of rival factions and in the end the Church as a whole tired of both, repudiated their authority, and, coming together in a self-styled General Council at Pisa (1409), elected a third pope of its own, Alexander V.

The Church did not by any means acquiesce passively in the division. From the day when first it realized that the division existed, schemes for a reunion were put forward and discussed on both sides. And as the schemes had to justify themselves by reference to theological principles, some strange new ideas began to circulate, and this under the guarantee of most respectable signatures. The idea that a General Council should be summoned to deal with the matter was natural enough, and it was a fairly common idea. The partisans of the idea next began to explain that the real ultimate authority in the Church was in the episcopate as a body, and that General Councils were superior to the popes. One of the most famous men of the day, John Gerson, Chancellor of the University of Paris, went a step further. Not bishops alone, but priests, and even all the baptised, were the real source of the papal authority. Power resides in the Church as a whole, and lawful election only communicates it. As the Church has a right to elect so it has a right to correct, and to punish, even to depose the pope if necessary. In a General Council every Catholic has a right to vote.

Another current of opinion resigned itself to the division as showing God's will in the matter—or the division would never have come about. Why only two popes, this argument proceeded, why not one for each country?

The general movement to bring the division to an and really began with the election of Gregory XII in 1406, for the Roman cardinals in the conclave had all sworn that whichever of them was elected would be willing to resign if the Avignon pope—Benedict XIII—would do the same. The way would then be open for a single united election of a pope whom both sides—and therefore the whole Church—would acknowledge. On his election Gregory XII solemnly renewed his oath.

The next two years were spent in negotiations to arrange a meeting between the two popes, to fix a place and name the day. Benedict was shifty and dishonest, Gregory, though straightforward, vacillating. They never met, though at one time only a day's march separated them. "One was a land animal that could not face the sea," said a contemporary wit, "the other a sea animal that would die on the land," and when the king of Naples captured Rome, none rejoiced more than Gregory XII, for now he had a better argument than ever for his inability to meet his rival (1408).

The king of France now abandoned the Avignon pope and declared himself neutral. The University of Paris did the same, and besought the two sets of cardinals to come together and work for reunion. Within a few weeks this had happened, and the majority of the cardinals of both popes met in a common assembly. They summoned a council which met at Pisa, and each of the popes summoned a council also. But while the councils called by the two popes were miserable fiascos, to Pisa there came, besides the twenty-four cardinals, numerous bishops and three hundred doctors in theology and canon law. The new theories about the constitution of the Church were now to have their chance.

Both popes were cited to Pisa, and when they failed to appear, were condemned in their absence for schism, heresy, and perjury, and deposed. Then the cardinals elected the archbishop of Milan, a one-time supporter of the Roman pope. He took the name of Alexander V. Next the council proceeded to enact a series of decrees for the reform of ecclesiastical life, all greatly to the profit of the traditional authority of the bishops.

The situation was now, in some respects, worse than ever. There were three popes instead of two, and, in the end, it was the third pope, the one of the three who was most certainly not pope, whom practically the whole of Christendom obeyed, Benedict possessing no supporters outside the little Spanish town where he now dwelt, and Gregory only an allegiance of Italian princes that varied with their political hopes.

Pope Alexander lasted only ten months, and then the Pisan party elected to succeed him Baldassare Cossa, who took the name of John XXIII. He was a man so bad and so utterly unworthy of any ecclesiastical office—an ecclesiastical financier who had the name of having once been a pirate and was now a trader in indulgences—that in the end the emperor Sigismund intervened and set in motion the train of events which at last saved the Church.

As pope, John XXIII showed none of the political ability which had won him the tiara. He stumbled for three years from one blunder to another, alienating all his supporters in turn. Had not the emperor, Sigismund, now forced upon him the convocation of a new council, the Church might not improbably have seen a new division and yet a fourth claimant in the papacy.

This council which met at Constance (November, 1414) is the strangest in all Church history from its composition, its procedure, and the nature of what was effected through it. The full effect of the chaos of forty years was now seen. All the wildest theories about the source of ecclesiastical authority seemed likely to be realised when there descended on the town (in addition to the 185 bishops) 300 doctors in theology and law, 18,000 other ecclesiastics, and a vast multitude of lay potentates, of princes, and of representatives of towns and corporations, to the number of more than a hundred thousand. The dominant figure was the emperor, and he it was who was to save the situation at the critical moment when John XXIII, realising that he had now to face a trial, and almost certainly deposition, fled from the town intending to revoke his convocation, declare the council null, and raise a counter-movement. The pope was arrested and placed under guard and the council proceeded.

All the doctors had a vote, as well as the bishops, and the decisions were taken, not by counting individual votes, but the votes of the nations, into five of which the council was divided—Italy, France, England, Germany, and Spain, having each one vote. The cardinals had no authority beyond what any other individual member of their nation possessed.

The pope was tried on a variety of charges and then condemned for simony, the maladministration of Church property, and unfaithful stewardship in things spiritual as well as temporal. On May 29, 1415, he was deposed, and six days later he accepted his sentence.

Meanwhile, the Roman pope, Gregory XII—now eighty-nine years of age—was still holding out at Rimini. He had refused the emperor's invitation to the council and the council's citation likewise. But finally he decided to abdicate, and to recognise the council as an assembly convoked by the emperor. On June 15, 1415, his proxies arrived at Constance, accredited not to the council but to the emperor, and on July 4 they read Gregory's bulls to the council.

By the first he solemnly convoked the council and next, to the council thus convoked, he announced his resignation. The council formally thanked him and notified to him his appointment as cardinal-bishop of Porto, for which the ex-pope made a grateful recognition of his thanks and an act of obedience to the council.

There still remained, in distant Spain, the heir of the pope who had begun the schism: Pedro de Luna, Benedict XIII. He remained obdurate to the last, and to the council's condemnation of him (July 26, 1417) replied with a renewed excommunication and threats of deposition to the princes. His supporters had now shrunk to his household servants and a handful of guards.

Then on St. Martin's Day, November 11, 1417, the conclave—consisting of twenty-three cardinals and five prelates from each of the six nations—elected as pope the cardinal Odo Colonna. He took the name of Martin V. The schism was ended. The whole Church was united in obedience to one pope.

But this same council that had brought the schism to an end had sown the seeds of much future dissension. Whatever the niceties of Canon Law that had safeguarded the legitimacy of its liquidation of a complex problem, the fact remained that the Council of Constance had judged two claimants to the papacy and condemned them, and that it had also elected a new pope. And it had also declared, in explicit terms, that General Councils were superior to popes, and it had provided that every five years this General Council should reassemble and the pope, in some measure, give to it an account of his stewardship. As far as the wishes of the Council of Constance went, a revolution had been achieved, and the Church for the future was to be governed in a parliamentary way, and not by the absolute, divinely given authority of its head, the Vicar of Christ. The forty years that followed the council were to see the successive popes —Martin V, Eugene IV, and Nicholas V—wholly taken up with the effort to destroy this new theory and to control the councils which it bred and inspired. The full fruits of the mischief were only reaped in the long-drawn-out dissensions of the Council of Basle (1431–1449).

Meanwhile the cause of reform suffered a setback impossible to measure. And, in these same years, a new Islamic renaissance conquered province after province from the Christian empire in the east, conquered territory even in Europe, and so prepared the way for the most resounding feat of all, the conquest of Constantinople in 1453. Against this menace to the very existence of Europe, the popes strove repeatedly to organise the princes of the west, but their appeals fell on deaf ears. The supranational prestige of the papacy in political matters had disappeared, and with it Europe's one effective guardian against anti-European dangers. The princes had refused to fight Islam on the Jordan and in Syria. Now they would have to face it on the Danube, in Germany, and in Italy.

Martin V (1417–1431) gave himself chiefly to the work of restoring Rome—a city of ruins with a population reduced to a bare ten thousand—and of slowly regaining hold on the Papal States. The Avignon experience, and the history of the years of the schism, had proved very clearly that a pope who was not in reality a sovereign tended very speedily to appear a subject, and his power to be the instrument of some sovereign's policy. With the General Council Martin V had comparatively little trouble. It was summoned, as Constance had provided, and met at Pavia on April 23, 1423. The plague broke out and it was transferred to Siena. But the attendance was so poor that to proceed would have been folly. The pope gladly seized the excuse and dissolved it. The second council he summoned he did not live to see assemble. It fell to his successor, Eugene IV (1431–1447), a nephew of Gregory XII, to deal with it. This was the famous Council of Basle. From the beginning it showed a strong determination to master the pope and to continue the mischievous work of Pisa and Constance, and the pope's alternations of impulsive violence and weak surrender played into its hands. He had in fact none of the diplomatic gifts of his predecessor. He dissolved the council and it refused to separate. The council next suspended the pope and then deposed him. The pope excommunicated the council, negotiations were opened, and finally, there was a compromise, the pope yielding to the point of withdrawing the dissolution. Next the council proposed to set up a new permanent system to supervise the pope and the Roman *Curia.* But Eugene here stood firm and transferred the council to Ferrara first (1438) and then to Florence (1439). A tiny group refused to move. They hung on at Basle and once more deposed Eugene and in his stead elected the duke of Savoy, "Felix V."

At Florence, meanwhile, an affair of the first importance was going forward, the great scheme on which Eugene had been steadily working for years, the reunion of the schismatic churches of the East, the Greeks, the Armenians, and the Jacobites. And a resounding answer was given to the theological innovators by the definition of the papal primacy over the whole Church as a thing divinely instituted (1439).

These two first popes after the restoration of unity were men of admirable life and keen reformers. Everywhere there began to be evident the beginnings of better days. The new congregation of St. Justina reorganised the life of the Benedictine monasteries of Italy. The Canons-Regular in Holland produced the new congregation of Windesheim whence was to come that new school of piety of which Thomas à Kempis and the *Imitation of Christ* are perhaps the best-known fruits. In the Franciscan Order, too, a renewal of the primitive life began, orthodox this time and free from extravagances of pride, and blessed by the popes, whose leaders were such saints as Bernardine of Siena—one of the greatest popular preachers ever known—and John Capistran, who was later to rouse Hungary so successfully to the defeat of the Turks. A like work of restoration was done for the Franciscan nuns by the Burgundian, St. Colette. The Order of Preachers received new vigour from the discipline of St. Catherine of Siena, and in St. Antoninus, archbishop of Florence, it gave to the Church a model ruler, a reformer, and one of the first of the specialised moral theologians.

Everywhere, in Spain, in Germany, in France, and in Italy, by their legates and by the provincil councils these summoned, the popes pressed the restoration of the ravaged Catholic life, and in Florence in 1436 Eugene IV founded the first seminary—a house of study and clerical discipline for the formation of those whose vocation was to the secular clergy. Last, but not least, of their merits, both Martin V and Eugene IV chose excellent cardinals, and while they increased the privileges and the jurisdiction of the Sacred College, they raised it, by their careful nominations, to a higher place in the Church than it had known for a hundred years.

But how far were the popes to be free, in this post-schism world, to exercise the fulness of their powers over the local churches and so carry out the needed reforms? Here was the crux of the whole business. The years of dissensions had been a great opportunity for the princes, and the embarrassment of the popes an occasion of lay profit. The king of France, and the princes of Germany, too, adopted the anti-papal decrees of the Council of Basle, and, without in any way repudiating the Roman Primacy, began to act very much as local popes in regard to the legislation of the local councils, to the administration of the churches, and the appointments of bishops. Against their declarations—the Pragmatic Sanctions of Bourges (1438) and Mainz (1439)—the popes for years dared do no more than protest.

The first half of this fifteenth century saw a very real revival of popular piety. While the curious medieval reluctance towards frequent communion continued, there was now, more than ever, a deep devotion to the life of Our Lord in its more pathetic aspects. Spirituality and religious art began to make a direct appeal to the emotions in all that regards the Passion and death of Our Lord, and the sufferings of His mother. It is now there begin to appear the statues of Our Lord crowned with thorns, the pictures representing the laying on the Cross, or His waiting, bleeding and lacerated, while the executioners make it ready. It is about this time, too, that the feast of Our Lady's seven sorrows is first celebrated.

Sometimes this new devotion develops in such a way that the vision of the sufferings risks obscuring the more important truth of the life-giving sacrifice wrought through them. Devotion and dogma do not always go hand in hand. There begins to be, in some cases, a mischievous divorce between theology and piety. From this tendency, it is to be noted, the three great preachers of the age— St. Vincent Ferrer, St. Bernardine, and St. John Capistran —are wholly free, although never in history have any preachers so moved the masses of mankind by their realisation of the details of the sufferings of the Passion.

This growing divorce of Catholic thought and popular Catholic piety—whence inevitably there will proceed a mechanical practice of religion, a reliance on practices alone, and endless superstitions—is no doubt related to the fact that, in the century since St. Thomas, there has been a growing tendency among Catholic philosophers to belittle the rôle of reason. It is not the system and the spirit of St. Thomas that dominate the thought of the fourteenth century, but the sceptical, agnostic spirit of Occam. We can have no really reasonable gurantee, such is the conclusion to which tends, for the most elementary truths of natural religion. There is no absolute in morals except the will of God. Philosophy becomes more and more a mental gymnastic, ingenious but sterile, futility itself. The mentality it fosters is abhorrent to the pious, and rightly so, for such self-satisfaction is at the very antipodes of the Christian ideal. So the theologian ceases to nourish himself with the necessary mental food, and theology ceases to nourish piety. Thought and prayer threaten to go their separate ways.

One interesting evidence of the decline of theology is the popularity of John Wycliffe, the day's one real heretic. This English scholar-priest would rebuild Christianity on the sole basis of pious meditation on the Scriptures. The papacy, hierarchy, priesthood, and sacraments are all so much human invention. The one certitude is Holy Scripture, the one thing really necessary is to have the scriptures preached. Indulgences, confession, the Mass should be renounced. And the Church should return to its first state of simple poverty. This revolutionary doctrine, preached in England by the Lollards for some forty years (1376–1415), continued to linger in corners of the country for the next century. It was also carried into Bohemia, and in John Hus it found not only a most able apostle, but its chief martyr. The national anti-German movement of the Czechs found in the heresy an additional means of self-expression, and Hus, ever since his death, has been the great hero of his race.

Something of this same idea that sacraments are not really necessary for perfection, or rather that the one thing necessary in a spiritual life is a man's own prayer and meditation on the scriptures, is to be found also in the book called *The German Theology* which had a certain vogue through all the later fifteenth century and whose influence can be seen in Erasmus and in Luther.

Here were sources of future trouble, reasons for the ultimate failure of their own efforts at reform, that might well have caused anxiety to Martin V or Eugene IV, had it been any more possible for them than it is for us to read the future in the present. A further, most potent, source of ill was the Pagan spirit that accompanied the new revival of learning and letters, the movement called the Renaissance *par excellence*.

This fifteenth-century revival differed from its predecessors—the much greater revivals of the twelfth and thirteenth centuries—first of all in this that it was an artistic rather than a philosophical movement. It was the literature, as such, of the Greeks and Latins that was now of importance. Ideas, not of course neglected or ignored, were yet of secondary importance to the form in which they were expressed. The real concern of the revival was with the imagination and the critical, artist's faculties, and therefore directly effective upon the emotions. One inevitable consequence of this preoccupation with the individual and the personal, was a new exaltation of man. The purely human was now set up and revered, adored even, as never since the days of the old Paganism. Nothing could have been more speedily fatal to Christian life, even in all its vigour, than the encouragement of such a spirit. The popes who came to be the leading patrons of the poets, prose-writers, and artists in whom the movement had its being, did not, it is true, set themselves to encourage that spirit. But they were too easy in accepting—because of their artistic usefulness—the services of men wholly tainted with it, and this at a time when Christian traditions were but painfully struggling to life again after a century and a half of decay.

Gradually, inevitably, the amoral spirit of the revived

Paganism gained a hold in the Church, halting effectively the whole reform movement and divorcing the papacy from it. For the final achievement of the neo-Pagans was the most unexpected thing of all, namely to bring about the moral collapse of the very centre of the Christian world. Pope Nicholas V (1447–1455) had desired to see Rome the centre of the new learning, the new culture, the new art. Fifty years after his time it was all this, and it was also the centre of all the new vices, and the popes were among their foremost practitioners. And this continued for some forty years, so that Pope Adrian VI (1521–1523), who lived all through the period,[5] could preface his reform with the deliberate statement that the Roman Church had been the first source of all the evils which good men were everywhere lamenting.

The immediate successor of Eugene IV was Nicholas V, who—as Tommaso Parentucelli—had been one of the leaders of the new classical scholarship, who as a theologian skilled in Greek had played an important part in the reunion council of 1438, and as priest and bishop had shown himself a man of unblemished life. His short reign —immortal by the pope's generous patronage to scholars and artists, a patronage of which the Vatican Library and the new St. Peter's are monuments that still survive— was yet one long struggle with the forces that worked against the pope's independence. To secure peace at home from the intrigues of neighbouring princes—there were several attempts at revolution in Rome in these years, and a serious plot to assassinate the pope and the cardinals—Nicholas set himself to sow discord among his foes, a policy which was to recoil on its author and on his successors.

The first of these, Calixtus III (1455–1458), was involved in an Italian war immediately on his election. Pius II (1458–1464), too, found an unavoidable Italian war absorbing the energy he would have preferred to give to the recovery of Constantinople. This pope, as Aeneas Sylvius Piccolomini, had been a singularly typical figure of the humanist revival. He had been a supporter of the Council of Basle, and an opponent of Eugene IV, and his

[5] He was born 1459.

private life had been as scandalous as that of many another of these humanists. Then he had reformed, made his submission to the pope, received Holy Orders, and turned his genius to the service of religion. He has an immortal place among the popes as the last of the crusaders. Here he continued faithfully the policy of Calixtus III, who had professed himself ready to sell manuscripts and chalices alike to provide funds for the recovery of Constantinople. Pius II pleaded, exhorted, negotiated with the Catholic princes for the whole of his brief reign. At last he assembled an army and a fleet—the best he could do, but insufficient, indeed, to meet those of the mighty genius who ruled the Turks, Mahomet II—and he died at Ancona as he arrived there, a broken old man, to take his share in the fatigues of the expedition.

Pius II, too, had to face seditions and rebellions in his own States, and he was unable to gather from his subjects even the taxes levied for defence. By the end of the next pontificate—that of Paul II (1464–1471), a Venetian and another scholarly Renaissance type—the papacy was, however, strong enough to earn the respectful distrust of all its neighbours.

Sixtus IV (1471–1484)—Francesco della Rovere—had consequently to meet an opposition stronger than any that had yet shown itself. It is with his reign that there begins the new captivity of the papacy, its enslavement in political methods to the spirit of the secular princes of the age. The spiritual arm of the Church is proved to be of no avail against the spirits of wickedness in high places, and the popes, henceforth, frankly resort to the secular weapons of diplomacy and statecraft. The practice was to cost them dear, nor were they by any means always successful in it.

Sixtus IV is commonly held to bear a heavy part of the responsibility for the scandals of the next sixty years. He lowered the whole tone of the Sacred College by his nominations, and he made over the high places of the papal administration to his relations—unworthy relations—to a degree hitherto unheard of.

The Sacred College was still a very small body. Rarely were there as many as twenty voters in a fifteenth-century conclave. Whence an anxiety on the part of the princes to gain the red hat for some of their own subjects and so help to determine elections, and, ultimately, new concessions of Church money or jurisdiction. The popes are compelled at times to yield to this pressure, and a vested anti-papal interest begins to form in the very college of cardinals. It is only a strong pope who is master in his own house, and even the strongest popes—until the *coup d'état* of Leo X in 1517, creating thirty-one cardinals at once—find the Sacred College at times beyond their strength.

At every vacancy henceforward, the cardinals bind themselves by a pact to limit the power of the pope about to be elected, now devising to themselves a new share of the Church's wealth, now reviving the heresy-tainted notion of periodical General Councils to supervise the pope. The astonishing thing—given human nature and such a world—is that the popes of such a time ever resisted. None ever fell to the temptation to carry out the capitulations, to join with his colleagues and patrons of cardinalitial days in a joint sack of the Church's spirituals for the sake of gain. The worst of cardinals, once he was elected pope, developed a new loyalty to his office, a loyalty set grotesquely, it may be, in the disorder of his personal immorality, but none the less real for all its setting. One arm against disloyal cardinals was for the popes to nominate their own relatives to the Sacred College. So out of the nine creations of Calixtus III three were nephews, and three again out of the ten creations of Paul II.

Sixtus IV, then, did not so much invent a new principle as give an existing principle a new development. Thanks to the character of almost all his creations, the Sacred College was speedily transformed—and decidedly for the worse, a transformation, however, in which the necessities of politics had at least as great a share as the pope's inordinate love of his relations. Now for the first time bad men are admitted to the Sacred College, and in what numbers! And their creator—ex-general of the Franciscans, learned, simple, industrious—is himself above reproach in his own life! Of his thirty-four cardinals no less than six are relations, nephews, and cousins. They are given all the chief offices, and wealth—in the shape of benefices—is poured out on them unstintingly. One alone—Giuliano della Rovere—held eight bishoprics in four different countries, besides various abbeys! Others of his kin who remained in the lay state the pope promoted to those civil and military offices which he could not trust to the disloyal Roman nobility. One nephew became prefect of Rome, upon another he conferred Imola as a fief when he had obtained its restitution from the duke of Milan. The pope's own family installed in the chief places of Church and State, reigning as his vassals in the papal fiefs, and allied by marriages to the neighbouring princes, such were the main lines of the new régime gradually developed by Sixtus IV to secure peace abroad and order, security, at home.

Order at home the policy did indeed secure, order of a sort. But the very system almost immediately turned against itself, for the successor of any pope who had thus made over so many offices to relatives, was faced with a permanent opposition of the very worst kind. For the future there is a new element in all conclaves—the struggle of the office holders to prevent the election of a pope likely to displace them. From now on they make a solid block in the Sacred College, this group of relatives powerful under the last pope and, almost inevitably, in bitter opposition to his successor. Sixtus IV dead, the della Rovere influence managed indeed to elect his successor—a victory that did not fall to it twice—and under Alexander VI a feud of della Rovere against Borgia was one of the chief political features of the time.

The sheer badness of the nephews of Sixtus IV involved the Holy See in a succession of discreditable and scandalous episodes, the terrible conspiracy of the Pazzi, for example, with the murder of Giuliano de' Medici, and the disastrous war against Venice that closed the pontificate.

Then came the simoniacal election of Innocent VIII (1484–1492), made by cardinals all of whom Sixtus had created, made chiefly by his ablest nephew the Cardinal Giuliano della Rovere, one day to be himself simoniacally elected pope as Julius II, and to publish the decree making such elections henceforth impossible.

With Innocent VIII the papacy descends lower still. Not that his own personal life as pope was reprehensible. He was indeed weak and vacillating, the tool of subordinates, and this is always evil enough in any ruler. But he is the first pope to acknowledge the natural children born to him in days gone by, to give them the place a married prince naturally gives his children, and to use them in the diplomatic game for the furtherance of the papal policies. His son he married to the daughter of Lorenzo de' Medici, thus sealing a pact with the great Florentine banker-prince who for years had been the papacy's bitterest foe.

The conclave which followed Innocent's death sank lower even than that which had elected him. For the majority chose, heavily bribed thereto, the Cardinal Rodrigo Borgia, an able administrator indeed, but a man whose life, after forty years in the Sacred College, was still as openly scandalous as when, a young cardinal of twenty-eight, Pius II had rebuked him for it. This is the man notorious as Alexander VI.

He reigned for eleven years (1492–1503), years which are a turning-point in the history of Europe, for they saw the discovery of America and the first emergence of Spain as a single united kingdom, after the final expulsion of the Mahometans in 1492; and with the emergence of Spain came the beginning of that duel between France and Spain for the control of Italy that was to go on for another century and a half. Inevitably the papacy was to be involved in that long fight, partly because the popes were Italian princes and partly because the necessity the papacy is eternally under, of being manifestly free from the domination of any particular State, made it impossible for the popes to wish to see either France or Spain really master of any considerable portion of Italy, whether of the kingdom of Naples to the south or of the duchy of Milan to the north. That the same power should ever come to control both, must, for the popes, seem to be the end of everything. Hence the eternal vacillation of the papacy, supporting Spain or France in turn, to secure that the rival does not crush it, and then, on the victory of its ally, working to prevent the destruction of the power it has just been fighting. And for all this—armies, fleets, diplomacy—money is needed, and always more money, and all the resources and methods of the modern State are employed to raise the money, and the methods are applied to ecclesiastical finances and to spiritual goods too.

Alexander VI was the first pope to whom it fell to face face a French invasion of Italy, and a resulting Franco-Spanish war.

With Alexander's death in 1503 the peculiarly immoral life of the papal court came to an end. The cardinals elected as his successor an admirable man, Cardinal Francesco Piccolomini,[6] but he reigned only a matter of weeks. They then chose Giuliano della Rovere, Pope Julius II, who speedily showed himself one of the most vigorous of all European rulers. In Julius II (1503–1513) the Holy See had what, given the new system, it had long needed —a pope who was a first-class diplomatist and a good general in the field, a strong and capable organiser, fierce, ruthless, and inflexible. With him the Roman barons were finally crushed and the papal States for the first time really organised with the pope as their effective ruler. Julius II, too, though his reign was free from much that had degraded Rome in his predecessor's time, furthered his policy by marriage alliances. He married one niece to a powerful chief of the house of Colonna, a nephew to one of the Orsini, while a second Orsini married one of the pope's own natural daughters. But this pope aimed at much more than the aggrandisement of his own family. It was Julius who ruled, and whatever the rank to which he promoted relatives—he introduced four nephews into the Sacred College—it was for the service they could render the Church that they were promoted.

Given the system of Church government—the system traditional for now fifty years—Julius II was an excellent pope; if in addition we recall that it was precisely in his reign that the Holy See had first really to meet the political peril of the great national States, we should say, the pope the time called for. Naples was henceforward but a province of the new Spanish empire. To the north the duchy of Milan was little more than a French province, and Venice, inevitably hostile to a pope who proposed to wrest from it the papal lands it had occupied so long, was at the height of its international importance.

The pope broke Venice by an alliance with France and the emperor—only to find the French a greater menace

---

[6] Pius III.

now than ever Venice had been. He began to negotiate an anti-French league, and the French king retorted by calling up once more the ghost of the Council of Constance. The emperor joined him, and with five cardinals in support, in May, 1511, they convoked a "General Council" to meet at Pisa, to reform the Church in its head and its members. Immediately in France and in Germany all the latent anti-Roman spirit found a voice. Julius had absolutely nothing to protect him except the dignity of the papacy. A century after Constance the papacy, the problem of its political independence still unsolved, was still at the mercy of the Catholic princes, and threatened with a new schism which the schismatics essayed to justify in the name of Constance and by the theories Constance had blessed.

The pope replied to the schismatics by summoning a council himself—the Fifth Council of the Lateran, which opened in May, 1512. Diplomacy won over Venice, diplomacy detached the emperor from his anti-papal alliance with the French, who, their best general slain at Ravenna (1512), were driven out of Italy by the pope's allies with an ease that gave the victory an air of the miraculous. The schismatic council collapsed with the political fortunes of its chief patron and—without any formal dissolution—it disappeared from the scene. Pope Julius died in this moment of triumph, and the reconciliation with the French king and the schismatic cardinals was left to his successor.

The successor of Pope Julius was the cardinal Giovanni de' Medici, Pope Leo X (1513–1521). The record of his career epitomises the time in all its tendencies. He had received the red hat from Pope Innocent VIII at the age of thirteen—part of the pact of peace between the pope and his father, the powerful ruler of Florence, the hitherto anti-papal Lorenzo. In his own first consistory Leo gave the red hat to a grandson of Innocent VIII, who was also his own nephew, for—a second item of the pact—Giovanni de' Medici's sister had married that Pope's natural son. Another relative to receive the red hat at the same consistory was the pope's first cousin Giulio de' Medici, the natural son of an uncle stabbed to death during Mass, years before, in Florence, by assassins who, though not commissioned thereto by the pope of the day, were certainly in his service and did the deed for his benefit. Three other nephews and another first cousin complete the list of near relatives—six in all—created cardinals by this pope.

As the Cardinal de' Medici, Leo X, after the death of his father, had been the head of his family. A revolution drove them from Florence in 1494, and as he kept the clan together during the exile, so he continued to lead them when, in 1512, an incident of the general political change-over, they came back into power. The fact that it was the head of the newly restored ruling family of Florence whom the cardinals elected pope in 1513 added yet another complication to the maze of papal diplomacy. Medici popes were to rule for the next twenty years, and, in fighting for the Holy See, never for a moment did they lose sight of the interests of the family principality. The pope's difficulties continued to be Cæsar's opportunity, and one result of the great French victory of 1515 was a Concordat, which is not unfairly described as the most extensive concession to Cæsar of ecclesiastical jurisdiction the age had ever known—concession of rights of nomination so far-reaching that, for administrative purposes, the papacy practically ceased to function in France except by the grace of the kings of France.

For the best part of twenty years (1513-1521 and 1523–1534), the vacillating Medici diplomacy was free to work its infinity of harm to the prestige of the Holy See, and to leave it the least trusted of all States among diplomats and princes. It was in the midst of the greatest of Leo X's anxieties, the approaching election of the young king of Spain (king also of Naples, ruler of the newly discovered Americas, ruler of the Netherlands, and Burgundy) as Holy Roman Emperor, that the last of his troubles showed itself—the revolt of Martin Luther. Little wonder if the pope underestimated the importance of this latest disturbance in a Church already distraught. Leo's policy turned him from France to the emperor, and then as the news of the first successes of the new alliance reached him, prematurely he died, December 1521, still four years short of fifty.

7

The Revolt of the Protestants, 1517–1648

THE CATHOLIC Church in the opening years of the sixteenth century, a hundred years after the termination of the schism, was, then, grievously sick in head and in members. Even the best of physicians would scarcely have known where to begin the cure. And then there appeared what the last two hundred years of European life—secular and religious alike—had lacked, a personality of genius. This was Martin Luther, an Augustinian friar, professor of theology in the university of Wittenberg, and his destructive genius achieved the most sweeping rejection of traditional doctrine and practice in religion that the world had seen since Marcion or Arius.

Luther summed up in his person all the good and all the bad, all that was most characteristically German, in a way no man of his race had summed it up hitherto or has summed it up since. He was Germany. Tender-hearted and brutal, sentimental, muddle-headed, self-contradictory, obscure, assured and dogmatic, arrogant, not too well informed on any one of the matters that occupied him—save the eternally all-important matter of human nature, its aspirations and, especially, its weaknesses and the temporarily important fact of the countless scandals in ecclesiastical life—he had but to lift up his mighty voice—"I, Dr. Martin Luther"—and he was answered by an approving shout from German Catholicism that rocked the Church to its very foundations.

Like many a hundred others of his time, Luther was a

INCLUDING ADOLPH HITLER

friar who should never have been a friar, and under the surface of his over-busy monastic life lay unfathomable deeps of anxiety, fruit of the endless struggle to keep his vows and of the difficulty of remaining God's intimate and friend. His devotional life was subjective—like that of all his age, and of a great part of mankind ever since. His knowledge of theology was superficial in the extreme. His only guides were the scholastics of the decay, Nominalist in tendency, and, in fact, convinced of the impossibility of any synthesis of reason and faith. From these barren sources Luther turned to Holy Scripture and to St. Augustine and gradually fashioned a way out of his difficulties. Man's sins—the illuminating discovery assured him—are not man's fault. They need not, do not, form a barrier between God and his own soul. They are due to an essential, all-embracing corruption of his nature which is the consequence of Adam's sin. Not only can man not help sinning, he cannot even do good though he wishes it. His actions must be sinful, though it is not his fault that they are so. From the penalties due in justice for this mass of sinfulness, man is saved by God's grace, and the condition of his receiving God's grace is Faith, i.e., that man shall believe God wills to save him and shall put his confidence therein. Such is the revolutionary theory technically called Justification by Faith Alone. If it is true then the whole traditional structure of Christianity is a needless empty show, the Mass, the sacraments, the sacrificing priesthood, the teaching hierarchy, the papacy, practices of penance, asceticism, habits of self-restraint, prayer itself. Nay, these things are a hindrance, an enormous sham, a terrible system of lies, and therefore to be utterly swept away and destroyed.

Luther's opportunity was the arrival at Wittenberg, in October, 1517, of the preachers of an unusually scandalous papal indulgence.[1] He proposed a debate on the indul-

---

[1] Scandalous, that is to say, in the way it was preached, the way in which the money was collected and by reason of the object to which much of the money was destined, viz. the repayment to money-lenders of the enormous sum and the interest on it, which the young archbishop of Mainz had had to pay at Rome for his dispensation to be, at the same time, archbishop of Magdeburg.

24,000 GOLD PIECES

gence system and the whole popular mechanical conception of salvation through pious gestures and sanctioned practices. The controversy thus opened continued until the summer of 1518, Luther revealing himself as a preacher of genius and, by his onslaught on the papacy as a financial machine, winning an immense following throughout Germany.

From Rome came the order to be silent and make his submission. Luther mocked at it in a great sermon on "the sham called excommunication." The true Church, he explained, is invisible. Next he was given sixty days in which to appear at Rome. Then Rome despatched Cardinal Cajetan, one of the greatest of all theologians, an exemplary Dominican, to settle the matter, to procure Luther's submission or his arrest and transportation to Rome.

And here begins the history of what not only saved Luther but made Lutheranism as a going concern, a permanently established religious organisation, namely the intervention of the Catholic princes, protecting the heretic from the pope. The thing had not been done successfully since the days of Arius. It had indeed been attempted, three hundred years before Luther, by the Counts of Provence, on behalf of the Albigenses, and it has been narrated how the pope organised a crusade and broke the protector. Now it was attempted again, and this time successfully. The day for crusades was ended. Expediency and politics, not principle, governed the movement of Catholic armies. Even the pope did not wish to offend Luther's sovereign. And to the very end the Catholic princes would not support the emperor in a war against the Lutheran princes, lest a Catholic victory might help towards the restoration of the imperial power in the empire which they dreaded more than anything else.

The political situation favoured Luther and, his genius expanding, the movement marched from success to success. From preaching he turned to writing and discovered himself as a pamphleteer, and soon everyone in Germany was reading the little books, which the new invention of printing spread as no books had ever been spread before, books written in a resounding popular way, full of good phrases, and a breezy insouciance where the decencies were concerned, that was more effective than any argument.

From protecting Luther the princes turned, on his invitation, to patronising the movement and in 1526 it became a kind of department of State, the first organized Protestant Church, controlled by the prince, who had, ere this, confiscated all the ecclesiastical property, broken up the monasteries and convents—which, it must be admitted, the most of the monks and the nuns quitted with scandalous rapidity to join the new movement, only too often, as preachers and the wives of preachers. Within ten years of the Wittenberg challenge Germany was a scene of religious chaos, Catholicism apparently submerged, and the trouble had captured Scandinavia and was threatening Poland, too.

Switzerland, too, had its religious revolution, and from a French Lutheran refugee in Switzerland—John Calvin—there was to come, in the generation after Luther, a further development that would sweep a great part of France, the Low Countries, and Scotland away from the Church altogether, a militant, crusading religion that had eliminated all the softness and indulgence from Lutheranism, and had developed to the full the doctrine latent in it, which Luther never really faced, namely that God creates some men to save them, and others that by damning them He may show forth His justice. There are thus two kinds of men, the elect and the reprobate, and they are such by creation and the positive act of God. Calvinism repudiated State patronage of religion. It regarded the State in terms of the human beings who directed it, and these, elect or reprobate, were under the Church. Not the haughtiest papal theorist of the thirteenth century could have taught these first Calvinists anything about the primacy of the spiritual. And, in Geneva, Calvin's influence established a model for all States, a republic where the Calvinist ministers ruled and judged and punished all and every the frailties and sins of mankind, as they fancied God would one day judge and punish for eternity. In Geneva Calvin established a great college, and here were trained the Calvinist ministers—many of them ex-priests and religious —whose labours won thousands of converts to the sect.

The third main element in the Reformation tragedy was

English. England had resisted Lutheranism in the most orthodox way, the king himself, Henry VIII (1509–1547), disputing with Luther and receiving from Leo X in acknowledgment of his book, *The Defence of the Seven Sacraments*, the title of Defender of the Faith. But ten years later, although Henry's faith was still the same, he was beginning to plan a schism. The occasion of this was the king's desire that Rome should declare his marriage null and void, and his growing realisation that, in Rome's eyes, the marriage was good and valid. The only way out would be a repudiation of the papal primacy over the universal Church. If the popes were not universal primates then the local episcopate had as much authority as the popes had claimed. The question of the marriage could be left to the English bishops to decide, and Henry had no doubt what their decision would be.

Between 1531 and 1535, the closing years of the pontificate of Clement VII (1523–1534), the English reformation went through all its essential acts. The papal supremacy was repudiated and the king declared to be the Supreme Head on earth of the Church of Christ, so far as England was concerned. To this new doctrine all subjects were to swear acknowledgment. The penalty for refusal was death, and soon a gallant minority, Carthusians, monks, a few secular priests, the bishop of Rochester, John Fisher, and Sir Thomas More, the late Lord High Chancellor, went to the scaffold sooner than abjure their faith. And upon England there came a reign of terror that lasted for some years.

The repudiation of the papal primacy—already defined at Florence in 1439—apart, Henry VIII remained fairly orthodox for the rest of his life and an enemy of the new doctrines. Nevertheless it was among the new heretics that he had found his chief instruments, and it was in accordance with their spirit that he dissolved the monasteries, broke up the chantries—confiscating their revenues, of course—and had the Bible officially translated into English, and copies of it placed in all the churches. He died in 1547, leaving a boy of nine to succeed him.

During the six years' reign of Edward VI (1547–1553) the heretical party among the late king's counsellors gained the upper hand and the continental reformation gained its first real hold. The Mass was now forbidden and a substitute, non-sacrificial rite officially devised and imposed in its place. To Edward succeeded his elder sister Mary, a proved Catholic, and with her advent there came a return to Catholicism and a vigorous persecution of heresy (1553–1558).

Mary was, however, childless and the younger daughter of Henry VIII who succeeded her, Elizabeth (1558–1603), returned to the new religion. The Marian restoration was undone and the Protestant régime, part Calvinist, part Lutheran, of the time of Edward VI was again set up. The Catholic bishops were all deprived and imprisoned. A new hierarchy was created. The sovereign was once more declared supreme in matters ecclesiastical and the Mass again forbidden and the Edwardian Communion Service reimposed. The penalty for refusal of the new oaths was death and whoever said Mass was liable to imprisonment for life. All were obliged under penalty of heavy fines to attend the new religious services every Sunday and Holy Day. All priests were bound, under penalty of life imprisonment, to perform the services. The time would come when to say Mass or to hear Mass or even to be a priest would entail death.

It was in 1517 that Luther first moved. By 1560 the religious revolution was, in its main lines, complete and Europe roughly resettled on the foundations where it still rests. Ireland, Spain, Italy, southern Germany, and Poland were Catholic. France and the Low Countries were still torn between the tendencies. The rest of Christendom had revolted and established itself in permanent opposition to the Catholic Church—to use a popular term, it was Protestant.

The great revolution is now universally called the Reformation, but, if to reform means to correct abuses in a system, to set right what is wrong, to restore good habits, the name is misleading. What Luther, Calvin, and the rest did was not to reform the Catholic system in which they were bred, but to build up new systems, systems based on their revolutionary theological theories. The Catholic Church, however, did not disappear. The loss of so many millions of its faithful did not destroy it, and within the Catholic Church the movement to root out abuses, to tighten up the administration, to overhaul the whole mechanism, and the beliefs to protect which the machinery existed, the movement that had never wholly ceased, even under the worst popes, now began to carry all before it. Such a movement is undoubtedly a reformation in the fullest sense of the term, and the reformation of the Catholic Church in the sixteenth century was the greatest triumph of the spiritual over the material, of man's better parts over his far too long triumphant lower parts, that the world has ever seen. The initial problem of sinfulness it met, not by denying man's responsibility, with Luther, but by acknowledging it and that most fully. The sole cure, it was declared, lay in repentance, and amendment of life. The means were prayer, penance, and closer union with God upon whose grace, truly, all does depend. The new religion solved the difficulty of religious practice by making concessions to human weakness. But the Catholic Church kept the ideal at its eternal height, and with a policy of "No surrender" fought off the natural human tendency to lower it.

This great restoration of Catholic spirituality is commonly called the Counter-Reformation, and if by this is meant that it was the Church's reply to the challenge of the Reformers we may accept the term.

This renewal of spiritual life was chiefly the work of a succession of seven great popes—Paul III (1534–1549), Julius III (1550–1555), Paul IV (1555–1559), Pius IV (1559–1565), St. Pius V (1566–1572), Gregory XIII (1572–1585), and Sixtus V (1585–1590). These were truly the commanders of the faithful, and to their assistance there came a whole pleiad of really great saints. These saints, in the religious orders they founded or reformed, and in the many souls their sanctity otherwise influenced, provided an army of new executors for the new papal policies, which, with the great Council of Trent, are the supreme achievement of these sixty years.

The popes continued to be, in many respects, the children of the age in which they fought to restore Catholic ideals, and they continued to make use of all the means open to them, the secular weapons of diplomacy and even war, and not merely the war of defence. There is thus a political side to the activities of these popes of the Counter-Reformation, and not infrequently it greatly complicates the story of their achievement. And, it must be added, the popes who were the pioneers of the reform were children of the Renaissance too, and more than one of the habits of earlier life continued to harass them, if not in their own personal life, in their public conduct of the Church's political activities. Paul III, for example, in the midst of all the intricate diplomacy which his plan to call a General Council necessitated, never lost sight of his ambition to establish his family among the reigning princes of Italy.

It was in 1534 that Paul III—Alessandro Farnese—was elected, seventeen years after Luther's campaign began and fourteen since his solemn condemnation and excommunication by Leo X. While it is not much of an exaggeration to say that Leo had to be pushed into any real activity against Luther—so little did he appreciate the importance of what was happening, so tied were his hands already with the complications of the political situation in Germany—he had nevertheless made a beginning of uniting the princes to suppress the heresiarch. The Diet of Worms, which saw Luther's electric defiance, saw also the manifest division of the Catholics, the bishops wholly indifferent or, as the Papal Legate reported, trembling like rabbits before a trap. It was due very largely to the bishops that the emperor, anxious for vigorous action, was left in a minority of one.

Leo X died in December of 1521, so unexpectedly—he was only forty-six—and so laden with debt, that the news caused a financial panic. His successor was a homely, decent Dutchman, a one-time professor at Louvain and a model priest, the Cardinal Adrian of Utrecht. Reading the memoranda drawn up by him by two of the reformers in the Sacred College—the German, Schinner, and the Italian, Lorenzo Campeggio [2]—one seizes immediately the causes of much of the evil, and at the same time one can understand why the reform was so long beginning. The ill practice of generations had, by this, produced a vested

---

[2] This cardinal went to England six years later to preside, with Wolsey, at the trial of Henry VIII's nullity suit.

interest in the maintenance of the abuses. And if the dirt were removed, could the wall still stand? The sale of offices, the cardinals urge, should cease, and the number of officials be reduced. There should be fixed salaries and lower fees. No benefices should be granted without the consent of the lawful patron. No man should hold more than one benefice, no one should be given an abbey as a mere claim to an income. Indulgences should be restricted. The pope should not override the decisions of his courts. Cardinals should have fixed incomes and none of them should be bishops. Nor should any more concessions of jurisdiction be made to princes.

The pope began by telling the cardinals that "The Roman scandals were the talk of the world." The Sacred College had met him at the papal frontier and it had to be explained to him that they were the cardinals, for in dress and manners they were simply Renaissance princes. Almost single-handed Adrian VI set himself to the task, and first began to de-monetise the Church, which Leo X had run like a bank. Ten thousand applications for favours, privileges, and appointments awaited the new pope. He granted just one. "All are trembling here," the Venetian ambassador wrote home; "the cardinals are shaving their beards." From the court his predecessor had left him, a rotten mass of parasites, prostitutes, bravos, and bullies, came howls of rage against the "niggard" pope, and presently libels and plots to murder him.

The pope persisted, and then the plague broke out and the rottenness fled from Rome, the worldly cardinals leading the retreat. All concessions to princes of the right to appoint to lesser benefices, made since 1492, Adrian VI now revoked, and at the same time he sent a new legate to prosecute the task of saving Germany for Catholicism. He was charged to say in the pope's name that the heresy was a scourge due especially to the sins of the prelates and clergy, and that the malady had crept down from the pope to the hierarchy and from the bishops to the people. It was a simple, candid confession, and meant as an assurance of the pope's real will to reform the Church. But for the Lutheran propaganda it was simply a papal testimony of the truth of all it had been urging. The Diet of Nuremberg, to which the legates spoke, refused to put the anti-Lutheran decrees into execution, declaring them to be "impracticable," and it was the vote of the Catholic clergy which so decided the Diet, for they held the majority of the seats. The German higher clergy were for the most part utterly indifferent to the progress of Lutheranism, as they had for generations been utterly indifferent to the fortunes of Catholicism. This inertia was to be one of Rome's major difficulties for the next seventy years.

Adrian VI reigned for all too short a time. Just twelve months and two weeks after his landing at Ostia he was dead (September 14, 1523), and with Clement VII (Giuliano de' Medici), the cousin of Leo X, the tide of evil returned—though not indeed in such force as before, for Clement was not, in any way, personally vicious. But the rude vigour of reform was halted, and indeed reform in the radical spirit of the Dutch pope was not again attempted until Paul IV, thirty years later.

The eleven years' reign of Clement VII (1523–1534) was one long disaster. The pope had been an admirable archbishop of Florence and one of the very few prelates who took the reform decrees of the Fifth Lateran Council (1512–1517) at all seriously. But he was timorous and vacillating and, though so young as forty-five at his election, he lacked energy.

He began by sending to Germany the ablest canonist in the *curia*, Adrian VI's old adviser, Campeggio (February, 1524). A national council was held under his presidency at Ratisbon and many reforms decreed, while the legate also succeeded in forming the Union of Ratisbon by which the Catholic princes pledged themselves to resist further innovations. Then came the rising of the peasants and its bloody suppression. This, Rome was so ill-informed as to interpret as the defeat of Luther, and the pope wrote to Philip of Hesse a message of congratulation—unaware that this prince had been a Lutheran for two years.

Then international politics, the eternal papal oscillation between France and the Hapsburgs, intervened. The pope was soon at war with the Faith's one champion in Germany, the emperor, and in 1527 an imperial army—half Lutheran, half Spanish—took Rome and sacked it with a barbarity rare even in those days. For some months the pope was the emperor's prisoner.

Briefs to Germany are fewer and fewer during the next few years, and for a time communications wholly ceased. They were resumed once Clement VII and Charles V had come to terms, and now, once more, the demand began to be made for a General Council. To Clement the very idea of a council was abhorrent. He had fears that it would mean, in addition to his present anxieties, the new strain of division among Catholics as to the respective rôles of council and pope. Better that affairs should continue to drag on in Germany, as during the last few years, than the risk that new divisions should arise over the council question. However, he had to make a show of acquiescence, since the emperor was insistent, but he made it on condition that the Protestants should first return to their obedience, and next that they should promise, in advance, to abide by the council's decisions.

On such matters as the receiving of Holy Communion under both species, and the marriage of the clergy, the pope was willing to make concessions. But the emperor did not trust the pope, and, when the Protestant princes refused even to discuss a provisional return to obedience, the council scheme was at an end. What Rome had not yet recognised was that by now Protestantism was a vested interest, an organisation, and not merely a matter of the erroneous views of German theologians.

Matters were still in this unsatisfactory state when, September, 1534, Clement VII died.

The conclave that followed was almost the shortest on record. Within an hour or two the cardinals had elected, unanimously, Alessandro Farnese, Pope Paul III. He was a frail old man of sixty-six, shattered in health but, as Titian's marvellous portraits bear witness, with nothing abated of his intellectual power or his natural fire.

It was Innocent VIII who had given him his first promotion, and Alexander VI who had made his fortune, giving him the red hat at twenty-five, in none too creditable circumstances. He had lived until middle age the life of that corrupt court, had been a generous patron of the arts, and established a well-founded reputation as one of the most cultivated men of his time. And he had served

the Holy See admirably as an administrator and diplomatist. Then at fifty he had been converted, received Holy
Orders, and turned his great powers to the question of
reform. He had already been a candidate for the papacy
in the conclave of 1521 and again in 1523.

Once elected pope he lost no time. A new note began
to be heard in all the instructions from Rome to the
papal agents in Germany. Theology, and not merely, as
for far too long, politics and diplomacy was now the order
of the day. The experts on German affairs were summoned,
and to remedy the incredible ignorance of the Roman
Curia about the state of things beyond the Alps one of the
chief of these experts, Vergerio, was given a wandering
commission to tour Germany and to report. This mission
of Vergerio was but the first of a series that was to issue,
ultimately, in the establishment within the empire of a
system of several permanent ecclesiastical ambassadors,
the predecessors of the modern nunciatures, through which
the reforming papacy was chiefly to act. Here, as everywhere else, Paul III is showing himself an innovator.

At his first consistory the new pope announced that he
would call the long-desired council, and despite the emperor's hesitations—fearful that at this news the Lutherans
would revolt—the bull of summons actually appeared in
1536. The council was to meet at Mantua in May, 1537.
The Protestants, embarrassed by this undeniable evidence
of the papal will to reform and to be reformed, revolted,
and in the *Articles of Schmalkalden* their theologians
declared war once more on Catholicism, while their princes
handed back unopened the letters inviting them to the
council. The French chose this moment to renew their
war with the emperor, and announced the dangers of
travel during wartime as the reason why they could not
take part in the council.

Everything thus conspired to halt the pope, but he
stuck tenaciously to his purpose. Next the duke of Mantua,
at the last moment, four weeks only before the council
was to meet, refused the hospitality of his city. The pope
only turned to find a new meeting-place, and after months
of negotiations, he secured Vicenza from the republic of
Venice. The council was now summoned to meet there for

May, 1538. The agenda was prepared, the legates were named, the appointed day came. But at Vicenza, besides the legates, there appeared only five bishops. Of the rest of the Catholic episcopate not a sign, neither proxies, nor apologies. The pope, apparently, stood alone in his zeal to reform the Church. The German bishops remained in their stolid, worldly indifference. The French had been kept away largely through the intrigues of the English king, Henry VIII, and the excuse of the war. Paul III postponed the council for a year and employed the interval to reconcile the French and the emperor.

Then there arose the worst obstacle so far. The emperor was persuaded that a compromise with Protestantism was possible, and on the eve of the date appointed for the delayed opening of the council, he pledged himself to the Lutherans to summon a round-table conference for the arrangement of the doctrinal differences. It looked as though emperor and Lutherans were to come to an agreement and the pope to be presented with the *fait accompli*.

The situation taxed all the pope's powers. He had no choice but to suspend the council indefinitely—no repetition of the farce of 1538 could now be risked. Then he had, somehow, to control the new dangerous "reunion" policy before it had made an end of what little real Catholicism still lingered on in Germany. Catholic Germany must not come to decisions in matters of faith without consulting the Holy See, and yet Rome must not show itself dictatorial and throw these ill-instructed Catholics into the hands of the Lutherans. The task called for the most expert brains and the finest characters the papal service possessed. In Contarini and Morone, both of whom he had brought into that service, Paul III found ideal agents, ecclesiastics of unspotted fame, learned, shrewd, patient, charitable, resolute, and sympathetic to the needs that had bred the Lutheran doctrines. The great conference ended in failure. But it had served to delay the council for another three years, and to that extent the Lutherans had been successful. On the other hand the German Catholics had accepted the Holy See's leadership. Its prestige north of the Alps stood higher than for generations, and the Faith in Germany remained secure.

Paul III, undeterred by the successive failures of eight

years, took up once more the work of assembling the council.

Not for another four years was he successful. The council did finally come together in December, 1545, and not at Mantua or Vicenza but at Trent, an imperial city just beyond the Italian frontier, and when it met it owed nothing to king or emperor. It was truly the pope's council, and this because only the pope's patience, diplomatic skill and determination to reform the Church had brought it into being.

The emperor badly wanted the council, but he wanted it chiefly to reform abuses, and he feared nothing so much as clear definitions on the doctrinal points in dispute between Catholics and Protestants. For the sake of political unity he was prepared to compromise Catholic teaching. The pope insisted on the council's dogmatic rôle, and arranged that the two sides of the council's work should go forward simultaneously. Only the bishops were allowed a vote and the pope sent three cardinals to preside as his legates, del Monte (the future Julius III), Cervini (the future Marcellus II), and the Englishman, Reginald Pole. Commissions of expert theologians drafted the decrees, which were then discussed in private sessions by the bishops and finally, when a decision was reached, solemnly promulgated in a public session.

The whole body of Catholic teaching was discussed in the light of the Protestant criticism of it, and reaffirmed, decrees being published on Holy Scripture, Original Sin, Justification, the Sacraments in general, Baptism and Confirmation. At the same time new practical rules were made for the use of the Bible, for the teaching of Theology, the regulation of preaching, the abolition of the much-abused system of the preacher-collector for indulgences, and a host of regulations, with automatic penalties, for the reformation of episcopal life, and the better control of clerical life by the local bishops.

Down to the last the emperor objected to the dogmatic decrees, and to none more than to that on Justification. Once it was made clear that the Catholic teaching was divided by an abyss from the Protestant theory, there could be no hope of a diplomatic accommodation that would allow Catholic and Protestant to be members of the one

Church, and some such fantasy as this never ceased to haunt the imperial mind.

As the year 1546 wore on, the legates, uneasy about the menace of the emperor's influence, began to think of transferring the council to some town in Italy. The emperor, in reply, threatened to make his own arrangements with the Protestants.

Next, in February, 1547, the plague broke out in Trent and on March 11 the council voted, by a two-thirds majority, to move to Bologna, the imperialist cardinals and bishops protesting strongly.

Paul III was none too pleased at the transfer which, he guessed, would mean a serious interruption of the work in hand. Charles V was furious. He denounced the move as a papal trick and threatened to call a council of his own and to hold it in Rome.

Just ten days later than this the emperor gained the great victory of his reign, completely routing the Protestants at Mühlberg (April 24, 1547). His great enemy, Francis I of France, had died three weeks earlier, and Charles stood out for the moment, the master of Europe as no man had been its master since Charlemagne. If schism was to be avoided the pope must compromise, and the end of the long negotiations was the suspension of the council (February, 1548).

Paul III is the pope who created the Council of Trent. But Trent could never have functioned had the pope not already created a whole corps of new officials inspired by a zeal for reform, able and willing to undertake the highly technical and very laborious work which the direction of the council involved. And also, in the eleven years during which the pope's tenacity toiled to bring about the council, it toiled no less actively to reform his own household and the trained officials of the *curia*.

In one consistory after another Paul III gave the red hat to the most distinguished ecclesiastics of the day, even—in the case of Contarini, a Venetian Thomas More—to a layman. Never has there been wiser, readier, or more munificent recognition of the combination of talent and virtue. Never did the Sacred College show such an array of personality as during this pontificate.

While official Rome made merry over the new spirit,

the new cardinals worked, and in March, 1537, presented to the pope their ever-famous report, *The Advice of the Commission of Cardinals on the Reform of the Church set forth at the command of Pope Paul III*. Here in embryo is the whole of the reformation that Trent was later to enact.

To investigate, and to plan, and to decree reform was comparatively easy. It remained to get the decrees acted upon, and since the Curia was obstinate, and since the only alternative to slow persuasion was dismissal, and since to dismiss the trained civil service would have been merely to bring to a standstill the whole administration of the Church's government, the reform made slow progress. Paul III refused to be discouraged. He understood human nature too well to hope to remedy abuses by legislation only. He warned the cardinals that the difficulties were almost insuperable, he upheld their corrective activity ceaselessly, and he gave them new courage when they faltered before their task. Nor did the pope wait for the council to meet before tackling the work of reforming the Church in general. Hundreds of his briefs have been found directing the reform of monasteries and convents in every part of Europe. Luther's own order and the Dominicans were especially the object of the pope's vigilance. The new order of the Theatines, founded by St. Cajetan and Gian Pietro Carafa, whom Paul III made a cardinal, was given every encouragement, and it supplied the pope with a host of good men whom he set to rule and reform the long-neglected dioceses of Italy. He encouraged and blessed the great work of the first Ursuline nuns, and he blessed the beginnings of a greater work still when, in 1540, he approved the Society of Jesus.

The future of Catholicism was still hanging in the balance when Paul III died (November 10, 1549). His immense effort for reform had not yet had time to bear fruit, and now the old trouble between the two chiefs of Christendom, the pope and the emperor, was once more threatening to mar all. The point at issue, raised by the very summoning of the reforming council, was whether the pope was to be left free to choose the means by which the losses of the last thirty years should be repaired. Who was to direct the reformation of the Church? The pope or the emperor?

The emperor Charles V, who was also, it must be recalled, king of Spain, sovereign of the modern Belgium and Holland, and king of Naples, ruler of all southern Italy too, had recently, by the victory of Mühlberg (1547), made himself, to all appearance, master of Germany as no emperor had been master for centuries. Did he now aspire to dominate the Church as he dominated the State? It was no idle fear that thus disturbed the papacy. It was due, very largely, to the emperor's policy that the council had been for months suspended indefinitely. Would it ever meet again, and when it did, would the emperor still be a Catholic?

The conclave which followed the death of Paul III was thus the most notable for generations, from the critical hour at which it assembled. It was notable also from the number of cardinals who took part, fifty-one out of the fifty-four who composed the Sacred College, and from the length of time it occupied. Its ten weeks of internal excitement ended on March 8, 1550, with the election of Giovanni Maria del Monte, presiding legate at the Council of Trent. He took the name of Julius III.

The record of Julius III as a reformer stands high. In the first place he reassembled the great council, in which he had literally slaved for the best part of three years. All his first activities as pope were directed to the council, and it should be borne in mind that the position of the new pope was none too happy. He had not been the candidate of the reform party in the conclave. He had not, among the cardinals, any personal following on which he could count. He would have to manœuvre among the various parties without the aid of any party of his own. And the emperor had actually sent orders to his subjects among the cardinals to keep del Monte out. The king of France was no more than prepared to tolerate him.

It was an incredible surprise to Charles V when the pope put out of his mind the stormy scenes at Trent where, insulted and vilified by Charles' ambassadors, he had had to defend the council's liberty against the emperor's interference, and when he turned simply to seek the emperor's co-operation to set the council moving once more. Charles rose to the height of the pope's generosity, and while the French king refused in advance to acknowledge anything the council should decree, the preparations went steadily forward and on May 1, 1551, the first public session of the reassembled Fathers took place.

It was not until September that enough bishops arrived to make the council a reality, but from that moment the work went on admirably, daily meetings of theologians and canonists to prepare the material, and of the bishops to discuss and decide what the experts had put into form. So were gradually elaborated the decrees on the Holy Eucharist, on Penance, on Extreme Unction, and a whole series of reform decrees designed to improve the character of the episcopate and to strengthen the hands of the bishops in dealing with the ill-living cleric. The experience of the previous sessions under Paul III made the running of the council easier than before, but the greatest help of all, undoubtedly, was the presence in St. Peter's chair of the man who had been the council's first president. The trained wisdom and the experience of Julius III, his constant firm guidance and support, his determination to keep the bishop's working, are everywhere manifest in the details of the council's story.

The council continued its sessions for just two days short of a year, and then the sudden renewal of the religious war in Germany forced its suspension. Nor was there ever, in the lifetime of Julius III, any chance of its reassembly. But the reformer in the pope did not despair. He was now sixty-five, his health was breaking, and the gout had him continually in its grip. He had, moreover, become involved in a disastrous little war with the Farnese over their possession of Parma and this had greatly damaged his prestige and drained his resources. Reform, however, came before all other problems. The council might not be able to meet, but at least the preparatory work could continue. A great commission of experts was set up and kept permanently busy, investigating and examining the theological and practical problems that yet remained. They were still at work, amassing a vast store of ordered knowledge which would one day assist the council when (March 23, 1555) the pope succumbed to his long-standing ailment, the gout.

Julius III, like Paul III, had never lost entirely the habits of the semi-Pagan Renaissance world in which he had been bred. His successor, however, belonged to the straitest set of reformers, one of those to whom Paul III had given the red hat that he might be a leader of the reform movement. This was the cardinal Cervini who, with Julius III and Pole, had presided over the council. As pope he retained his own name, Marcellus, but the rejoicings that filled all at the news of his election were suddenly turned to sorrow, for within a month the new pope was dead.

The ensuing conclave brought to the papal throne an old man of seventy-nine, Gian Pietro Carafa, Pope Paul IV.

Across the sixteenth century his short pontificate (1555–1559) stretches like some high embankment. Through him, at last, the Paganism of the Renaissance is driven from the papacy, the last association of secularism with that high office broken. His elemental zeal, his fire, his wholehearted surrender of inexhaustible energy to the purpose in hand, his contempt for compromise and for half-measures, his entire devotion to the one purpose of purifying the Church and making it once more the fit instrument of God's service now, after fifty years of impatient looking on, found the fulness of opportunity.

His reign marked the end of that *flanerie* with worldliness which had dulled the achievement even of good popes. If Rome—papal Rome—bears to-day, and has borne for centuries, something of the appearance of a monastery, of the modern popes, whatever their faults as individuals and as popes, have all lived, primarily, as priests, in a setting of prayer and a certain religious decorum, this restoration of what should be is due, in the largest possible measure, to Paul IV. For he broke and broke for ever, and broke by the sheer violence of his wrath, all the long tradition in which worldliness in the highly placed cleric was taken as rather in the nature of things. Certainly never since his time has it shown itself with that naïve, unabashed impudence that, before him, had been for generations its very second nature. His violence smashed the pattern of austere living so deeply into the stuff of things that not even his worldly inclined opponents dared to destroy it when the inevitable reaction came.

The Roman mob, with the tacit consent of the authorities, might insult the monuments to him as the aged pope lay dying, but he had so firmly set the law of decent living upon its throne that no mob, nor any worldliness of high ecclesiastics, has since availed to cast it down.

His career had begun in the evil days of Alexander VI and he had lived in that court and not been stained thereby. He had been for years nuncio in London and then, for a still longer period, nuncio in Spain. He was by birth a Neapolitan, and second only to his passion for reform came a hatred of the Spaniards who now ruled his native land. It was a patriotism that would ultimately involve his pontificate in political disasters, which affected adversely his religious schemes too. He had been archbishop of Naples and had resigned this great see to found, with St. Cajetan, the order called the Theatines, and as a simple religious he had laboured for years in the slums of Rome and of Venice, preaching, catechising, and administering the sacraments. Paul III made him a cardinal and when the Inquisition was reorganised it was Carafa whom he placed at the head of it.

Never was there so iron a will, nor such rigidity, never, it must be added, such intolerance of any will but his own. He was a man to whom tact was treason, and of all the questions of the day, after those of heresy and the evil-living cleric, there was none moved him more than that of the hold of the Catholic princes over Church life and action. To end this he was ready to scrap everything, and unfortunately the only weapons he recognised as fit to use were such as had, centuries before, rusted into obsolescence. Paul IV was an Innocent IV born three centuries too late.

This vigorous reformer did not reassemble the council. All the studious care of Paul III and of Julius III to bring the Catholic kings to an acceptance of the papal policies, had irritated his austerity to the point of fury. Nor had he seen, in the history of the council—its delays, the endless negotiations, the compromises—any reason to alter his opinion that these methods were unworthy of the cause at stake and, moreover, fruitless. He had other methods, and while as cardinal he had not shrunk from rebuking the popes to their face for what was worldly in their way of life, now, like some grim Old Testament figure, he set himself, whip in hand, to speed up the pace of the improvement, at whose slow progress he had, for twenty-five years, assisted with impatient helplessness.

Soon there began to appear, not new laws—there were enough laws already, the pope declared—but orders for the observance of the old and commissions to ensure it. Dispensations for lack of due age in those elected bishops ceased to be given, and alienations of Church property were made null—the cardinals being severely lectured on this within the first few weeks of the reign. Trusty bishops, with Jesuits to assist them, were sent down into Sicily to reform the monasteries and convents of women. Others were despatched to Spain for a similar purpose. The practice of giving abbeys to non-religious, *in commendam,* as it was called, was abolished and the Penitentiary was forbidden to give dispensations. The greatest strictness began to be shown in the nominations of bishops, and in one day, of fifty-eight proposed, the pope rejected all.

The old complaint of religious who left their order to find other—clerical—employment, Paul IV met with a terrible law that deprived them of whatever benefices, incomes, degrees, or offices they had since acquired—and this no matter what their present rank—and ordered them back to their monasteries under pain of instant suspension. All dispensations allowing such monks and friars to pass to other orders were declared invalid, even though granted by the popes themselves. For the future only the hermit orders of the Carthusians and the Camaldolesi could validly receive such religious. Rome itself was the scene of raids, and these unfortunates were arrested by the score. Nor did their rank or dignity save them. Some went to prison, others to the galleys.

Bishops were ordered to resign all benefices other than their sees, and the new decrees requiring bishops to live in their sees were rigorously enforced. It was discovered that in Rome there were living 113 diocesan bishops. They ignored the first order to go home and then a second was made with the penalty of deposition, and the punishments already enacted for vagrant monks, if within a month they had not obeyed. Within six weeks the bishops had all departed.

Evil-living bishops were treated more severely still. One, the bishop of Polignano, was sentenced to life imprisonment with an annual punishment of three months' bread and water.

The whole financial side of the appointments was revised. Pallium fees were abolished, and the pope ended the long problem of the reform of the Dataria—which, it was held, the Holy See could not afford to reform, so greatly did it depend on the revenues that came in through it—by abolishing all the fees. That he lost immediately two-thirds of his revenue did not for an instant halt Paul IV. And he was no respecter of persons. Despite the excellent nominations to the Sacred College made by the popes since 1534, there were still not a few cardinals of the bad old type. The pope told the cardinals, who had so recently elected him, that there were none of them really to be trusted. To those not ordained he gave three months to receive the sacrament or resign. They were bidden to send in lists of the benefices they held, allowed to choose one, and the rest were considered as vacant and given away to others. In his own nominations the pope utterly refused to pay any attention at all to the wishes of the Catholic princes. He deliberately, and explicitly, set them aside—even the demands of the king of France when, in the war against Philip II of Spain, France was the pope's sole ally.

The end of the reign was, however, tragic. Political affairs, and the government of the papal States, Paul IV had left to his nephew, the cardinal Carlo Carafa, that he himself might be free to give all his time to Church matters and the reform. The nephew—a lesser Cesare Borgia—aimed at the establishment of the Carafa in some principality carved out of the States of the Church, as the della Rovere had been established and the Borgia and the Farnese. The pope, alone in Rome, was ignorant of the scoundrel his nephew was, and of the way things were going. Then one day he too understood. In a terrible scene he broke with his nephew and broke with the family for ever.

The wickedness had one good effect. The fury its discovery provoked ended for ever, not nepotism indeed, but nepotism on the grand scale. Never again did the relations of a pope attempt to establish themselves as a reigning princely family. A few months after this tragedy Paul IV died (August 18, 1559).

Not until Christmas Day were the cardinals able to agree on a successor to him. They chose Gian Angelo Medici, a Milanese, who called himself Pius IV. The new pope was a man of sixty, whose career had been useful rather than distinguished, for he had slowly worked his way through the Curia as a practising canonist. He was essentially a moderate, conciliatory in disposition, and gifted with great power of accommodation. Within two years his diplomacy had reconciled the Holy See with the Catholic princes and brought about the reopening of the council at Trent (January 18, 1562).

This time the council sat to a finish, and in the next two years it produced decrees on the remainder of the Church's teaching and a mass of reform legislation which was to set the pattern of Catholic life for the next three hundred years.

For his Secretary of State Pius IV—in many respects himself a Renaissance type—chose one of his nephews, Charles Borromeo, a young man of twenty-one, to whom he gave, along with the red hat, the see of Milan. In this young prelate there was given to the century of Trent the very perfection of the new type of bishop the council's decrees hoped to produce. The constructive reforms in the great archdiocese, and his province, to which St. Charles gave himself during twenty years, were to be the model application of Trent's legislation, inspiring, even to the very details, other bishops all over the world down to our own times.

Pius IV died in 1565, leaving to the Church as his legacy the completion of Trent and a peaceful understanding with the Catholic powers. His successor was the one pope of modern times who had been canonised, Michele Ghislieri, a Dominican, who took the name of Pius V.

It was thus to a man of saintly life, a model of piety and unworldliness, and a man as vigorous, not to say as ruthless, as Carafa himself, that it fell to inaugurate the practical application of the new legislation. St. Pius V made obedience to the decrees of the council the one rule of his life, and his six years' pontificate (1566–1572)

ensured that there should not befall the work done at
Trent that sterility which had been the fate of the council
that preceded it, the Fifth Lateran, in 1512–1517

St. Pius V and his two immediate successors—Gregory
XIII (1572–1585) and Sixtus V (1585–1590)—are the
popes who begin the offensive against the hitherto victorious heresy. They not only tone up the lives of Catholics by a vigorous enforcing of the decrees of Trent, everywhere founding colleges and seminaries for the education
of the new clergy, but they definitely enter the field of
national and international politics, ceaselessly endeavouring, by the new diplomatic service they create, to form
combinations of Catholic princes for the defeat of the
Protestants and the extirpation of heresy.

St. Pius V excommunicated and deposed Elizabeth of
England. Gregory XIII sent an army against her into
Ireland, and to the end of his reign worked against her
on the Continent. Sixtus V subsidised the Spanish Armada.
So it was in France, and in Germany also. Wherever there
was a hope of a Catholic offensive against the newly
established Protestant régimes, these popes were ready to
support with money if not with arms.

Their most lasting work was, however, the reformation
of Catholic life and the constructive application of the
decrees of Trent, and their chief auxiliaries here were the
new religious orders.

This renewal of spiritual life goes back to the first years
of the century. Its earliest signs are to be discerned, before
Germany had revolted, in the corrupted Rome of the reign
of Leo X, in the society called the *Oratory of Divine Love*
where prelates of the papal court, priests, and laymen
joined to pledge themselves to a more spiritual life. From
this little society Paul III, later, took six of his most famous
reforming cardinals, and from it there came also the
founders [3] of a new kind of religious order, the so-called
Theatines (1524). These were priests living under the
three vows but doing the work of parochial clergy, preaching, visiting the sick, and administering the sacraments, in
the slums of the great Italian cities. They had a singularly

---

[3] St. Cajetan and Gian Pietro Carafa (Pope Paul IV).

rigorous vow of poverty, for they were not even allowed to beg.

Two other contemporary new orders were the Barna-bites, founded by St. Anthony Zaccaria (1532) to give open-air missions in the towns of northern Italy, and the Somaschi, who founded orphanages and cared for the waifs and strays. These two orders were never of any great importance outside Italy, and the new Franciscan reform of St. Peter of Alcantara was, similarly, restricted to Spain. But there were several orders whose influence was to be world-wide.

The first in date of these was the Franciscan reform called the Capuchins, which began in the last days of the reign of Clement VII, and provided the popes of the next hundred and fifty years with an army of zealous, well-trained, popular preachers who did untold good work among the uneducated masses of Italy, of France, and of Germany. Not even the Jesuits had a greater share in the victories of the Counter-Reformation than these new Franciscans.

Spain, half-way through the century, was the scene of a great revival of the Carmelite Order and of the contem-plative life, that has gone on continuously ever since. Its agents were St. Teresa of Avila (1515–1582) and St. John of the Cross (1542–1591).

The most celebrated of all the new orders was also Spanish in its origin, the Society of Jesus. Here was not only a new order but a new kind of order, religious who dispensed with the customary foundations of community life and the common recitation in choir of the Divine Office. Wherever there was a Jesuit there was the order. All the individualism characteristic of the age was seized on by the new society and brought into the service of religion. The discipline of the order, that reflected the current authoritarian tendencies, was something new in its military strictness, and it produced the most perfectly subordinated instrument the papacy has ever had at its disposal. The training was long; a discipline of the will in the interests of the will of God, shown through what-ever orders the superior gave, was its main object. And the Jesuit was to be superbly educated in the best the Renaissance had to give. Wherever the Holy See needed them the Jesuits went, ready to do whatever work lay to hand. From the beginning they had a deserved reputation as preachers, controversialists, confessors, and school-masters, and willy-nilly, they soon became involved, like their masters the popes, in all the politico-religious activity of the later sixteenth century.

In the names of their first great saints, Ignatius Loyola, Francis Xavier, Francis Borgia, Peter Canisius, Aloysius Gonzaga, Robert Bellarmine, there is written the whole history of one side of the Counter-Reformation. St. Ignatius not only founded the society and gave it its superbly successful instrument, *The Spiritual Exercises*, but, as a spiritual director, his personality gradually reacted upon the whole spirituality of Catholicism. St. Peter Canisius was to Germany a second St. Boniface, and St. Robert Bellarmine gave a direction to Catholic theological life which it followed for another two centuries and more.

It is true that the rôle of the society has been exaggerated—alike by those who hate it and by its friends—for it has been, from the beginning, a sign of contradiction, and rarely written about with that practical serenity which is its own characteristic note. But without the Society of Jesus the Counter-Reformation would have been little more than a solemnity of pious resolutions.

A more hidden force than this militant company, and one just as vital to the ultimate success of Trent and all that Trent stood for, was the influence of the Florentine priest St. Philip Neri (1515–1595), who for forty years, from his obscure room in Rome, directed the salvation of the great world of the Curia. To his work, the personal direction of innumerable souls, as much as to the violence of Paul IV, is due the final banishment of sinful life from those high places. The terrible pope cast out devils, and in the clearance St. Philip Neri worked, simply, unostentatiously, jestingly almost, building a new type of spiritually minded clerical official, a new race, whence were to come nuncios, cardinals, legates, and popes. In the work of the Roman Oratory, which St. Philip founded, the best of the old humanist tradition is preserved, and a refuge provided for such religious spirits as the forbidding Theatines failed to attract, or the barrack square efficiency of the great Spanish company.

There was one important chapter in the programme prepared for Trent which the council did not dare really to attack, namely, the reform of the Catholic princes. The event was to show that nothing in all that the great council did was more important than this, and yet, had it proceeded to discuss the thorny questions bound up with it, the council would no doubt have involved the Church in as many schisms almost as there were princes. For under this heading the council would have been led to make definite and binding statements on the fulness of the papal authority in matters of public morality no less than private, to reassert the claims put forward, in how different circumstances by the great popes of the Middle Ages, to demand explicit recognition of the Church as, in its own sphere of faith and morals, a free and independent society, and to ask for that independence a definite assurance of protection. And for any prince in 1562 to give such assurance would have been to go against the whole trend of the political development of the time.

Impossible though this reform may have been at the moment, though it may be granted that to press it would have been worse than inopportune, the ultimate effects of the tendencies that then went unchecked were nothing short of disastrous. In the long run the absolutism of the Catholic princes was to ruin the influence of Catholicism in the south as truly the Protestants had ruined it in the north, and to inflict injuries on religion that are still felt as a real hindrance. And the failure to reform the public morality of the Catholic States, ultimately reacted on the papacy itself. It was on an unreformed temporal power that the papacy had to lean, and the price of support continued to be concession. Expediency, despite Paul IV and St. Pius V, crept back into the papal counsels. Something of the world survived here, and played its part in the life of the papal court, and in the conclaves. Once the life and death crisis of the sixteenth century was past, a mitigated worldliness reappeared in the papacy itself and a new nepotism that showered gold and the social rank of Roman princes on the papal relatives. It is now that there begins the great age of the families of Borghesi, Barberini, Pamfili, Chigi, and the rest, the well-endowed relatives of

Paul V (1605-1621), Urban VIII (1623-1644), Innocent X (1644-1655), and Alexander VII (1655-1667).

One of the best examples of the difficulty, and the menace even, which the Catholic prince could present to the reforming papacy, the Catholic prince zealous himself for reform, yet determined, by reason of his absolutist conception of his office, to control the reform itself, can be studied in the history of Philip II of Spain (1556-1598). For forty years he was almost the one prince on whose fidelity to the Faith unlimited reliance could be placed. Almost alone of the great princes, Catholic or Protestant, religion was to him a matter of deep, internal, personal conviction.

But the whole matter of ecclesiastical discipline the king strove to keep in his own hands. It is the royal power that will search out heretics, try them, and punish them. It is through the State that monasteries will be visited and reformed, and that the decrees of Trent—which the king has made the law of the land—will be enforced. The king had already the right to name all the bishops and through the machinery of the Inquisition he kept a strict control over all their actions. Not Henry VIII himself exercised a more complete supremacy in ecclesiastical matters—definitions of Faith apart—than this Most Catholic Majesty.

Pius IV was, by necessity as well as by nature, conciliatory, St. Pius V independent, Gregory XIII again conciliatory, seeing primarily in Philip II a convinced ally against the heretics of the north. But between Sixtus V and Philip, the dissensions produced by the pope's determination that the Holy See should be independent, more than once brought the king within reach of excommunication and Spain within sight of an interdict.

The crisis came in the two years that followed this pope's death. The king's policy of forcing his own nominees into the Sacred College had so far succeeded that he had now fourteen of his subjects cardinals, three of them his close relations. In the four conclaves of these two years—following the deaths of Sixtus V, August 27, 1590; of Urban VII, September 27, 1590; of Gregory XIV, October 13, 1591; and of Innocent IX, December 30, 1591—the king interfered as never before; his whole object being to secure the exclusion of any cardinal likely to prove an independent pope. In the second of these conclaves he sent the Sacred College an instruction barring no fewer than sixty-two of its members. In Gregory XIV he had the pope of his desires. But Providence intervened, and after the next short pontificate, the election of Clement VIII (1592–1605), whom Philip II had three times vetoed, gave the Church a pope with all the independence of Sixtus V and the suppleness of Pius IV. The worst menace of all, a papacy enslaved to the Catholic king of Spain, was averted.

Through all the last fifty years of the sixteenth century papal legates, Jesuits and Capuchins, toiled heroically in Germany, Switzerland, and Poland to save for Catholicism whatever the new heresies had not managed to capture, and to win back as much as possible of the lands that were lost. The measure of success they met was remarkable, though northern Germany and Scandinavia remained hostile to the end. The discouraged Catholics of southern Germany, so it seemed, needed only the experience of priests really devoted to their vocation, and competently instructed, in order to rally to the ancient faith. The greatest obstacle was still the high-born native prelates and the politically minded Catholic princes. When Charles V abdicated in 1556, the imperial title and the Germanic hereditary lands of his house did not pass to his son, Philip II (who now became ruler of Spain, the Netherlands, Milan, Naples, and the new American lands) but to his brother Ferdinand I. The new emperor, though a Catholic, was even more nervous than Charles V as to the effects on his plans for German unity of such an offensive as a genuine Catholic revival must entail. The old policy was renewed of a vague, indefinite understanding between the two religious forces that divided the empire.

Ferdinand died in 1564, and his son and successor, Maximilian II (1564–1576), was distinctly favourable to Protestantism. The long reign of the next emperor, his son the weak and eccentric Rudolf II (1576–1612), was a great disaster for the Church. The Protestants saw their opportunity and the compromise made at Augsburg in 1555 was so systematically violated that by the end of the century it seemed that the Reformers had only to make their demands, at the expense of the Catholics, for them to be granted. Rudolf's heir was his brother Mathias, and before the end of the reign the intrigues of Mathias had stripped him of all but the imperial title—a *de facto* change of ruler that, once again, brought no advantage to his Catholic subjects.

The one hope was in the next heir, the cousin of Mathias, Ferdinand, Duke of Styria, and in Ferdinand's co-operation with the line of Catholic Dukes of Bavaria who, for two generations, had been the political mainstay of the Counter-Reformation in Germany. Ferdinand, a pupil of the Jesuits, had shown himself resolute to the point of ruthlessness in resisting the Protestant penetration of his own Catholic State. He had closed all their schools and banished the teachers and the missionaries. When he was elected emperor, in 1618, he proposed to save the rest of his dominions in the same fashion. Naturally the election of so active a Catholic, who was also a ruler of proved competence, coming after fifty years of decadence and vacillation, was a challenge the Protestants did not ignore. They set up in opposition the Elector-Palatine, Frederick, a Calvinist prince whose wife was the daughter of James I of England. From this election came the terrible Thirty Years' War (1618–1648), the last great act in the Counter-Reformation, for it left both parties in Germany utterly exhausted, the population destroyed from a half to two-thirds, and whole areas of Germany little better than waste lands, through which the wolves roamed unhindered where once had been villages and towns.

The Thirty Years' War, never a purely religious war, ultimately became a purely political affair, in which France and the House of Hapsburg fought out yet another round of their age-old feud. Its religious effect was to confirm in Germany the rule adopted at Augsburg in 1555, that in religion the German people should follow the religion of their prince—and as there were in the empire no fewer than three hundred and forty-three independent sovereign princes this meant an incredible mosaic of varied, petty, religious tyrannies.

Against the adoption of this cynical, immoral, and essentially anti-religious principle the pope—Innocent X (1644–1655)—vehemently protested, denying all validity to the Treaties of Westphalia (1648) in which it was enshrined. Those Treaties, moreover, contained innumerable clauses which disposed of ecclesiastical property and of civil jurisdictions that belonged to the ecclesiastical princes. All this rearrangement, new dispossessions of the Church, and condonation of old dispossessions, was carried through without any reference whatever to the views or wishes of the pope. He was no more regarded at Westphalia in 1648 than at Versailles in 1919. Nor could he, even in 1648, do more than make his protest.

In this respect the Treaties of 1648 really mark the end of an epoch, or rather they are a definite sign that the ages in which the Catholic Church, through its head the pope, was a recognised force in the public life of Europe, had finally come to an end. After more than a thousand years the State was once more to transact its business as though the Church did not exist, and the Church would now, increasingly, be considered—by Catholic powers, too —as simply a collective association of those who held like beliefs in religious matters—no longer *the* Church but *a* church. The next hundred and forty years, from the Treaties of Westphalia to the French Revolution, are dominated by the development of this new, anti-Catholic principle, and in virtue of it, by reason of the denial implicit in it of the Church's authority as a moral guide in public affairs, the Catholic princes tend once more to enslave Catholicism, to stifle its own independent voice and, breaking the Church into a series of national bodies, make it, each in his own dominions, a mere organ of State. There is no denial of the classic Catholic doctrines of the Incarnation, the Redemption, of Grace, of the Sacraments, nor of the papal primacy. The princes, in these matters, pride themselves on their orthodoxy and continue to repress and to punish Protestantism. But in this other field, this practical denial of the Church's right to teach and to make herself heard, they are as dangerous to her existence as any Protestant.

At the same time there begins to show itself the inevitable second state of Protestantism, that is to say, a Christianity that rejects dogmatic belief altogether, that becomes an affair of mere "good will to men," that denies the existence (or the knowability) of the supernatural and becomes a mere cult of morality and benevolence.

This new development—Deism—sees in Catholicism its inevitable enemy, sees that if Catholicism lives it cannot itself survive, and the eighteenth century becomes the scene of a bitter fight, in which the Deists take the offensive and in which they have the advantage that the best intellects of the day are their allies.

Deism—and Freemasonry, the new international oathbound sect in which it finds corporate expression—are not by any means confined to Protestant Europe. In the first quarter of the eighteenth century, in the general reaction against religion that follows the death of Louis XIV (1643-1715), they gain a great hold on France, and thence spread to Spain and to the Spanish kingdom of Naples.

By the time the eighteenth century is half-way through its course, the Catholic Church is more isolated from European life than at any time in history. The Catholic kings see in it no more than a political instrument, the intellect of the day is leagued against it, its hold on the allegiance of the bishops and clergy in the Catholic countries is precarious and doubtful, and the need of a reform of religious life throughout these countries where Rome has been reduced to impotence, is once more urgent.

The final tragedy—and the proof of the shackles the princes have put upon the Church—is Pope Clement XIV's enforced suppression of Catholicism's best defenders, the Society of Jesus (1773). Catholicism has reached in the West the point at which it disappeared from the East—how can it survive in absolute States that are themselves Catholic, unless its ideals dominate these States? A solution to the riddle, a temporary release from the vicious circle, was provided by the Revolution, which broke the old absolutist monarchies, leaving the Church broken, too, it is true, but, for the first time in centuries, free once more, yet so little used to freedom that, for a century or so, she halts and stumbles somewhat in the unexpected light.

8

The Revolt of the Catholic Kings, 1648–1789

As THE empire and Spain were the theatres of the chief crises of Catholic history in the period 1517–1648, so in this later century and a half it is France that is the principal cause of the Church's anxiety.

The first developments of the Lutheran revolution left France scarcely moved at all. Gradually, through the twenty years that followed the condemnation of 1520, small groups of Protestants began to form in the various towns and then, in 1534, a vigorous offensive on their part, the placarding of attacks on the Mass, led to arrests, trials, and executions. From now onwards the king, Francis I (1515–1547), was actively hostile to the Reformers. None-the-less the movement spread, and especially once the French exile, Calvin, had developed his new religion which was French to its very bones. Under Francis I's successor, Henry II (1547–1559), Calvinism began to establish itself a little everywhere, and, despite the protestations of the papal nuncio, the heretics were rarely molested. Their chiefs began even to hope that, with a little tact and patience, the royal house would one day be Calvinist as so many German princes had become Lutheran. Then Henry II died, killed by accident in a tournament. He left a minor to succeed him—a minor who died in less than two years, to be succeeded by a still younger child, Charles IX (1560–1574). In the struggle of the different factions to control the regency, the religious division received a new importance. The political Calvinist came into existence to thwart the political Catholic. Whence, in very large part, the forty years or so of the so-called Wars of Religion (1562–1598).

This is the epoch of Catherine de Médici and Coligny, of the Guise and Henry of Navarre, of murders, treachery, and massacres without end—massacres of which one especially has received great publicity, since the victims were Calvinists, namely, the massacre of St. Bartholomew (August 24, 1572). Priests and religious had already been massacred in thousands, and repeatedly, by the fierce Calvinist zeal that hated them as idolaters—the Calvinist ministers being themselves, not infrequently, apostate priests and friars. To cut off a priest's ears became a kind of pastime and one Calvinist leader habitually wore a scarf made up of them.

Wherever the Calvinists triumphed churches were sacked, their treasures of art, the windows, the statuary, the sacred vessels, ruthlessly destroyed. More than twenty thousand churches in all were thus destroyed in France. The Calvinists were a minority whom the supineness of the Government allowed to impose itself on the country. In the end it was the simple patriotism and faith of the betrayed Catholic majority that saved France. The people rose in an endeavour to force the King into an activity worthy of his descent. Finally the last of the decadent Valois race, Henry III (1574–1589), was stabbed by a mad Dominican, and five years later the Protestant heir to the throne made his submission to the Church, Henry IV (1589–1610).

There now began in France a revival of Catholic life in all its forms such as the Church has rarely known, a revival which is in some respects the most brilliant passage of the whole Counter-Reformation epic.

In St. Francis de Sales (1567–1622), Bishop of Geneva from 1602 to 1622, Savoyard by birth, the French renaissance is baptised and humanism becomes devout. He founded the new order of the Visitation, and by his immense correspondence, no less than by his amazingly popular book, *L'Introduction à la Vie Dévote*, he did for the noblesse of the court and the noblesse of the robe something of what St. Philip Neri had done for the world of the Roman Curia. The saint's greater work, the *Traité sur l'amour de Dieu*, one of the masterpieces of mystical theology, may serve as a symbolic reminder of the general revival of the life of prayer, that now showed itself through all the religious orders and gave birth to a singularly rich popular literature. Everyone knows how in recent years a French historian secured for himself a place of the highest distinction by narrating the story of this aspect of seventeenth-century life, an aspect hitherto little known and yet the most important of all—and essentially characteristic of the whole Counter-Reformation.[1]

The crowded tableau there presented, besides containing the figures of innumerable preachers of retreats and missions, and of a host of saintly women who restored the family life of France no less than the life of its convents, is particularly attractive by reason of the group of reformers of clerical life which it contains. Such were, for example, the Cardinal de Bérulle, who founded the French Oratory, and developed a new devotion to the priesthood of Our Lord which bore practical fruit as the basis of a new ideal of priestly practice, and of the formation of innumerable priests in the many seminaries which the Oratorians founded and directed. Two other new orders also devoted themselves to this fundamentally important work of forming a new type of priest—fit minister of the reforms of Trent. There were the Eudistes founded by St. John Eudes, and, the most famous of all, the Company of St. Sulpice, founded by Jean Jacques Olier. Even through the worst days of the next two hundred years the Church of France reaped, from the work of these foundations, the benefit of a never-failing supply of well-instructed, well-formed parochial clergy, a body whom no episcopal negligence, worldliness, or bad example could ever really corrupt.

There is another saint who must be mentioned in this connection, though the founding of a new order of priests, missionaries to the country districts,[2] was but one of a se-

---

[1] Cf. Henri Bremond, *Histoire Littéraire du Sentiment Réligieux en France,* 10 vols. (English translation published by S.P.C.K.).

[2] Called in France Lazarists, in England and Ireland Vincentians; officially styled the Congregation of the Mission.

ries of the good works he inaugurated. This was St. Vincent de Paul (1576-1660), one of the greatest organisers of works of charity who ever lived, the founder, with St. Louise de Marillac, of the Sisters of Charity, and the first successful organiser, thereby, of an order of religious women devoted to active benevolence outside their cloisters.

The most extraordinary production, however, of these years so rich in practical devotion to the cause of God was the *Company of the Blessed Sacrament*. This was a kind of benevolent secret society—not oath-bound—which, though it included priests and bishops among its members, was under lay direction. The members assisted every form of Catholic activity, and not least they brought pressure to bear on dilatory bishops, and forced reforms where reforms were needed. It was the generosity of the members of this league that made possible many of the ventures of St. Vincent, and also the establishment of the great Parisian college of the Foreign Missions in 1663.[3]

The first great check to the revival was the spread of the movement called Jansenism, a movement whose basis was a heretical theory about grace and whose effect was to produce a kind of "calvinised" Catholicism.

The apostasies of the sixteenth century had naturally turned the minds of all Catholic theologians to an exhaustive study of the matters in dispute between the apostates and the Church they had left. Never since the days of St. Augustine and Pelagius had the subject of Grace been so actual. One very natural by-product, then, of the Calvinist and Lutheran controversy was the appearance of a new Catholic theory to explain how man's free will still remained free will when under the influence of Grace, and from the publication of this theory there developed a vigorous domestic controversy among Catholics, in which leading theologians of the new Society of Jesus and of the old Order of Preachers took opposite sides. The whole matter was thrashed out before Clement VIII. He died before publishing any decision, and his successor, Paul V,

[3] The *Missions Etrangères.*

ended the discussion by allowing each party to keep to its opinion, and forbidding either to stigmatise the other as heretical (1606).

Some years before this, however, a professor of Scripture of the University of Louvain, Michael Baius, had, from his study of St. Augustine, deduced a new theory of Grace which Rome had condemned, first in 1567 and then again in 1579. Baius accepted the Roman decisions, but, as the eternal problem of refuting the Calvinist theories and of further exploring the mystery of Grace continued to urge itself, so, too, there lingered in theological circles in the Low Countries something of the spirit of the solution given by Baius.

Fifty years after the death of Baius (1589) his ideas reappeared in a book called *Augustinus*, the work of Jansenius, once a professor of Holy Scripture at Louvain and then for a time Bishop of Ypres (1635–1638). The book was published by his friends two years after the author's death. But already for some years a French associate of Jansenius, a personage of great distinction, the Abbot of St. Cyran, had been translating the Dutchman's theories into the practical business of spiritual direction, giving the new doctrine a systematic application in the field of morality and ascetics.

The publication of the *Augustinus* supplied the new movement with its theoretical justification and this at an opportune moment. At Louvain Jansenism had been little more than the occasion of an academic, theologians' debate. In France it was from the beginning an organised faction, of priests, nuns, and layfolk, all well connected, wealthy, and influential. The battle now begun between this party of innovators and the Church, went on for the best part of a hundred years, and the crisis was soon complicated by further divisions, among the Catholics, as to the extent to which the papal primacy could lawfully control the Church in France, the controversy over the so-called "rights of the Gallican Church."

During this hundred years three subjects, of the greatest practical importance, are thus in debate in France: (1) the relation of grace to man's free will, (2) the function of the sacraments of Penance and the Holy Eucharist, and thence the whole question of the conduct of a truly

Christian life, (3) the relation of the papacy to the hierarchy of bishops.

Jansenius saw himself as a man raised up by Providence to save the Church from the Society of Jesus, which he disliked intensely, by reviving a long-forgotten primitive teaching on Grace and the true Christian life which only that teaching could produce. This teaching, he maintained, was enshrined in the works of St. Augustine, of which he, Jansenius, had an expert knowledge. It was a teaching theologians had lost sight of for centuries. Catholic critics were to describe the new system as "St. Augustine seen through Calvin's spectacles."

According to the new theory all the supernatural gifts with which God endowed the first man, and those other gifts called preternatural (i.e. immunity from death and sickness) were, in reality, natural to man. The effect of original sin is a radical corruption of human nature. Henceforth everything purely natural is evil. The human will, since Adam's fall, is powerless before the assault of concupiscence. It cannot avoid sin unless Grace is given it. Grace is all-powerful, is even irresistible. The soul, then, sways between the two pleasures of sin and of Grace. If God gives Grace, man avoids sin; if the Grace is not given, he cannot but sin. And the Grace is given only to a few, to the tiny minority of men whom God wills to save. For God does not at all will to save all men, nor did He die for all, but only for the minority He determined to save. This doctrine of predestination effectively killed the practice of prayer to the saints for their intercession or to Our Lady. The best homage to pay Our Lady, it was said, was "the hymn of silence."

As a theological theory Jansenism has an obvious place in the history of the general movement of Catholic thought to defend the traditional theories of Grace against Calvinism. This movement had produced new theories in explanation of the great problem how to conciliate the operation of Grace with man's free will, and these new theories had, in their turn, provoked fresh discussions among Catholics and opposition from those who held by the theories taught before Calvinism had made it appearance. There was, on the part of some of these Catholic opponents of the new Catholic theories, a tendency to bring the dispute to an end by the historical argument that the new theories were contrary to the classic writer on these problems, to wit St. Augustine. Jansenius is simply one—although the chief—of the many who have appealed to St. Augustine's writings in support of their opposition to later developments and who have excogitated that support at the cost of misunderstanding much else.

But linked closely with this heresy—which is simply the condemned theory of Baius, presented more completely and with a greater wealth of erudition—is the Jansenite practice in the use of the two sacraments of Penance and the Holy Eucharist. Here again the movement is not free, in its origins, from an undoubted desire to overturn practices which the Jesuits had done much to introduce and to foster.

At the time of the Council of Trent (and the foundation of the Society of Jesus—for the two things were contemporaneous) these sacraments were hardly ever received at all by the generality of the faithful. The Council proclaimed as the ideal that, at every Mass, all those present should receive Holy Communion, and taught explicitly that the effect of the sacrament is to purify man from venial sins and strengthen him against mortal sin. The immediate result of this decree was to produce, everywhere, apostles of the new ideal of frequent communion, the most striking of whom, perhaps, were St. Charles Borromeo and St. Philip Neri. The bishops of France also, very notably, addressed themselves to introduce the reform, and everywhere the new Society of Jesus was singularly loyal to the Tridentine decrees. These decrees, one may say, merely gave a higher sanction still to what had been from the beginning one of the main elements of the spiritual directions of its founder St. Ignatius.

To work against the new practice of frequent communion—and this, as yet, rarely meant more than monthly communion for people in the world, weekly communion for religious—was not only in harmony with Jansenist doctrine but in keeping with the Jansenist opposition to Jesuits wherever found. The Jansenist teaching on this point has to be read to be believed. "Not in bread alone doth man

live," Our Lord had said in reply to the devil's temptation, and the Jansenist used the text to justify his abstinence from receiving Holy Communion. Holy Communion should only be received when there was a certain
proportion between him who received and Him who was
received. It was a reward for the successful in virtue, and
to refuse the reward was more meritorious than to accept
it. "Your sadness that you have not been able to receive
Holy Communion during your illness," St. Cyran wrote
to a nun, "is a relic of your old wordly spirit, that worldly
devotion which made Confession and Communion the
chief things in life. I, too, used to feel like that, and it
used to be very hard for me not to say Mass every day.
. . . You will soon understand that you do more for your-
self by not going to Holy Communion than by going."

As to the sacrament of Penance the Jansenists taught
that without perfect contrition it was of no avail, and
they planned a revival of what they thought was the
practice of the early Church. Absolution should not be
given until the penance enjoined was completed, and the
old discipline of days, weeks, and months of bodily penance should be restored.

There was nothing humanly attractive about this gloomy
heresy, but there are always sufficient of mankind who,
in matters of religion, prefer to follow their imagination
or sentiments rather than use their critical intelligence or
follow the dictates of authority. The Jansenists were
gloomy, had every appearance of being more austere than
the rest of men. They were conscious of being an *élite*,
and the isolation from the common run of men, the solitary life which they urged on their adherents, had its
attractions too. In practice in their reaction to the directions of the pope, these super-Catholics—for such they
claimed to be—showed themselves the most shifty casuists
of the century. Never was there a heresy which had so
finished a technique in the arts of mental reservation and
deceit.

The history of the heresy is a history of endless condemnations, of submissions, of subterfuges by which the
heretic when condemned, submits and then explains away
the submission, is recondemned, submits again, appeals,
and submits, and always with a fresh reservation, some

new loophole through which he escapes to restate—still within the Church—his condemned theory. Then, as in so many cases, the Catholic king steps in, not, this time, directly to protect heresy, but fearful lest Rome's successful condemnation of it might lower his own prestige as the protector—the *de facto* chief—of French Catholicism.

To confine the recital to the Roman activities, the Holy Office condemned the *chef d'œuvre* of Jansenius in 1641 and Urban VIII confirmed this in 1642. The Jansenists first alleged that the bull was a forgery, and then, accepting it, explained that it did not condemn any particular theory the book contained. After seven years of controversy—during which the Holy See lost its most powerful supporter in the matter, the Cardinal de Richelieu—five propositions were extracted from the work, that summed up the essence of the heresy, and Rome was asked to condemn them. The pope—Innocent X (1644–1655)—in response to a counter-petition, set up a commission, and on its report, after two years of study, condemned the five propositions as heretical. Again the Jansenists accepted the papal sentence. They now, however, explained that though the five propositions were heretical they were not heretical as they appeared in Jansenius' book, or they did not appear there in the sense in which they were condemned. Whence new controversies, formularies to be signed, and finally in 1664 a very definitely drawn formulary decreed by Alexander VII (1655–1667). Four bishops strongly resisted this, and matters were fast approaching a new kind of crisis when the pope died (May 22, 1667).

It was now that the royal influence began to tell. The Jansenists had also gained in official circles, and when the new pope—Clement IX (1667–1699)—proposed to take up the matter where his predecessor had left it, nineteen of the bishops of France protested and declared publicly that any drastic action against their four colleagues would be "harmful to the interests and the safety of the State."

From this came the negotiations that produced what has been called the Peace of Clement IX. The Jansenist bishops consented to sign the formula—and then in their synods they made the declarations, orally, to their clergy, which explained away their submission. The pope was merely told that they had submitted. But rumours began to spread, and when they reached Rome Clement ordered new enquiries, and appointed a commission of cardinals for the purpose. In despair, apparently, at ever arriving at the facts, the commission recommended that the official report be taken as true, namely, that the bishops' submission was sincere and single-minded. In the bulls issued to seal the reconciliation this is explicitly stated, and the bishops are publicly praised for their real, complete, and unrestricted obedience to the Roman decisions.

There followed a period of thirty years during which the Jansenist controversy fell into the background, obscured by new difficulties and dangers.

The first of these troubles, and the more lasting, was a dispute between the King of France, Louis XIV (1643-1715), and the Holy See. It centered round the body of customs, privileges, and rights of the French kings in matters ecclesiastical, known collectively as the Liberties of the Gallican Church. The beginning of the trouble was Louis XIV's claim to extend to all the sees of France the right given by the Concordat of 1516 to enjoy the revenues of certain sees during a vacancy. When an appeal to Rome was made, Innocent XI (1676-1689) condemned the usurpation and threatened to use against Louis "the remedies which God had placed in our hands." The ultimate reply of the king was the adoption by the assembly of the clergy of France, in 1682, of a declaration: (1) that neither the popes nor the Church have any power over temporal princes as such; they cannot be deposed nor their subjects released from their oaths of allegiance; (2) the decrees of Constance on the superiority of the General Council to the pope still hold good; (3) the papal primacy must be exercised with due consideration for the customs of local churches; (4) the papal decrees, in matters of faith, are not irreformable until the whole Church has signified its assent to them.

These are the famous Four Articles of 1682, and the king gave orders that they should be taught in the seminaries and accepted by all who took degrees in theology.

The pope annulled all the proceedings of the assembly and refused to institute to vacant sees any who had taken part in the adoption of the articles. The king, in whose hands the nomination of the bishops lay, thereupon persisted in nominating none but members of the condemned assembly. The deadlock continued until there were no fewer than thirty-six sees vacant in France.

In 1687 a dispute about the rights of asylum enjoyed by the French embassy in Rome caused further bitterness, and the pope prepared to excommunicate the king—to which Louis would certainly have replied by breaking away from Catholicism.

It was not until 1693 that the crises ended. The king withdrew the edict imposing the articles on the seminaries, and the pope—Innocent XII (1691–1700)—instituted the bishops.

But the articles continued to be taught, and the mass of the clergy of France were formed by them, formed in a settled distrust of Rome, potential partisans of the king in any disputes that might henceforward arise. The articles had not indeed invented anything new, so far as Catholic thought in France was concerned, but they had given concrete and explicit form to what hitherto was but a vague, though widespread, tendency, and this explicit doctrine was henceforth taught universally to the parochial clergy. The Dominicans made a strong stand against it, so too did the Jesuits. The Society's loyalty to Roman principles during the coming century was, in fact, to be one of the reasons why it was marked down for destruction.

A further consequence of this dispute, of the fact that it had produced an explicit, formal assertion of anti-Roman and pro-regal teaching, was to popularise Gallicanism in all the countries where there was an absolute ruler who was Catholic, that is to say, everywhere in Catholic Europe.

While the dispute between Louis XIV and Innocent XI was at its height there appeared the new heresy called Quietism.

The pioneer of this movement was a Spanish priest, Michael Molinos, who had for many years been living in Rome and hence directing a whole army of pious souls, when, in May, 1685, he was arrested by the Inquisition.

The basis of his teaching and practical guidance in the spiritual life, prayer, and moral conduct was that man must annihilate all his powers. For the desire to be active in one's spiritual life is offensive to God. Man should not concern himself with thoughts either of reward or punishment, of death or eternity, of his own sins or of his virtues. Temptations he should ignore, not even making resistance to them, for this involves activity. Instead he should cultivate a habit and state of passive resignation. When the devil violently invades a man, and this is inevitable, the invasion should be suffered and also the sinful actions which result, the soul resigning itself to this as God's will for it at this moment. Nor need a man confess what he does on these occasions, for this "inward way" is not a thing subject to confession and it is by not confessing that the desire will be overcome. In fact, for the perfect soul God sometimes makes confession impossible.

The cultivation of these ideas and their application had led Molinos and his associates to an amazing life compounded of religious practice and sexual impurities. More than two hundred people in Rome, clerics, nuns, and layfolk, whom Molinos had directed, were implicated. More than twelve thousand letters from his "clients" were discovered, and not for another twenty years did the Inquisition come to the end of the business. Molinos himself, after a long trial, was, on September 3, 1687, sentenced to life imprisonment, having confessed not only to his own aberrations but to having taught that impure and carnal acts are licit to those who pray, for it is only the lower, sensual man that is affected by them.

This horrible business had its repercussions in France through a certain Madame Guyon, the penitent of a Barnabite disciple of Molinos. Let it be said immediately that this lady has never been proved guilty of any adherence to the immoral side of the Quietist movement. But she had developed theories of prayer and of the life of contemplation that were closely allied to those of Molinos, and by her personal influence—she was a woman of great charm and simplicity, and wholly absorbed in spiritual practices—and by her writings, she spread, fairly extensively, in the very heart of the governing classes of the country, the system called semi-Quietism. The bishops were alarmed and wherever she went they began to beseech her to quit their dioceses. Then, in 1686, she was arrested, and for a time imprisoned. After her release she made the acquaintance of the great man through whose friendship she achieved most, and indeed is chiefly known. This was François de la Mother Fénelon, soon to be tutor to the heir to the throne and archbishop of Cambrai.

In the next eight years (1686–1694) Madame Guyon's influence as a spiritual force touched its maximum. Then in 1694 the bishops moved once more. Her theories were condemned and Fénelon, too, was compelled to sign the condemnation. It was the end of the movement.

But the most mischievous feature of the whole affair was the suspicion it threw on the contemplative life as a whole. Jansenism had already done immense harm to the practice of prayer and now the reaction against all the forms of Quietism completed the damage. At the moment when, more than any other, the Catholicism of the key province of the Church needed the strength that only the life of contemplation can give, it was the tragedy of history that this life shrank to very small proportions, and religion, even for holy souls, took on too often the appearance of being no more than a divinely aided effort towards moral perfection.

It was in 1696 that the condemnation of Madame Guyon ended the effective propagation of her troublesome theories and then, five years later, Jansenism revived as an active disturbing element of Catholic life.

In the thirty years that followed the Peace of Clement IX, out-and-out Jansenism had practically disappeared. It was no longer, in all its fulness, the creed of the Jansenist party. The party did indeed continue to exist and to assert that the Church was not infallible in its declaration that Jansenius taught, in the *Augustinus,* the doctrine it had condemned. The party also continued faithful to its first rigorism in the use of the sacraments and in its archæological spiritual preferences. And these sterile theories and ways of life continued to affect, beyond the party properly so called, Catholics whose faith was whole and orthodox but who were temperamentally inclined to what one might, popularly, style a Puritan view of life. There was thus permanently a penumbra of "Jansenised"

Catholics, that included bishops, priests, religious, and layfolk.

About 1701 the whole business flared up once more, apropos of discussions as to the lawfulness of a Catholic holding the Jansenist view that the papal teaching on the fact of Jansenius having taught Jansenism might be met with "a respectful silence." This new discussion moved Louis XIV, whose long seventy-two-years' reign still continued, to ask a decision from Rome, and in 1705 Clement XI (1700–1721) declared that "respectful silence" was not enough. The papal teaching must be accepted as true.

This decree did not end the Jansenist revival, for the new discussions had given fresh publicity to a book by an ex-Oratorian—Pasquier Quesnel (1634–1719)—which had already been a source of trouble. This was a reprint of the New Testament with moral reflections for every verse. Here, in a work of devotion, Quesnel, who was saturated with Jansenist theories, managed to insinuate the very essence of the condemned doctrine, hidden beneath the appearance of pious direction.

The book, when it first appeared in 1684, had been approved by Quesnel's bishop, de Noailles, then bishop of Chartres and now (1708) archbishop of Paris and a cardinal. When Clement XI proceeded to condemn the book, it was more than the cardinal's pride could stomach to revoke his own approbation. He did not oppose the pope outright, but asked for "explanations," and so began a new twenty years of the old warfare, condemnations—the most celebrated of them the bull *Unigenitus* in 1713—submissions, explanations, subterfuges and appeals, and a host of new quarrels as to how far the supporters of the appeal to a General Council (made by the cardinal in 1717), whom Clement XI in 1718 had excommunicated, could be given the last sacraments, and how far priests who refused to administer them could be punished. The conflict in this last stage was eagerly taken up by the courts of law called the *parlements*—the most famous of which was the Parlement de Paris—where the regalist lawyers saw in the controversy an opportunity to resist an alleged papal encroachment in the internal discipline of French Catholicism.

Cardinal de Noailles submitted in 1728, a few months

before his death, and with this Jansenism, as an organized thing, really died. But it survived in individuals, and it survived as a spirit in the ruling classes and the *parlements*, whom it inspired and encouraged in the long fight, which now began, to bring about the suppression of the Society of Jesus.

The basic principle of the sixteenth-century Reformers had been the right of private judgement. They refused to acknowledge the existence of such a thing as an impersonal teaching authority in religious matters. With the Bible at his disposal every man would come surely and safely to a knowledge of divine truth. From the first months of the movement there were, however, divergences among the Bible readers as to the meaning of what they read. With the centuries these divergences grew and the sects multiplied. Such a development was inevitable, and there being but one solution to whatever difficulties the sacred text or the remnants of the traditional doctrine presented—namely the honest opinion of the individual—it was no long time before sceptism as to the truths alleged to be taught by the Bible began to grow, scepticism as to such fundamental truths even as the very existence of God.

There had always been an undercurrent of atheism in Europe, even in the Middle Ages, an undercurrent closely connected with the cult of the natural sciences and allied to the practice of an unmoral life. The semi-pagan Renaissance of the fifteenth and early sixteenth centuries had been its hour of opportunity, and the breakdown of belief in religious authority throughout Europe brought about by the Lutheran-Calvinist revolution finally set it free to develop, scarcely hindered now save by convention.

The two countries where atheism first really developed, as a kind of philosophical reflection on life, were Holland and England. Religion, the only kind of religion Europe had known for twelve hundred years, that is to say, a collection of doctrines and practices held to have been revealed by God to man, these new thinkers rejected entirely. The only religion they acknowledged as reasonable was natural religion, a religion that included no doctrine save what the unaided reason could discover and whose sole end was the practice of natural virtue. This is the system called Deism, and its first inventors were Englishmen of the seventeenth century. In the last years of this century and the opening years of the eighteenth, the Deists began to attack revealed religion as it showed itself in the different sects and, once the movement passed the Channel, it began a war of destruction on the Catholic Church. Its greatest asset was the capture of the chief writers of the day, scientists, philosophers, and publicists, and among them one of the greatest propagandists who has ever lived, the brilliant, cynical, unprincipled and immoral Voltaire.

In this France, where Catholicism lay helpless, racked with the Jansenist controversy, cut off from Rome by its Gallicanism, shackled by its long connection with the State, oppressed by a hierarchy too often incompetent and not infrequently worldly, a France whose ruling classes were more and more given over to immorality, the mockery of Voltaire, in a single generation, put the Church in the position of the defendant. Catholicism was summoned to explain what right it had to live. Hated, derided, it was henceforward, for the best intellect of France and therefore for the intellect of the world, an infamy, and not to be endured.

The French deists and atheists availed themselves of every possible literary weapon, and they secured a hearing in thousands of minds where no serious work of theology or apologetics would ever gain entry. The Jansenist had been a solemn and serious opponent and could be fought off, intellectually, without any great difficulty. But the mockery of these new foes, the pioneers of the modern popular assault on traditional faith and conventional morality, could not be met with the weapons of learning. They had the first laugh, and the crowd that laughed with them was already beyond the reach of dialectic. For the hour when the crowd turned to reflect, the movement provided a great compendium of knowledge, the first Encyclopædia, and there the civilisation of the eighteenth century found a kind of universal popular educator by which to initiate itself into all the sciences and general history, and so written that at every turn the universality of human knowledge was made to tell against religion, and especially against the Catholic Church.

Against these philosophers, the Encyclopædists, poets, dramatists, and social reformers, who practised and recommend every licentious habit, Voltaire, Diderot, D'Alembert, Rousseau, and the rest, and who in this age, when to be civilised was to be French, and when in every part of Europe French thought and French ways of life were eagerly, enthusiastically followed, writers who fashioned the ways of the whole world, as no writers had done since the time of Erasmus: against these spirits of wickedness the Church was not well armed. Her best defenders were the Jesuits, equipped as they were, not only with a sound theological training and a solid spiritual foundation, but with a practical skill in the use of language that made them masters of a classic modern style. From about 1750 the Deist attack on Catholicism becomes an attack on the Jesuits and in that attack the Deists find powerful allies who are Catholics.

In the year 1770 there were 23,000 members of the Society of Jesus, priests, students, lay brothers, and novices, and in addition to their European houses they administered two hundred and seventy-three foreign mission stations. It was in Portugal that the assault gained its first victory. The king, Joseph I, a man whose faculties had rotted through years of debauchery, was the puppet of his minister, the Marquis de Pombal, an adventurer who, by manipulation of the finances and the creation of innumerable monopolies—notably in the wine trade—had piled up an enormous fortune. The details of his long maladministration, the wreck of the military system, of the schools, and of the universities, due to him, his savage repression of all criticism, are nowadays a commonplace of history. In the Jesuits he saw the one power that might, through a possible revival of its influence with the royal family, overturn him as suddenly as he had been elevated. When a Jesuit attacked the monopolies he resolved to strike.

His method was to lay an accusation before the pope —Benedict XIV (1740–1758)—denouncing the Society for sharing in commercial enterprises—a charge based on the fact that the Jesuits sold the produce of the great Indian settlements which they had created in Paraguay. The pope consented to an enquiry. It was conducted by the Cardinal-Patriarch of Libon, Saldanha. Within a fortnight, without hearing a single Jesuit in explanation or defence, he found the Society guilty.

The aged pope died the very day after the Jesuits received notice of the commission. It was to his successor, Clement XIII (1758–1769), that the Jesuits appealed against the way it had gone to work. Pombal, fearing a more energetic policy at Rome would rally the king to the Society, resorted to forgery and produced for the king a Roman decision confirming Saldanha's condemnation. The pope discovered the trick and the forgery was burnt at Rome by the public executioner. Pombal, it seemed, must now be dismissed. But at this moment the king of Portugal was attacked, as he returned from a rendezvous with the wife of one of his nobles, by the injured husband. The shot missed, but the affair was the excuse for an announcement of a widespread plot, hundreds were arrested, and, of course, the Jesuits were implicated. On January 12, 1759, all the Jesuits of Portugal were arrested and most of them shipped off to the papal States and landed on the coast with no more than their cassocks and breviaries. Their houses, colleges, and lands were confiscated, and when the nuncio protested he was expelled, too, and the Portuguese ambassador recalled from Rome.

It was next the turn of the French provinces of the Society. "When we have destroyed the Jesuits," wrote Voltaire in 1761 to a kindred spirit, "we shall have easy work with the Infamy" [i.e. the Catholic Church]. In France, from about 1750, there had been added to the Jansenists, the Gallicans, and the Philosophers, all bitterly hostile to the Jesuits, a new force, namely the king's mistress, Madame de Pompadour, who never forgave the Society the refusal of its members who filled the office of confessor to Louis XV (1715–1774) to countenance her adulterous relations with the king. At the critical moment all would depend on the king, and the mistress would, in that moment, have her revenge.

The occasion of the suppression in France was the financial failure of the Jesuit mission in Martinique, due to the capture of its cargoes by English ships in the opening weeks of the Seven Years' War (1756). The deficit was something like a million pounds, and the principal creditor applied for his money to the Jesuit who was Procurator-General for the Missions.

This official declined responsibility, alleging—what apparently was true enough—that the administrator of the mission in Martinique, Fr. Lavalette, had acted without authorisation in his transactions, and also that each house of the society was solely responsible for its own debts.

The creditor then sued the society and the courts found it liable and ordered it to pay. The Jesuits appealed to the highest court of all—that Parlement de Paris where, for a good hundred years or more, had sat the most influential of their many foes. Once again the case went against them, and not only were they ordered to pay, but the high court seized the opportunity to make an official enquiry into the kind of thing the society was, commanding that its Constitutions be laid before the court. Through the whole of 1761 and 1762, invited or provoked or stimulated by this attack from the Parlement de Paris, every accusation ever made against the society, or against individual Jesuits, was raked up and in broadsheets and pamphlets given new life, while their repetition in the official documents of the process gave these stories, for the indifferent, uncritical, general public, a kind of authenticity. On April 6, 1762, the decision was given that the society, being little better than an association of criminals, responsible for all the schisms and the heresies that ever were, blasphemous and impious in its doctrines, should be suppressed.

Then for two years more the battle continued, first in the *parlements* of the different provinces of France and then in the conscience of the king, whose signature was necessary to give legal force to these edicts. After a long siege Louis XV capitulated and in November, 1764, signed the decree extinguishing the society's legal existence and handing over its members to the jurisdiction of the local bishops.

How far the king acted against what still survived of his better self his own words to his minister, Choiseul, remain to prove. "I have not myself any cordial love for the Jesuits, but all the heretics have always detested them. I say no more on this point. For the peace of my realm, if I expel them, against my inclinations, I will not, at any rate, have it believed that I agree with all that the *parlements* have done and said against them. . . . I say no more or I should say too much."

The suppression was carried out in spite of the protests of the bishops of France and their clergy, and finally of the pope himself. Clement XIII showed himself a most energetic protector. He protested against the edicts of the Parlement de Paris and when the final act came and Louis XV signed the decree, he published, in the bull *Apostolicum* (January 9, 1765), a most eloquent defence of the society, a kind of formal recognition of the totality of what it had done for the Church and a new approbation of the principles of the institution and of its many good works.

"You congratulate me about Russia, congratulate me too about Spain," Voltaire wrote in 1768 to a free-thinking Protestant friend, the Calvinist minister Vernes. He went on to speak of his other friend, the count of Aranda, Prime Minister of Spain, who "in one year has got the Spaniards moving further than Frenchmen have moved in twenty years." Aranda's achievement was the suppression of the Society of Jesus in the empire where of all Catholic countries it was most flourishing, Spain, and this in the reign of a king, Charles III (1759–1788), who was taken universally as a model of Catholic life. "Tu quoque fili mi," the broken-hearted pope wrote to him.

The suppression in Spain was the most mysterious of all, and how the king lent himself to it has never been made clear. In March, 1766, there were serious riots at Madrid and throughout the other great cities. It was alleged that the actual authors of this political movement, whose real object was to protest against the undue influence of the Neapolitans brought in by the king since 1759, were the Jesuits, and in October an enquiry began. The whole affair was conducted with unusual secrecy. The names of the witnesses, the nature of the evidence were never revealed. Nor were the accused heard in their defence. And all the records of the enquiry were destroyed, once the king had studied them. By February, 1767, the decision was taken and it was arranged that it should be announced without any reasons given. Sealed orders were sent out to be opened on the night of April

2, 1767. On the morning of the 3rd, in accordance with the instructions, every Jesuit in the Spanish Empire was arrested, marched to the appointed port, put aboard ship and conveyed to the papal States. The king merely announced that grave motives of state, that must for ever remain locked in his royal breast, necessitated and justified this course of action.

In November the king of Naples, the king of Spain's son, acted in similar fashion and in the following January (1768) the duke of Parma, the king of Spain's nephew, followed suit.

It now remained to force on the pope the suppression of the society as a whole. There were still ten thousand Jesuits in the Austrian dominions, in Germany, and in the northern Italian kingdom of Sardinia, for these sovereigns had not been hostile to the society. The new campaign, against the pope, began immediately, and its leader was Charles III of Spain. The pope was firm against any suggestions, against the threat (1768) that the Bourbon powers would dethrone him and partition his States, and against the actual capture of Avignon, Benevento, and Ponte Corvo.

In January, 1769, the three powers, France, Spain, and Naples, made a joint official demand for the suppression of the society. Clement XIII utterly and absolutely refused. It was his last act. The long strain of his eleven years' fight with this decadent Bourbon Catholicism had broken him at last, and while the three powers planned a blockade of Rome and an insurrection that would drive the pope away, on February 2, 1769, he died.

There is no space here to tell of the intrigues that occupied the long weeks of the ensuing conclave (February 15–May 18). It resulted in the election of the Conventual Franciscan, Lorenzo Ganganelli, who took the name of Clement XIV. Had he, as the price of his election, promised the suppression? It has been asserted by serious and competent historians, but would seem not to be true. Certainly from the very first week of the reign the attack on his will to defend the innocent society began. Maria-Teresa, the empress of Austria, ceased to uphold the Jesuits. The king of Sardinia, also friendly to them, died and gradually Clement yielded. The Bourbons drafted the decree and on July 21, 1773, Clement XIV signed it, the brief *Dominus ac Redemptor*. He did not judge the society nor pass sentence on it. The decree recited merely how from all time the Jesuits had been a sign of contradiction, and set forth many of the things accused against them. For the sake of peace, since there could not be peace while they lived, the pope suppressed the order.

With the partition of Poland, begun almost that very year (1772), the suppression of the Jesuits is the great crime that ushers in the new age of Liberalism. The intrigues, the lies, the blasphemy, the licentiousness, the tyranny from which it springs, characterised the Liberal movement against religion through the next hundred years, till it achieved its next spectacular triumph, the abolition of the temporal power of the popes and the destruction of their States (1870).

The story of these fifteen years (1758–1773) is a terrifying demonstration of how little Catholicism really survived in these Catholic absolutist monarchies that the Council of Trent had hoped, but not dared to reform and recall to their duty. Within two centuries they had brought the very papacy to its knees. And there were other triumphs, not so brutally violent, but equally significant, in the non-Bourbon States. Space must be found for a mention of the German movement called Febronianism and its Italian repercussions in the Synod of Pistoia (1786), and for a summary description of the reforms of the emperor Joseph II (1765–1790).

Febronius was the *nom de plume* of John Nicholas van Hontheim, bishop-auxiliary to the prince bishop of Trèves. He was a canonist and a pupil of the most famous perhaps of all the Gallican canonists, the Louvain professor, Van Espen. In 1763, as a contribution to the movement to reconcile Protestants and Catholics, he published a work called *The Status of the Church and the Lawful Power of the Roman Pontiff*. Here all the theories associated with the Council of Constance, and set forth in the Gallican articles of 1682, were stated once more and in still more radical form. Jurisdiction, it was declared, belonged to the Church as a whole and the pope was subject to the Church. The primacy was not necessarily attached to the see of Rome and the Church could, if necessary, make any other bishop pope. The papal primacy is in fact an administrative office rather than a source of jurisdiction. From this analysis of theory Febronius passed to the facts, and explained their contradiction of his theory by the assertion that during the last thousand years the popes had gradually usurped many of the powers properly belonging to the diocesan bishops. The pope, he also declares explicitly, is not infallible. The real primate in the Church is the General Council, without which the pope cannot issue decrees on faith nor decrees that affect the discipline of the Church as a whole. Nor can the pope lawfully receive appeals from the whole Church.

The practical conclusion of the book is that the usurpation must end, the primitive discipline be restored, and to bring this about Catholic rulers are invited to resist the pope's decrees, and bishops to call in the civil ruler to protect them against the pope.

The book was condemned by Rome within a year of its publication (February 27, 1764), but though ten bishops were found in Germany to obey the pope and suppress it, the next year (1765) saw two new editions and it was speedily translated into German, French, Italian, Spanish, and Portuguese. Between 1770 and 1774 Febronius issued three supplementary volumes defending his theses against the condemnation and in 1777 he published a handy abridgement of the work. By the year 1780 the new ideas were well diffused throughout what part of Europe still called itself Catholic.

Pius VI (1775–1799), the successor to the much-tried Clement XIV, not content with the condemnation of the book, summoned its author to retract what he had written, and in 1778 Febronius made a kind of disavowal. But the mischief was done, and the work proved a most useful tool for the Austrian canonists who were now engaged in enslaving Catholicism to the State in the dominions of Joseph II.

The book also afforded a literary setting for an antipapal demonstration on the part of the German prince-bishop. The electors of Cologne, Mainz, and Trèves met at Coblenz in 1769 and publicly proclaimed their grievances against the Roman *Curia* for its "usurpations" on jurisdiction.

Eleven years after this ecclesiastical demonstration the succession of Joseph II to the full rulership of the empire seemed likely to bring about the translation into fact of the whole Febronian programme. The new emperor was a Liberal, sympathetic to all the characteristic ideas of the eighteenth century, determined to reform the whole of his administration, to abolish ancient servitudes and to build up a modern State of educated, free citizens. The complex variety of customs and jurisdictions and laws was to be replaced by the uniformity of an efficient, highly centralised governmental machine. The chief agents of the policy were the chancellor, Von Kaunitz, a friend of Voltaire, and Van Sweten, the minister for education (if an anticipatory description be permitted), who was a Jansenist.

To Joseph II the Church was primarily a department of State whose office was the promotion of moral order. In the life of the Church the emperor shall be supreme, and now, in one edict after another, the bishops were forbidden to receive or take account of papal decrees without the emperor's consent, forbidden to communicate with Rome, even to ask faculties from Rome, and forbidden to issue pastoral letters, until the imperial censor had approved them. Useless monasteries and convents (i.e. those of the contemplative orders) were suppressed, 318 in all out of a total number of 915. The Third Orders, too, were suppressed, and the confraternities, and all the wealth of the Church combined into a single central fund, which the State would administer for the benefit of religion. Parishes were re-arranged on a basis of one church for every seven hundred people, and it was laid down as a guiding rule that no man should need to live more than an hour from any church and that no more than a single church was needed in that radius. State examinations were to determine clerical promotions, and in place of the various diocesan seminaries and the houses of study of the monastic orders, the emperor founded twelve new State seminaries, in which alone the clergy, secular and regular, were to be trained. The directors and staffs of these seminaries were carefully chosen from the Liberals among the clergy—not a few of them were Freemasons—and a current of Liberal thought was thereby introduced into Austrian ecclesiastical life which continued to be a force until well on into the nineteenth century. "My brother the sacristan," as the free-thinking king of Prussia nicknamed the emperor, went into still greater detail. The number of candles to be lit on the altar for Mass, the prayers to be used, the hymns to be sung were carefully fixed by imperial decree. There was to be but one Mass daily in every church, and this must be said at the High Altar—all other altars were to be removed. Masses were allowed at funerals but not upon anniversaries. The breviary was carefully censored and such feasts as that of St. Gregory VII were forbidden. Sermons on Christian Doctrine were not allowed, the Litany of Loreto was forbidden, and the Rosary too. The monstrance must not be used for exposition of the Blessed Sacrament.

Pius VI, alarmed for the future of Catholicism in Austria, whose ruler was, by his own admission, seriously thinking of a formal breach with Rome and the establishment of a national church, took the unusual step of personally visiting the emperor to plead the cause of religious unity. He arrived in Vienna in March, 1782, and for a month the discussion proceeded. The emperor would not retract what he had already decreed, but he gave the pope a promise not to interfere in matters of Catholic belief and not to do anything that would bring in question the primacy of the Roman See.

In Spain, Sardinia, Venice, and in Naples especially, the reforms of Joseph II began to be copied. The king of Naples now explicitly repudiated the seven-hundred-year-old papal suzerainty and, claiming the right to fill the vacant sees independently of the pope's approval, brought it about that by 1790 more than half of the sees of his kingdom were without a bishop.

In Germany, in 1786, the prince-bishops came together once more, at Ems, to protest against the Roman "usurpations." One of them, the elector-archbishop of Cologne, was Joseph II's brother, and the manifesto is practically a demand that the Church in Germany be recognised as independent of Rome, and an assertion that, in practice, bishops have no earthly superior. The occasion of this rebellion was the establishment of a nunciature at the Bavarian court. These princely ecclesiastics habitually ignored the obligations of their office, and it was the papal nuncios who administered the episcopal sacraments in their dioceses. The establishment of yet another nunciature, and the coming into their territories of yet another episcopally minded prelate from Rome, was resented by these mitred princelings.

Just one month after the declaration of Ems the same impatience of the supernatural flared, much nearer to Rome, in the synod called by the bishop of Pistoia in Tuscany. Here the sovereign, the grand duke Leopold, was also a brother of Joseph II and the synod was intended to inaugurate in Tuscany a movement of "reform" similar to that now in progress in northern Italy and Austria. The bishops of Tuscany, however, refused to support their colleague of Pistoia, and except in an antipapal demonstration, and a further testimony of the poverty of the Faith in the Catholic princes, the synod had no lasting importance.

It is not hard to understand the French historian who writes: "God now saved the Church by sending the French Revolution to destroy princely absolutism." Certainly by 1790, outside the States of the Church and the new United States of America, there was not a single country in the world where the Catholic religion was free to live fully its own life, and not a single Catholic country where there seemed any prospect but of further enslavement and gradual emasculation.

Before the effects of the Revolution are considered, however, something must be said of the other side to the sombre picture of Catholicism in these hundred and forty years (1648–1789), of the continuous supernatural intervention which kept the Faith in being, and which is most strikingly shown in the lives of the great saints and the development of devotion. Three saints in particular must be noticed, St. Margaret Mary Alacoque (1647–1690), St. Paul of the Cross (1694–1775), and St. Alphonsus Liguori (1696–1787).

St. Margaret Mary was a nun of the Order of the Visitation founded by St. Francis de Sales, a member of the community at Paray-le-Monial in Burgundy. In this convent our Lord appeared several times to the saint between the years 1673 and 1675, instructing her to be the herald of a new devotion which should recall to the Church both His love for sinners and the fact of His justice. The devotion was to centre round the contemplation of the Sacred Heart of Jesus and the saint was expressly bidden to proclaim to the world the passionate love of this Sacred Heart for men. In one of these apparitions Our Lord appeared to her with His five wounds radiating light like five suns and the heart in His breast exposed and in flames, the centre and source of all the light. The saint was bidden to establish the practice of especially honouring the Sacred Heart of Jesus on the first Friday of every month, and herself to spend the last hour of every Thursday in a vigil of prayer "in part to appease the divine wrath beseeching mercy for sinners, in part to soften in some sort the bitterness I felt at being abandoned by my apostles." The words of Our Lord at the apparition during the octave of Corpus Christi in 1675 resume the whole meaning and spirit of what the new devotion was meant to promote, "Behold this heart that has so loved men, that has never spared to exhaust and consume itself to prove its love. And in return, from the greater part of mankind, I receive only ungratefulness, scorn, irreverence, sacrilege, and coldness in the very sacrament of love itself. What touches Me even more is this, that it is those whose hearts are consecrated to Me who treat Me thus. Wherefore it is that I ask you that the first Friday following the octave of Corpus Christi shall be dedicated to a special feast in honour of My heart, making honourable reparation for the insults It has received during the times It has been exposed upon the altar. And I promise you that My heart will expand, to pour forth most abundantly the influences of its holy love upon those who pay it this honour, and who labour to have this honour paid it."

The new devotion made very slow progress. The community of Paray were themselves hesitant for long. Gradually it conquered the covenants of the order, and in two spiritual Jesuits, the Blessed Claude de la Colombière and Fr. Jean Croiset, it possessed active apostles to make it known outside.[4] Blessed Claude died in 1682, St. Margaret Mary in 1690, and it was upon Fr. Croiset's efforts that the first really adverse criticisms fell. It was the moment of the universal alarm about Quietism and the beginnings of the general suspicion of mysticism. Here, it appeared, was yet another spiritual novelty, and in 1704 Fr. Croiset's book, *The Devotion to the Sacred Heart,* was put on the Index. The requests for the establishment of the feast were refused in 1696 and again thirty years later. It was not until 1765 that Clement XIII, in the midst of his efforts to save the Society of Jesus from the Catholic princes, issued the decree that placed it in the calendar.

Italy, in the generation that saw these first efforts to establish the devotion to the Sacred Heart, was the witness of a great spiritual revival led by the Franciscan Observant St. Leonard of Porto Maurizio (1676–1751). From about the year 1710 he was continuously *en route,* preaching, and especially in Tuscany, Genoa, Corsica, and in Rome. By his sermons he did much to restore the practice of daily prayer, and, in an age that tended to minimise the necessity of sacraments, he preached constantly and consistently the use of the mass. In his attachment to these two themes and in the extreme austerity of his life St. Leonard is a kind of precursor of St. Alphonsus, for whom, indeed, he is *"the* great missionary of the century."

St. Alphonsus had other gifts, which made his influence felt in a wider field, but another saint, who like St. Alphonsus is a founder of a new order, holds a place midway between him and St. Leonard. This is Paul Danei, St. Paul of the Cross (1694–1775), the founder of the Passionists. St. Paul is primarily a great mystic, a man of incredible penances and of ceaseless prayer, whose whole life is marked by visions and special revelations that centre around devotion to the Passion of Our Lord. It is a life which is the very antithesis of Jansenism. Like St. Leonard it was from the Italy of the north that he came, and it was here that he principally worked. The order he

---

[4] One of the first places where the devotion was preached was the royal palace in London, where Blessed Claude officiated for a time (1676) as chaplain to the Catholic Duchess of York, Mary of Modena.

founded had for its object the preaching of the meaning of the Passion. The Passionist gave himself to a union with Christ suffering, and in this spirit preached his mission, and wherever he preached he was vowed to preach on the Passion.

St. Alphonsus is perhaps best known as the founder of the Redemptorists, an order founded for the single object of giving missions, that is of preaching organised courses of sermons to bring sinners back to the right way and to strengthen the faithful in their loyalty to it. The founder was the one great Catholic personality of his time. He was of noble birth, a Neapolitan, partly Spanish in blood, and already a leading figure at the Bar when, in 1723, he turned to his new life as priest and preacher of missions. The congregations he had in view were the neglected peasantry of the Neapolitan country-sides. The new order founded in 1732, had a definite plan of action and a high standard of studies. In their monasteries the Redemptorists led a life as rigorous as that of a Carthusian.

St. Alphonsus made, and kept, a vow never to waste a moment of time, and when, after nearly twenty years of missionary activity and religious life, he began to write (1745) his literary output was prodigious. There are in the list of his works innumerable books of popular devotion, still reprinted and still familiar to every Catholic such as the *Visits to the Blessed Sacrament* and the *Way of Salvation*. There are also the saint's hymns, for he was no mean poet, and a competent musician. There is a mass of anti-Jansenist writings and a host of books, great and small, in reply to the attacks of the philosophers on Catholic doctrine and practice. Finally there is the work which has set him among the Doctors of the Church, his *Moral Theology*, one of the great works whose appearance truly marks the beginning of a new age. None has done more, not merely to rout Jansenism as a system of morals, but to put an end to the Jansenist influence upon orthodox Catholic moralists and spiritual directors, than St. Alphonsus. This, and the establishment of a new positive tradition in the science of Moral Theology, gives him a great claim on the gratitude of all later generations of Catholics.

His order of Redemptorists had to face the full strength

of the regalist theories in Naples and the interference of Charles III's all-powerful minister, Tanucci, who did much to hamper its early growth. It was but a kind of divine revenge for this that the order produced in St. Clement Hofbauer (1751–1820) not only the apostle of the Catholic revival in Austria in the generation that followed Joseph II, but the successful leader of the opposition to the attempt to impose a new regalism after the Napoleonic wars.

Meanwhile Redemptorists and Passionists continue, with Dominicans, Franciscans, and Jesuits, to be among the most familiar of all the forces which, in modern Catholicism, work together to maintain and extend the primacy of the spiritual.

9

The Assault of Liberalism,
1789–1878

IT IS not unfair to say that the French Revolution fell upon the ruling authorities in the Church like a bolt from a summer sky. To Pius VI the long train of events since 1758 had taught everything save the one thing that mattered, namely that sooner or later both the absolutist monarchies and the papacy that could not learn how to be independent of them, would alike be the victims of the new philosophy's aggression. The papacy had capitulated even to the criminal injustice of the suppression of the most loyal servants of the cause of God, and had lowered itself to praise publicly as an ideal Christian monarch the wretched, lust-ridden king of France who had been one of its own chief tormentors. Now the papacy was itself to undergo a long castigation of eighty years (1789–1870), and then to be renewed, the old worldliness burnt out by new suffering religiously borne. And in the universal turmoil of the quarter of a century that followed the destruction of the Bastille (July 14, 1789), the last remains would be destroyed of the material structure that had enshrined the Catholicism of the Middle Ages. In France, first of all, and then in all the countries which fell under French influence, in Germany, Italy, and Spain, the great princely abbeys disappeared, never to rise again, except as religious houses, and there disappeared, too, the unmitigated, irreformable scandal of the prince-bishop. The good suffered with the bad, for the revolutionaries were not inspired by love for the good, but rather with an iconoclastic zeal to destroy the whole fabric of Catholicism. The semi-sacred States of the Church were ruthlessly occupied in 1798 by the new absolutist State the Revolution had thrown up, and the aged pope carried into captivity, to die in his prison eighteen months later (1799).

The same fate of captivity was in 1808 to befall his successor Pius VII (1800–1823), and in the sufferings of these two popes, the easy, dilettante worldliness of the eighteenth-century régime was to be atoned for, and the foundations to be laid of that devotion to the person of the reigning pope which, for seventy years now, had been so marked a feature of Catholic life, and a source of such power to the modern papacy.

Pius VII returned to his capital in 1815 to face the task of rebuilding a church everywhere in ruins, and a church that had lost in the catastrophe all that immense organisation of the religious orders which, for a thousand years, had been the papacy's finest instrument of government. Not since the time of St. Gregory the Great had there been so few Benedectine abbeys. The Dominicans had suffered so hardly that it would be sixty years again before they were a force. Newman, in 1846, would be able to speak of their ideal as magnificent but unfortunately dead. To this day the Canons-Regular have not recovered from the agony of those years of revolution and war. And these were the orders with whose prosperity was bound up—for it was one great basis of their prosperity—the public performance of the sacred liturgy and the proclamation thereby that Catholic piety is a social thing and Catholics not merely a collection of pious individuals working out their own salvation under their own particular chosen directors. The Catholicism of the next century was to be greatly hampered in its development by this lack of monks. It was to be a serious weakness that this important side of Catholic life was unrepresented in the restoration tableau.

The monastic orders had shrunk almost to nothing and the influence of the liturgy with them. Another grave loss was the disappearance of all the universities. They had been Catholic, and often papal, foundations. In all of them there had been a faculty of theology, and round this mistress science their whole intellectual life had turned. Now they were gone, and when restored they would be restored as State universities, academies for the exploration and exposition of natural truths alone. Education, the formation of the Catholic mind in the new Catholic Europe, would suffer immeasurably, and religious formation be to its intellectual development an extra something added on. There would be the further mischievous effect that henceforth not universities but seminaries would set the tone of theological life. The leaders of Catholic thought would not be the professional thinkers whom a university produces, but technicians, those to whom the important work of training the future clergy is committed and who, among other things, teach them theology. The effect of this destruction of the faculties of theology in the universities of Catholic Europe, the disappearance of the old Salamanca, Alcala, Coimbra, Bologna, Douai, Louvain, and Paris, is a theme that still awaits its historian. Louvain was indeed restored in 1834, but the healthy interplay of the theological intellects of half a score of Catholic universities, the nineteenth century was never, alas, to know.[1]

This is the debit side of the account. There were, however, in the new age, some most promising new assets. There was the new goodwill of the Catholics generally throughout the world, their new attachment to the papacy, and their new appreciation of the value of a religion independent of the State's enslaving patronage. The old tradition of the primacy of the spiritual in the eternally necessary alliance of spiritual and temporal had renewed its life throughout the Church. The absolutist monarchies, as they existed before 1789, had gone for ever. Where they still existed, as in Austria, a country destined to be the papacy's evil-angel [2] for yet another thirty years, they existed under the eyes of a new Europe and a new Catholicism, as hostile to their claim to regulate the spiritual as the Liberals were hostile to their claim to political absolutism.

[1] Readers of Newman will recall the innumerable occasions on which the absence of Catholic universities is the occasion of his sorrowful comment.

[2] In purely political matters.

There were also a host of new active religious orders of women, and particularly of orders devoted to teaching, upon whose zeal and self-sacrifice the system of free popular education, destroyed by the Revolution, would be restored in France and Belgium and Germany.

Finally there were the Jesuits, for in 1814 Pius VII had called the great society back to life, and because of its flexible organisation, it was to be the chief auxiliary of the popes in the Catholic restoration of the next sixty years.

The great effect of the Revolution had been to destroy for ever the unquestioned reign of absolutism. But in 1815 the defeat of the revolutionary French State entailed a general restoration of the absolutist monarchies, a restoration qualified in some cases by the grants of certain constitutional rights to subjects. This settlement caused grave dissatisfatcion in every country in Europe, for in every country there was, by 1815, a strong body of Liberals, a party which had made the principles of 1789 its gospel and which, after the experience of seeing them in action for twenty years and more, would not bear patiently any limitation of the practical expression of those principles. The settlement of 1815 would endure just so long as the conflict between the restored kings and the Liberals among their subjects could be averted.

Speaking generally, the first thirty years (1815-1848) is a period during which the Absolutist kings seek to regain lost ground and the Liberals to overturn the settlement of 1815. The first Liberal risings, in Spain and in Italy, are easily repressed. But the Liberal success in overturning the restored Bourbon kings of France (1830), and, allied with the Catholics, in establishing the kingdom of Belgium, marks the beginning of a great change. In Spain during the thirties, and in Portugal, too, there is a civil war between Liberals and Absolutists and the period culminates in the year of revolutions, 1848, which sees a Liberal revolution triumph in almost every capital in Europe. From 1848 to 1870 Liberalism touches its apogee, and in the movement which unites the whole of Italy under the rule of the House of Savoy, it achieves the most spectacular and symbolic triumph of all.

The popes are temporal sovereigns and, as temporal sovereigns, are Absolutists. They cannot but be concerned with, and affected by, this political duel between Liberalism and Absolutism. But Liberalism concerns them in another way, for it has also a moral side. It is a system which proposes to battle with all the evils that afflict mankind, and in this fight not only does it not propose to avail itself of the spiritual system which is the Catholic Church, but it denies that system all legal existence, consenting merely to tolerate the profession and practice of Catholicism by the private citizen. Still worse, Liberalism denies the right of the Catholic Church to be a system having views on the morality of public life. Politics is something independent of morals. It has a code of right and wrong that is its own, and the Church must take the action of the State as it finds it. The position is complicated, and the crisis rendered inevitable, by the fact that it is in States where the mass of the people are Catholics that the Liberal movement is most active. Finally, some of the fundamental postulates of Liberalism are irreconcilable with Catholic teaching and some of the institutions most characteristic of the Liberal State are such as it is impossible for the Church to approve. And, unfortunately, the Liberals are almost everywhere the only party really interested in the material betterment of mankind and the correction of social abuses.

The Church everywhere fights Liberalism—in the sense just described—and at the same time there still faces the Church the menace of the Absolutist kings. These she no longer endures with the gentle deprecation of the eighteenth century, but fights with the beginnings of new vigour, and especially does the restored Catholicism of these years fight for the liberty of the Church in the lands outside Europe, in the States of South America which until lately were the colonies of Spain in active revolt against the mother country.

The period ends—1870—with the papacy finally routed as a temporal power, destroyed in this respect by the Liberal States. The downfall of the papal States in 1870 is a kind of symbol that the process begun at Westphalia in 1648 has reached its climax. At the same time, the Vatican Council of that same year testifies to the final triumph within the Church itself of the old Roman conception of the papal office. Henceforth there will be no Gallicanism, even in name, even as a school of ecclesiastical politics. And, the most remarkable thing of all, there will be a new type of pope, a new mentality will direct the fortunes of the Church henceforth. The popes of the nineteenth-century restoration (1800–1878)[3] are all of them good men, and several are men of real ability. But they are all men of the eighteenth century, or rather of the absolutist age of which that century is popularly the symbol. None of them really understood the new world which the Revolution had produced, understood either how to fight it or how to convert it. But on the death of Pius IX (1846–1878) there was elected a pope supremely gifted in political understanding as in the diplomatic gifts. This was Leo XIII (1878–1903), the greatest papal ruler since Paul III (1534–1549), a traditionalist and a conservative who thought in modern terms and spoke in the modern idiom, and whose long reign is the beginning of a new age of Catholic history, the age in which we live, an age which as yet is in the state of transition and whose revolutionary character is only beginning to be apparent to us.

The French Revolution was an affair of such complex magnitude that it is not possible, here, to do more than make a list of the principle events in so far as they directly affected the Church.

The States-General, summoned (for the first time since 1614) to advise Louis XVI in the general crisis of national affairs, met on May 4, 1789. It was a body of three "orders," Clergy, Nobility, and the "Third Estate." The representatives of the first order had been elected by a system that gave every parish priest a vote, while abbeys and monasteries had but a single vote each, and chapters one vote for every ten canons. It was thus the parish priests of France who determined the election, and of the 296 clergy representatives, 208 were parish priests and only 47 bishops. It was again the parish priests who settled that the States-General should transform itself into a National Assembly (June 22, 1789), and on the following August 4, by vote of the assembly the Church of

---

[3] Pius VII (1800-1823), Leo XII (1823-1829), Pius VIII (1829-1830), Gregory XVI (1831-1846), Pius IX (1846-1878).

France lost all its legal privileges and exemptions. On October 10 Talleyrand, still bishop of Autun, proposed that the nation should take over the Church's property—two thousand million francs capital, seventy million a year revenue—and on November 2, by 568 votes to 346, the assembly so decreed. Next the sale of the property was ordered and inventories were drawn up (January, 1790), while in February commissioners were sent to "liberate" the monks and the nuns. By the end of this year all the communities had disappeared,[4] and the greater part of the properties were in process of being sold up.

The Assembly next proceeded to the fatal measure which divorced the Church inevitably from the movement of reform, for it touched not upon property, but ecclesiastical jurisdiction, and the ultimate foundation of all, the Roman primacy. This measure was the *Civil Constitution* of the Clergy, the work of the innumerable Gallican lawyers who were the legacy of the Parlements to the Assembly. They now had their chance, these Gallican Jansenists, to revenge themselves on the authors of the bull *Unigenitus* and the rest, and to put the pope out of French ecclesiastical life altogether. What they achieved was to divide the national life of France as it had never been divided before, with a division that still endures. The dioceses of France were to be rearranged and the bishops henceforth elected by the people. The archbishop would confirm the election and consecrate the elect, the new bishop would then write a respectful letter to notify the pope of his succession (July 12, 1790). Louis XVI, advised by his bishops, signed the decree. He wrote to Rome asking for its approbation and the nuncia at Paris wrote in the same sense. It was long before Pius VI ventured on a public judgement. Privately he exhorted the king to refuse his signature, and meanwhile signs of resistance began to show in France itself. In October ninety-three bishops denounced the law, and in reply to this opposition the Assembly (November 27) decreed that all ecclesiastics should take an oath to observe the Constitution. High authorities were still torn between disapprobation

---

[4] Half of the monks went without compulsion, but the whole body of the nuns stood firm to the last.

and the fear that a definite declaration would result in the loss of France to the Church. Finally, before the pope made up his mind, the king signed the decree establishing the oath, again on episcopal advice (December 26). And now, all over France, there were scenes that might have recalled the inauguration of the royal supremacy in the England of Henry VIII. The clergy, left without any guidance, except their own knowledge, were almost evenly divided. Those who refused the oath were dispossessed of their livings, and, while this was in progress all over the country, the news arrived that the pope had at last replied (April 10, 1791) by a condemnation of the Constitution and a prohibition to take the oath. Furthermore, those who had sworn were to retract within forty days under pain of suspension from their functions.

The position was clear at last, and a persecution began of the non-juring clergy and their adherents. Catholics everywhere refused the ministrations of the Government priests and bishops, and by a series of new measures the clergy faithful to the Roman decisions were tracked down, imprisoned, exiled, and, once the era of blood opened, sent to the guillotine. In September, 1792, there were massacres of priest-prisoners all over France, and, more mercifully, wholesale deportations.

Nor was the Revolution as it advanced more tender to its own creation, the Constitutional Church. It stripped it of all its sacred vessels, all its statues and pictures, forbade the wearing of ecclesiastical dress, interfered with the liturgy, abolished the celibacy of the clergy. Finally it set up in place of Catholicism the cult of Reason, and an actress was enthroned as the Goddess of Reason on the high altar of the cathedral of Paris (1793).

For yet another six years the fortunes of Catholicism rose and fell with every change of the political régime. The Mass, for most of this time, was proscribed and the non-juring clergy had no legal existence. Thousands of priests were deported, hundreds perished in the prisons. In 1797 the milder régime of the Directoire allowed some twelve thousand priests to return, but within a few months the old savagery had once more the upper hand. It was now that the final vandalism functioned, and the great abbey church of Cluny, the second largest church in the world, was razed to the ground, and the cathedrals of Arras, Liége, Cambrai, and Burges, while that of Antwerp was only saved by the arrival of the man who was to change all, Napoleon.

It was the *coup d'état* of November 9, 1799, that placed Napoleon in power, and on the morrow of the battle of Marengo (June 14, 1800), which assured his position definitely, he sent a message to the newly elected pope, Pius VII, that he was prepared to reinstate Catholicism in France and to make some arrangement regarding the Church's future endowment.

Pius VII, a "young" pope of fifty-eight, who had already, as Bishop of Imola, met the revolution in the person of Napoleon himself, and was willing to recognise that the pre-1789 world had gone once and for all, hastened to accept the offer to negotiate. The outcome of the meeting of these two personalities was the Concordat of 1801 which immediately settled the restoration of religion in France, Belgium, Holland, Switzerland, and northern Italy, regulated the fortunes of Catholicism in France down to 1906, and served as a model for the general relations between Rome and the different States through the whole nineteenth century.

It was not, of course, any zeal for religion that urged Napoleon. "Did I rule Jews," he explained, "I should be rebuilding the temple of Solomon." He wished to restore Catholicism in order to remove a division that was slowly killing the nation, and the restored Church, he intended, should be an additional instrument of his absolute government. At Rome the pope's concern was the restoration of Catholic life, of opportunities for Mass and the sacraments, for the recruiting of new priests to fill the depleted ranks in a country where well over half the clergy of 1789 had disappeared by death, schism, and apostasy, and where, in the meantime, none had been ordained.

The settlement was in some respects revolutionary. The 133 ancient sees were swept away and 60 new sees erected to replace them. The remnants of the old hierarchy were asked by Rome to resign and all save thirteen did so— these thirteen the pope deposed. The pope agreed to convalidate the marriages made by so many of the clergy who had apostatised during the years of trouble, and also to accept among the new bishops some of the bishops elected and consecrated under the Civil Constitution of the Clergy. Catholicism was not declared to be the official religion of the country, but the authority of the bishop in his diocese was recognised and supported by the State—to which was restored the right of nomination previously enjoyed by the kings of France. The clergy, in compensation for the loss of their property, were to receive a small salary. The full free exercise of the Catholic religion was guaranteed, chapters and seminaries were restored, and the cathedrals and churches given back to the bishops.

To this Concordat Napoleon added, and by a trick won the consent of the legate Cardinal Caprara for, a further set of articles in which the old claims of the Gallican theologians reappeared, limiting the exercise of the papal power in France. The pope protested and, after a kind of disavowal by Talleyrand, the matter was considered arranged—to give further trouble later on, inevitably.

It was on Easter Sunday, 1802, that the Concordat was published, and the three consuls who now ruled France assisted at a solemn Mass of thanksgiving at Notre Dame.

In the next ten years Napoleon marched from triumph to triumph, dispossessing ancient kings and seating his relatives on the different vacant thrones. Between 1806 and 1808 his armies occupied one town after another of the papal State and by a decree of May 17, 1809, the State was annexed to the empire. Pius VII replied by excommunicating the emperor and then on July 5 he was arrested and carried off into a captivity that lasted the best part of six years and did not end until the abdication of the emperor in 1814.

In most centuries since the conversion of Clovis France has been the key province of Catholicism. This was to be true of the nineteenth century also, and the survey of the history of the Catholic restoration may very well begin with France. Under the restored Bourbons, Louis XVIII (1814–1824) and Charles X (1824–1830), who accepted the ecclesiastical settlement of 1801, the bishops gladly leaned on the monarchy for support and, in one crisis, came near to a fresh crisis thereby with the pope, Leo XII (1823–1829). But the outstanding figure in the

French Church during these years was not a bishop but a priest who was a writer of genius, the Abbé de La Mennais. This gifted publicist saw in the alliance of Church and State the source of all that was wrong in the ecclesiastical world of his time. The French revolution of 1830 was for him the beginning of a new age. Under the new Orleanist Liberal monarchy, the Church, free of the State, would exert the fulness of its influence. This premature attempt to reconcile Catholicism and the Revolution aroused the bitterest antagonism. The bishops of France were seriously alarmed, and when the prophet attempted to gain the favour of the pope—Gregory XVI (1831–1846)—for his solution of a problem that, in fact, he oversimplified, the end soon came. In a famous encyclical, *Mirari Vos* (August 15, 1832), the theories were condemned, though La Mennais was not mentioned nor his equally famous collaborators, the Comte de Montalembert and Henri Lacordaire. For La Mennais the shock of disavowel by Rome was too much. He left the Church to become its bitter critic.

The discussion which he had done so much to enliven between Gallicans and Ultramontanes (as the anti-Gallican party came to be called) went on with increasing bitterness for the next forty years, discussions indeed on matters of discipline and policy and the right attitude of Catholicism towards the new age, never discussions on defined doctrines, but discussions which embittered Catholic life at the time and weakened it for the generation immediately following. These forty years saw three more revolutions in France, and the political divisions in the nation to which these are witness also had their inevitable effect in dividing the Catholic forces in the struggle for real religious liberty. By the time Pius IX died (1878) these divisions were bearing all their fruit, and the Catholics of France soon found themselves face to face with the development of the Third Republic into the classic example of a persecuting Liberal State, and bereft of real leadership, ecclesiastical or lay—a misfortune that was to deprive the masterly guidance of Leo XIII of half its value.

The entry of the French revolutionary armies into Germany in 1792 found the Church there, to all appearances, on the verge of a serious breach with Rome. But the prince-bishops fled before the victors, and their political importance disappeared for ever—and with it the menace to Catholic unity. "Now we are free," cried their subjects, "and we'll once more have the Mass in Latin." Twenty years later, the wars at last over, a grave problem of religious reconstruction had to be faced. The treaties of 1815 confirmed Napoleon's great reform which had reduced the number of independent States in Germany from 303 to 38. The ecclesiastical principalities were not restored at the Congress of Vienna, and, as a result of the transfers of population, hundreds of thousands of Catholics now found themselves under Protestant rulers. It was at once a danger and a blessing that there were but five bishops in all Germany, four of them men eighty years of age. The first instinctive move in these highest ecclesiastical circles in Germany was to plan a national independent Church. Thanks in very great measure to the Redemptorist, St. Clement Hofbauer, this peril was averted. The Church had also to thank the calculation of the German princes, who hoped to get from Rome concessions that would ensure them an easier control of ecclesiastical life than could be attained were there a single national church for the whole of the thirty-eight States.

Napoleon had shown the princes the way and his Concordat was the model for a whole series now negotiated between the Holy See and the different princes, Bavaria in 1817, Prussia in 1821, Hanover in 1824, and the Rhine principalities in 1827. All these princes strove to play the trick devised by Napoleon, namely to follow up the Concordat by laws that gave them additional powers in Church affairs, and in each case this brought about a serious crisis which it taxed all the diplomatic powers of the Holy See to surmount. The Concordats had one admirable, if unexpected, effect throughout Germany. They were a practical recognition by all the princes, Protestant as well as Catholic, that the Holy See is the effective primate of the whole Church. Gallicanism in Germany, Josephism, here received a blow from which it never recovered.

There now began an amazing revival of Catholic life

throughout the States of Germany, a revival all the more singular in that it came from below. Its leaders were not bishops, nor always ecclesiastics, but distinguished scholars, writers, and publicists, and many of them were converts. It was on the labours of Stolberg, Schlegel, Görres, and Möhler, that the new Catholicism was built up. The theological studies of a new generation of scholars, among whom was Ignatius Döllinger, gave the revival an intellectual basis that made German Catholicism for fifty years a thing apart and gave the Church a prestige among this learning-loving race which it had never enjoyed before. And the romantic movement, the new interest in the culture of the Middle Ages, also worked powerfully in favour of the Catholic revival.

It was one of the blessings of this Catholic revival that it proceeded independently of State patronage and independently of the fortunes of any particular political party. In Bavaria, it is true, it owed much to the personal interest of the king, Ludwig I (1825–1848), but even here it was never a government-directed restoration. In other States the revival had, very often, to make its way against the opposition of the State bureaucracy, determined to oppose any tendencies that accentuated the differences between Catholicism and Protestantism and eager to patronise a religious indifferentism that might result in a featureless common "Christianity." Differences on the practical question of mixed marriages finally brought about, in Prussia, a miniature persecution, the archbishop of Cologne and the Bishop of Poznan both being imprisoned when they resisted the Government's commands to ignore the Roman instructions on this subject (1837).

The new spirit shown by these bishops acted very powerfully through the whole episcopate, and Rome was sufficiently encouraged to order the one bishop who still showed the old servility to resign his see. Already the Prussian Government was beginning to hesitate before the task of coercing its millions of new Catholic subjects when, in 1840, the accession of a new king, Frederick William IV, gave it a chance to renew negotiations without loss of prestige. The result was a concession of religious liberty, of real independence of the State such as Catholics had never before known, and which for thirty years made the

Prussian system a model that the Catholics of the other German States strove to have imitated.

In Austria, no longer since 1815 enjoying an uncontested primacy in German affairs, the Catholic revival made little headway. The bishops, still for the most part courtier prelates, chosen from the nobility, preferred the Josephist system which connived at the irregularities of their lives and protected them from Roman "interference," and while Catholics in other parts of Germany were laying the foundations of a tradition of Catholic citizenship and of the apostolate in social matters, the Austrian Church remained in its chosen stagnation, content merely to provide a kind of religious setting for the political system.

The year of revolutions, 1848, saw a new departure of immense importance, not for Germany alone, but for the whole Church. This was the Congress of Mainz. With the appearance throughout Europe of Constitutions establishing everywhere something of a parliamentary system, Catholicism gained a new asset, the Catholic voters, and the bishops a new responsibility, namely to educate the voters for their civic functions and to organise them in the exercise of them. It was the Catholics of Germany who first grasped the new possibilities and understood the way in which they could be realised, and it is the glory of the new German episcopate that, half a century before the rest of the Church, it welcomed and blessed the new initiative and thereby secured, not indeed a right to direct it, but the wholehearted confidence of the army of enthusiasts who had set it in motion. At Mainz there was founded for the first time a union of Catholics to promote Catholic ideals in social life. "This association," its programme declared, "cannot limit itself to the purely educational object of the Church's legal freedom nor to education itself. On the contrary, it must strive to reawaken and to put new life into Catholic public opinion, it must spread this and Catholic moral ideals, must plant these in the whole field of the national life, and so prepare to solve the great problem of the day, the social problem." This was forty years and more before Leo XIII's *Rerum Novarum!* Here was the beginning of a wonderful movement, which soon in Ketteler, bishop of Mainz, possessed a leader of genius.

The union of Germany under Prussian leadership was consummated by the war of 1870. For the Catholics this national triumph was not without its price. Bismarck, who had planned it, was anti-Catholic, and had already shown this. Now, master of a united Germany, he set himself to put German Catholicism in its place as an institution subject to the State. The liberality of the old Prussian constitution was not to inspire the régime of the new German Empire. The first manœuvre was to attempt, through Rome, to break up the political party, the *Centrum*, in which most of the German Catholics were organised. Here Bismarck failed, and next, by a series of laws passed between 1871 and 1875, he abolished the Church's control of its own schools, expelled the Jesuits and other religious orders, took over the seminaries, claimed the right to appoint the clergy, and finally punished with severe imprisonment the clergy who violated any of these various regulations.

The Catholics made an admirable resistance. Soon hundreds of priests were in prison and with them the archbishops of Poznan and Cologne and the bishop of Trèves. The persecution lasted in full vigour for seven years. Then fear of the rising power of the Socialists halted Bismarck a little. The strength of the Centre Party and the skill of its great leader, Windthorst, began to tell, and when Leo XIII was elected (1878) the Chancellor was already willing to make terms. Gradually the persecuting laws were repealed, and by the accession of the emperor William II (1888) the German Church was fast rebuilding its vast system of schools, colleges, hospitals, universities, its innumerable societies, study clubs and social organisations, that made it in the early years of this century a model for the whole Catholic world.

Nowhere, in the century that followed the French Revolution, did the fight of Catholicism with the principles of the Revolution show itself so bitter as in Italy, and the reason for this was, of course, the political complication that in Italy the popes were also temporal sovereigns.

Italy had, for centuries and centuries, been nothing more than "a geographical expression." There were seven Italian States, and the State of the Church, running northeast from Rome, cut the peninsula in half. To the south of this papal State was Naples, where in 1815 the Bourbons were restored. In the north lay the Hapsburg duchies of Tuscany and Parma, Lombardy and Venetia, which were provinces of the Austro-Hungarian empire, and the kingdom of Sardinia. This last kingdom had for its rulers the most Italian-minded of all these princes and the most ambitious. It was, from about 1830, the only kingdom of which Liberalism had any hopes, and from 1848, when it had gone to war with its powerful Austrian neighbour, in a desperate attempt to expel the Austrians from Italian soil, Sardinia became inseperably associated with the cause of Liberalism—of anti-clericalism, therefore—and of Italian unity.

In the ten years between its two wars with Austria, the defeat of 1849 and the triumph of 1859, this State, whence was organised the revolution which in 1860 dispossessed all the lesser Italian rulers (including the pope) carried through a programme of drastic anti-religious legislation. Monasteries were suppressed, religious orders expelled, priests and bishops imprisoned for resistance to, and even for criticism of, the new laws. It was to be the tragedy of the new national movement in Italy—the *Risorgimento*—that its promoters attacked not merely the popes as, in their temporal sovereignty, a political obstacle to the scheme, but Catholicism itself, and to make their attack more effective they called to their assistance all the secret societies, and especially the Freemasons. The inevitable result was half a century of extremely bitter controversy and an immense loss of souls to the Church.

It was only with the greatest difficulty that the powers were persuaded, at the Congress of Vienna in 1814, to restore the papal State. For years it had been a part of Napoleon's empire, and during all those years Austria had coveted the succession to Napoleon. But the diplomacy of Consalvi, Cardinal-Secretary of State to Pius VII, had succeeded, and from 1815, part of the price of their independence, the popes had to face the insoluble problem how to govern a country whose intelligentsia, whose whole educated class, was hopelessly and finally alienated from their whole political system and ideals. The root of the trouble, as Consalvi himself noted, was the natural objection of the layman to being governed by priests. And in this State the whole administration, it is scarcely an exaggeration to say, from the sovereign to the very clerks in the public offices, was clerical. And it was inefficient. Taxes were indeed light, but industry and commerce were non-existent, and an immense proportion of the people lived systematically by begging. Nowhere did the secret societies gain recruits more readily, and they gained recruits from all classes, even from the clergy and the religious orders. The memory of the efficient government of the French, of the advantages to be gained from a definite, uniform system of law, of a time when all were equal before the law, and the petty tyranny of the small official could find correction from the courts, all these persisted and hardened men's minds against the paternal admonitions, the spiritual favours, and the excommunications, which were all that popes like Leo XII (1823–1829), Pius VIII (1829–1830), and Gregory XVI (1831–1846) had to oppose to the revolutionary propaganda. If ever this should issue in an insurrection the popes would be powerless, unless some friendly neighbour came to their aid with troops. One such friendly neighbour was Austria, which, under the guidance of its great Chancellor, Prince Metternich, had consecrated itself, since 1815, to the task of repressing Liberalism wherever it showed itself. Consalvi had feared the final results of dependence on Austria. He understood only too well that the old spirit of Joseph II still survived, and skillfully he managed to keep the papal foreign policy independent. But he died in 1824, and his successors threw themselves gladly into Austria's arms, obsessed with the sole idea that Liberalism must at all costs be crushed.

In 1831 the rebellion came, a serious affair that had Bologna for its centre. The pope appealed to Austria and an army was sent which restored his authority and settled down in permanent occupation of the disturbed provinces. The French, jealous of the Austrian intervention, uninvited, sent a fleet and an army to the papal port of Ancona and occupied it for as long as the Austrians remained in the north. A State that had to tolerate such a condition of things, to call in foreign armies to protect itself from its own subjects, was clearly doomed.

The successor to Gregory XVI was Pius IX (1846–

1878), a kindly, well-meaning prelate, friendly, even to the revolutionaries, and willing to introduce reforms. The first two years of his reign saw concessions that amounted to a revolution, and that filled most of the cardinals and permanent officials with horror. One of the pope's greatest difficulties was their sulky refusal to co-operate with him. Nevertheless, railways were constructed, tariffs reduced, monopolies restricted, the law courts reorganised, the press censorship abolished, commercial treaties made with foreign States, local councils set up, and an amnesty granted for all political offences. The Romans "were presented in two years with as large a measure of constitutional progress as the English had won arduously in two centuries." [5]

Pius IX was in no sense a man of the world. He had not the political gifts, nor could he be called a statesman. And between the Liberals—who hailed his reforms with joy, proclaimed him one of themselves, and planned to use him to promote Liberalism under the guise of Italian patriotism—and the clerical reactionaries, he was destined soon to be lost as a temporal sovereign.

The crisis came in 1848, when Sardinia marched against Austria. The pope, who as a sovereign had no quarrel with Austria, refused to play the part of "liberator" for which the Liberals had cast him. Whereupon they turned against him, permanently, and stirred up a revolution in Rome itself. In November, 1848, the pope was forced to flee and the Roman Republic was proclaimed. It lasted until the following July when a French army captured Rome and restored the papal power. Pius IX was cured of any leanings to promote political reforms, and for the rest of the reign it was a French garrison in Rome that ensured the pope's independence and his safety.

Ten years later (1859) there was another war with Austria; France now allied with Sardinia. The French emperor, Napoleon III, once the war was over, allowed the Sardinian minister, Camillo Cavour, a free hand, and between Cavour and Garibaldi the unity of Italy was accomplished (1860), all the princes being dispossessed of their territory, save that Austria still retained Venetia, and that the pope was left his capital and the district

---

[5] F. A. Simpson, *Louis Napoleon and the Recovery of France* (1923), p. 57.

around it called the Patrimony of St. Peter. Ten years later still, the Franco-Prussian war brought about the withdrawal of the French garrison from Rome. The Italian troops marched in and the temporal power of the pope was finally ended (September 20, 1870).

For the popes this event had a much more serious consequence than any loss of territory or revenue. All men are either sovereigns or subjects to sovereigns. The pope could not, for the sake of the Church he rules, consent to be a subject, or he would thereby—in the eyes of the world —make his sovereign the real ruler of the Catholic Church. If the Italians would not recognise explicitly that the pope is a sovereign, what could the pope do to make clear to the world his independence of the Italian Government? He could at least refuse all recognition to the *fait accompli* of 1870, and let no opportunity pass of protesting against the violence done to him and against the ambiguous position to which that violence had reduced him. This is the meaning of that rôle of "Prisoner of the Vatican" which the popes adopted for the next fifty-nine years, the sole disproof possible to them of any belief that the pope had now no choice but to be the king of Italy's chaplain.

The reign of Pius IX (1846–1878), the longest in the annals of the papacy, was, in the political sense, a succession of disasters, a time in which many troubles, already ripening before the pope was elected, came to their unpleasant maturity. And it was a reign marked by serious losses to the public position of Catholicism in almost every country of Europe. But in the purely religious sense these same years were years of immense recovery and new gains. They are the years in which the many new teaching orders of women begin effectively to re-Christianise the education of women in France, Spain, Belgium, Germany, and Italy. They are the years in which, slowly, and as by a series of miracles, two great orders of Benedictions and the Preaching Friars come back to life. The principal figures in each case are Frenchmen, Dom Guéranger for the Benedectines and Lacordaire and Jandel for the Dominicans.

France is also the scene of the heroic life of St. Jean Marie Vianney (1786–1859), the Curé of Ars, and of many apparitions of Our Lady (1830, 1846, 1858, 1871), the best known of which are the series at Lourdes in 1858 to the child who became St. Bernadette Soubirous. Italy has St. John Bosco and St. Joseph Cottolengo to show, and the young Passionist St. Gabriel of the Sorrows.

And the recognition of the papal primacy reaches a new fulness in the final stages of the movement for the definition of the dogma of the Immaculate Conception. This was proclaimed by Pius IX (December 8, 1854), by a personal act, in response to the urgency of all the bishops of the Catholic world. The most striking evidence, however, as to the Church's essential independence of all but the grace of her divine Founder and her divine Guide, was the General Council of the Vatican (summoned for December 8, 1869). Here the episcopate of the whole world gathered in numbers never known before, and after defining in singularly reassuring fashion the traditional Catholic belief in the value of reason and of its rights in the field of religion, it passed to define anew the universal primacy of the Roman Pontiff in the Church of Christ, and also that in the exercise of his teaching office as Supreme teacher of the whole Church he enjoys that infallibility which was promised by Our Lord to the Church itself.

The long discussions between neo-Gallicans and Ultramontanes, in which, on both sides, exaggerations had abounded, were ended now for ever. The Church could face the problems of the new age with a new internal unity, undistracted by the last legacy of old dissensions, the last tradition of a particularly mischievous piece of Renaissance theology. After four hundred and fifty years the Church was finally rid of the misery of the Great Schism and of the mistakes of Constance.

The outbreak of the Franco-Prussian war brought the Council to an end long before its work was finished. But many of the reforms to discuss which it was principally convened, have been put into operation by later popes, Leo XIII (1878-1903), Pius X (1903-1914), Benedict XV (1914-1922), and Pius XI (1922-1939), and find permanent legal statement in the Code of Canon Law, compiled at the command of Pius X and promulgated (1917) by Benedict XV.

10

The Missionary Church

So FAR this history has been almost wholly a history of Catholicism in the lands that once formed part of the Roman Empire. Those lands were, and for many generations continued to be, conterminous with the known world. Beyond them, or, to be more accurate, beyond the lands that lay on their frontiers, stretched the eastern countries, India, China, and the rest, about which little certain was known but the fact that they existed. As for America, its very existence was not so much as suspected. But towards the end of the fifteenth century, and within little more than fifty years, the courage of the seamen of Portugal and Spain discovered all these lands to Europe. With the overwhelming effect of these discoveries on European life in all its phases we are not concerned in a sketch of Church history, but for the Catholic Church the importance of the matter lay in this, that in the very years when Protestantism was disputing her hold on so much of Europe, another spiritual empire was opening to her in the new world. The possibilities were understood from the first, and every part of the Catholic organism moved instinctively in a great urge of spiritual conquest.

Between 1493 and 1550 the Spaniards and the Portuguese had made themselves masters of central and southern America, of states and peoples that had developed a certain elaborate civilisation, no less than of "Indians" wholly primitive in life and in religion. Priests had

257

accompanied the original expeditions as chaplains, and from the moment that the conquest was assured, everywhere an army of priests appeared to begin preaching of the Gospel to the natives. Franciscans, Dominicans, and Augustinians, in the early years, Jesuits in the latter half of the century, and secular clergy, too, began to build up a new Catholicism from California to the Argentine. The first sees were established almost as soon as the news of the conquest reached Rome. Schools were founded, hospitals, convents, and, in 1553, at Mexico, the first university.

The conquest, or rather the exploitation of the conquered, had about it all the evil features that have always, before and since, distinguished such affairs. But in these countries, where even the worst of the oppressors owed allegiance to Catholic ideals, and where kings never failed to proclaim the ideals, the missionaries, from the very beginning, made a great fight for their helpless native flock. In this they were encouraged and strengthened by the steady attitude of the popes, the famous bull of Paul III in 1537 marking a new age, with its declaration that the Indians were as much human beings as their new lords, and enjoyed the same natural rights, which their lords must respect. And the missionary effort to save these native races had yet other powerful auxiliaries in the professors of the Catholic universities at home. The most notable of all these was the Dominican, Francis of Victoria (1480–1546) who, with a directness in his critical analysis of the fundamental rights of the crown that throws a flood of light on the liberty of thought enjoyed in the Spain of Charles V, set forth in detail the natural rights of the Indians and the limitations of the royal power in their regard.

The end of the sixteenth century saw Catholicism everywhere established in this new world, and everywhere fighting the evils it had fought so long in the old world. And with the fight came the first American saints, the heroic archbishop of Lima, St. Toribio de Mogrovejo (1538–1616), the great Franciscan missionary St. Francis of Solano (1549–1610), whose preaching, marked by a renewal of the miracle of Pentecost, converted the Indians of the Chaco by thousands, and the Dominican nun, St.

Rose of Lima (1586–1617), who was actually born on American soil, as was also her contemporary, the half-caste son of a noble Spanish debauchee, Blessed Martin de la Porres, a Dominican lay brother.

The effort to free the native from the oppression of his masters, and from the worse plague of their atrocious example, led finally, in South America, to the foundation by the Jesuits of the famous "reductions" of Paraguay. These were settlements of hundreds of Indians each. The centre was the church with its missionaries and its nuns, its school, and its hospital. The whole village lived its natural life under the directing care of the fathers. The work was divided out and supervised, and the whole community cared for in a paternal régime which, more nearly than anything ever seen before or since, realised the fulness of what the Gospel can do for life, for public life as for private life. It was the City of God really built on earth. By 1750 there were nearly 100,000 Indians living in these Jesuit-directed settlements, inhabitants truly of an "earthly paradise." In all the hideous story of the suppression of the great Society, no chapters make more painful reading than those which describe how the poor Indians were robbed of their Jesuit protectors, to meet now, inevitably, the fate to which the invincible native simplicity had long before this doomed all their fellows, to be the serfs of a decadent civilisation.

While members of all these religious orders were thus labouring for the conversion of the natives in the European empires of the new Western world, their brethren were attempting a still more arduous task in the East. Here, without any effective protection from their own State, and often in the teeth of hostility from the native State, they were endeavouring to convert to the Faith heathens possessed of a culture more ancient than anything Europe could boast, the Indians, the Chinese, and the Japanese.

When the Portuguese, in the opening years of the sixteenth century, made their first settlement in India they found there some small groups of Christians. These were the scattered remnants of the churches established, centuries before, by Nestorians from Persia, and by the end

of the century, at the synod of Diamper (1599) a reunion was effected between them and the Apostolic See.
The Portuguese brought in their train Franciscans and
Dominicans, and these hardy friars, pushing well beyond
the safe limits of the settlements, did their best to evangelise the natives. In 1541 the movement received the great
assistance of the visit of St. Francis Xavier, one of the
first companions of St. Ignatius Loyola, perhaps the
brightest spirit of that chosen band, whom the founder
had gladly sacrificed for the missions at the demand of
the king of Portugal. Steadily, all through the next fifty
years, the mission proceeded and Jesuits penetrated even
to the court of the Mogul Akbar himself.

In Japan the dangers were greater. Here St. Francis
Xavier was himself the pioneer (1549), and when he left,
two years later, to make an attempt to enter China, there
was a body of 3,000 Japanese Catholics. By 1582 they had
grown to 200,000 and possessed 250 churches. Then came
the first jealous hostility of the State, but despite this the
numbers of the Catholics rapidly increased and in 1597
there were 300,000 of them. This was the year that saw
the first martyrdom, 26 priests and laymen being crucified
together at Nagasaki.

An interval of peace followed this outburst, during
which still more missioners arrived, drawn from all the
religious orders and including secular clergy also. Protestantism first showed itself in 1609, with Dutch traders, and
then, four years later, came English merchants. In 1616
the persecution was renewed, an edict ordering the complete extermination of all Catholics and prescribing an
annual violation of the crucifix by all Japanese. Nagasaki was
once more the scene of a great holocaust in 1622 when
52 martyrs suffered together on the same day. Fifteen
years later 37,000 Catholics were massacred, and in 1640
Japan sealed itself against Catholics from abroad.

Despite the ban and its terrible sanctions Dominicans
and Jesuits were never lacking to attempt to enter the forbidden land. Some were successful and, speedily taken,
were put to death with inhuman tortures.

In the nineteenth century the efforts were renewed, and
after 1858 missionaries were allowed in the open ports
to serve churches for foreign residents. Then in 1865

came the great marvel of Japanese Catholicism, when a band of 15 Japanese made known to the missionaries that they were Catholics, and that there were some 30,000 altogether who, without priests or sacraments (save Baptism) had contrived for 200 years and more to keep alive the Catholic tradition. They recognised the missionaries to be Catholics like themselves by three things, their acknowledgment of the authority of the pope, their devotion to Our Lady, and the celibacy of the clergy. This was the beginning of the Catholicism of modern Japan. To-day there are about 104,000 Catholics, and of the clergy who serve them one bishop and about 100 priests are Japanese.

The first Christians whom China ever knew were Nestorians from Persia, who appeared there in the seventh century and established a flourishing church with many bishops. It was from this source that Kubla Khan derived what Christian blood flowed in his veins, and the Chinese Nestorians became so powerful in the sect that, in the thirteenth century, they gave a patriarch to the mother church in Persia. It is from that same thirteenth century that the Catholic mission to China dates. Its origin was the attempt of Innocent IV, preoccupied—even in the midst of his struggle with the emperor—with the liberation of the East from the Turks, to form an alliance with the Mongols who, under Genghis Khan, were harassing the Turkish power from the far east. It was the Franciscan envoys of this pope who first revealed to Europe the existence of this ancient civilisation. The diplomatic mission was followed by attempts to convert the Mongols, the actors in which were Dominican and Franciscan bishops. The mission endured for a hundred years and more until, with the fall of the Mongols in 1368, it came to an end in circumstances of which we know little.

The modern mission to China really begins with the arrival of the great Jesuit astronomer, Matteo Ricci, in 1568, and Jesuits of the same type, learned in the mathematical sciences, played a great part in its development. The story of their successful penetration into the very heart of the Chinese culture, and thereby of the governing class, of their intimate relations with the emperors, of their rank at court as astronomers, and their propaganda for the Faith, is one of the strangest and most interesting chapters in all the fascinating history of the Catholic Missions.

The Jesuits were not the only missionaries. Franciscans and Dominicans shared their labours, and from the end of the seventeenth century Louis XIV began to send out priests from the newly founded seminary of the Missions Étrangères at Paris. The Lazarists or Vincentians also began to take a share in the work, and after the suppression of the Jesuits they were made responsible for the Jesuit missions, too.

The mission in China did not lack difficulties. The Manchu conquest in 1644 was a considerable setback, and half-way through the eighteenth century the persecution began to be systematic. There were new edicts and new martyrdoms all through the early part of the nineteenth century, down to 1870. Nowhere, however, in the last century, has there been greater Christian heroism than in Korea, where the story of martyrdoms recalls the worst days of the Roman persecutions, the tortures inflicted on the victims outrunning in horror even the wildest legendary accounts. In recent years many of these nineteenth-century martyrs, natives and Europeans, bishops, priests, and laymen, have been beatified.

To complete the tale of the missionary activities of the modern Church something must be said about Africa. Here it was the Portuguese who were the pioneers, and through them that the Jesuits went to the west coast settlements in 1596 and the Dominicans to Mozambique in 1614. Jesuits also made their way, in the time of St. Ignatius himself, to Abyssinia, and though the mission did not realise all that was hoped, it gave many martyrs to the Church in the seventeenth century.

It is with the nineteenth century that the real exploration of Africa begins and also the systematic missionary activity that makes it to-day almost the principal field of missionary work, with more than a hundred bishops, thousands of priests taken from thirty-four religious orders, and still more missionary nuns. It is the needs of Africa which have given rise to some of the greatest of the new purely missionary, orders such as the Fathers of the Holy Ghost (1842), the Society for the African Missions (1859), the White Fathers of Cardinal Lavigerie (1868), the Missionaries of Scheut (1868), and the English Society of St. Joseph (1866).

While it is invidious to compare the missionary effort of one country with that of another, no one will deny the primacy of France in this respect, and it was in France, too, that was devised and organised (and for nearly a hundred years administered) the good work which is the principal support of all these missions throughout the world, namely the Association for the Propagation of the Faith, founded by Pauline Marie Jarriot at Lyons in 1835.

The nineteenth century, the century of Catholic losses and trials in all the Catholic countries of Europe, is then, at the same time, the century in which the Faith has at last been carried to every part of the earth. Everywhere, now, it has at least made its appearance, and everywhere the immense work is in hand to convert the two-thirds of the peoples of the world who as yet remain pagan. It is this same century that has seen the races of northern Europe occupy the new western world as the sixteenth century saw the races of southern Europe similarly swarming. Canada—save for French-speaking Quebec, strongly Catholic since the early seventeenth century—Africa, and Australasia have been the field chiefly of English and Irish and Scottish emigration and settlement, during the last century, and what Catholics have settled there in that time have been preponderatingly Irish or of Irish descent.

In the United States of America, which is very largely another creation of the nineteenth-century expansion of Europe, every race has seen opportunity for emigration, and every race that has settled there has taken its religion with it. Of the present population of 137 millions, something like 20 millions are, it is estimated, Catholic. These are, by descent, chiefly Irish, German, Slavonic, and Italian. When these States wrested their independence from England (1783) they were under the spiritual jurisdiction of the Catholic bishop in London. In 1789 the first American see was erected at Baltimore, and a member of the recently suppressed Society of Jesus, John Carroll, was named as bishop. Through the hundred and fifty years since, the hierarchy has never ceased to grow, and there are now 106 sees in all.

One last important feature of the history of the Church

in the ninety years between the Revolution and the election of Leo XIII may be noticed here, for it has a certain affinity with the missionary effort just described. This is the growth within the Church, during that time, of a considerable English-speaking population. In 1789 this was utterly negligible. It is doubtful if there were so many as half a million English-speaking Catholics, and of these not fifty thousand were of English blood. English Catholics are still not a numerous body, but Catholics who speak the English language must, to-day, number close on 50 millions, one-sixth of the total Church.

In England, on the accession of Queen Elizabeth (1558–1603) the work of restoration accomplished by her sister Mary was completely destroyed. The old anti-papal laws of Henry VIII were re-enacted, the doctrine of the royal supremacy revived, the Mass once more forbidden, and a new religion set up with a new *Book of Common Prayer* (1559) for its rule of worship, the *Thirty-Nine Articles* (1563) for an official code of belief to mark it off from the old religion, and acts of parliament for the basis of the change with appropriate penalties for all who resisted. These penalties went as far as death for refusing the Oath of Supremacy.

The bishops were all deposed and a new, self-consecrated hierarchy of heretics took their place. The clergy, for the most part, accepted the situation. Later (1568), a Lancashire priest, Dr. William Allen, founded in the university city of Douai a college to train writers and controversialists. Six years later this college began to send priests into England, to take the place of the few priests faithful to the old religion, whose ranks death was beginning to thin. This was four years after St. Pius V had excommunicated and deposed Elizabeth—an act that gave her government occasion to enact that anyone returning to the Catholic Faith should suffer death, and likewise the priest who "reconciled" such an apostate. The advent of the well-trained, zealous priests from the seminary at Douai, the finest fruit of the Counter-Reformation, was likely to harass the government's religious schemes far more than the distant papal diplomacy, and the reaction was sharp and severe. In 1577 Douai had its first martyr, Cuthbert Mayne, put to death at Launceston, in conformity with the new laws, for the crime of bringing into England "Agnus Deis" and a bull proclaiming the Jubilee. There were two more executions in 1578.

In 1580 two English Jesuits were sent into England as missionaries, Robert Persons and Edmund Campion,[1] and the next twelve months saw the most active concerted effort yet made to rally the English to the Faith. Its immediate result was yet another spate of anti-Catholic legislation, new penalties, more arrests, and the spectacular trial of Edmund Campion and a dozen others, for high treason, plotting to murder the Queen.

There were plots in plenty, really genuine plots, plots even to murder Elizabeth, and that one pope at least had knowledge of one such plot seems certain. But in such plots, and in the more presentable business of the papal diplomatic activity against Protestantism, none of these men had ever hand or share, and the records of their trials remain to show it. That the Government should resort to the old device of bogus plots to convict its opponents has nothing peculiarly shocking about it. It is an iniquity that modern governments still resort to. But the reaction to the trial of Edmund Campion and his fellows was such that the Government had to find a new way of dealing with the missionaries of whom, by now, there were a couple of hundred in the country. It was therefore made high treason for a priest ordained abroad merely to come into England, and a felony punishable by death to harbour or shelter him. At the same time the fines levied, since 1559, on all who did not every Sunday attend the new religious service were increased to a ruinous amount.

Under the double pressure of fines and the gallows (and the torture chambers in the Tower and elsewhere), and with the increasing popular identification of Catholicism with the national enemy Spain, the number of faithful professed Catholics shrank steadily. The partial relief that came in the reign of Charles I (1625–1649) and Charles II (1660–1685) came too late to make any real difference, and even a shrewder man than the Catholic James II (1685–1688) could hardly have won for Catholics more than a suspension in practice of the bloodier

---

[1] This is what is called in all the books "the Jesuit Invasion."

laws against them. The new religion had been a vested interest since Henry VIII shared out the plunder from the abbeys with the anti-clerical gentry and the wealthier merchant classes. By the time of James II it had long been a national interest. Thence, for another century the decline went steeply down, until, by 1780, there were no more than 60,000 Catholics in England altogether, and the signs were that these, too, would disappear.

A variety of causes joined to save this remnant of the ancient Church. The Government began slowly to remove the penalties enacted for practising Catholicism, and to open once more to Catholics the learned professions—the law, medicine, schoolmastering—from which they had so long been barred. Slowly, from this moment, conversions began to be made. Then the French Revolution threw into this country thousands of refugee priests and, partly charity, partly political wisdom, the country made much of them and came to see a new usefulness in "popery"—for so, almost universally, Catholicism appeared, and was spoken of—as an ally against the Revolution. Finally there now began (from about 1790) a new Irish immigration into the new industrial England of the north—a small affair in comparison with the tidal wave of 1847–1850, but a much bigger thing than any known so far and an immigration of skilled workers.

Steadily through the first forty years of this nineteenth century the numbers crept up. The 60,000 of 1780 were half a million by 1840. Then came the great Irish famine of 1846–1847. Within three years the poor plague-stricken refugees had doubled the Catholic population of England. It was from this moment that Catholicism in England began to present that Irish appearance which, for most Englishmen, it still possesses.

Rome had allowed the old hierarchy, that dated from St. Gregory the Great, to die out. Then, after a hundred and twenty years, it had once more sent a succession of bishops into the country with the title of Vicars of the Apostolic See—one in 1685 and four in 1688. This number had been doubled in 1840 and then, in 1850, the hierarchy of diocesan bishops had been restored.

These Irish, who from about 1847 began to swell the numbers, and ultimately the political importance, of Catholics in England,[2] came from the one country where the State-supported Reformation had failed to conquer. In Ireland as in England it had behind it all the resources of the State, but the Irish remained Catholic. Ireland was, of course, in Henry VII's day and in Elizabeth's also, for the most part only nominally subject to the English king's jurisdiction. But from the reign of Elizabeth the plan began to be adopted of extirpating the Catholic Irish in the interests of the Protestant English (and later of the Scots) introduced as colonists. Midway through the seventeenth century came Oliver Cromwell, and his bloodthirsty hatred of Catholicism subjected the Irish to a persecution whose thoroughness has had scarcely an equal in modern times. His wars all but exterminated the race, but what was left of it still clung to the Faith. After Cromwell came the comparative respite of the later Stuarts and then, in reaction after the temporary Catholic régime of 1687–1691, the inhuman penal code of William of Orange, of Anne, and of the first two Hanoverian kings. This was a deliberate, carefully drawn plan to force the apostasy of the Irish by a complete social, economic, and cultural blockade. To remain loyal to Catholicism was voluntarily to reduce oneself to the status of the savage. Literally nothing was left to the Irish Catholic who remained in Ireland—whence thousands fled abroad—but what consolation and strength he could draw from his religion.

But the race survived even this disastrous century and its faith survived, too. From 1774 the heavy burden of the laws began to be lifted, and despite the social strength of the dominant Protestant minority, the Church came slowly to the fulness of its life again. One consequence of this was that through all the nineteenth century when, after 1846 especially, social conditions in Ireland drove the Irish overseas in an endless exodus to all the new countries of the world as well as to England, they carried with them the Catholic Faith, and to-day, in the United States and Canada, Australia and South Africa, there are millions of Catholics of Irish blood, and Irish priests by the thousand, and nearly one-third of the total episcopate of the Catholic Church bear Irish names.

---

[2] The same phenomenon is to be noted in the English colonies, and very notably in Australia.

11

The Contemporary Scene, 1878–1946

WITH THE election of Leo XIII, on February 20, 1878, a new age—as it is now universally realised —began in the Church's history. Pius IX had openly said, some little time before his death, that his methods and his policy had had their day, and that his successor would need to alter the whole direction of the papal action. The new pope not only understood this thoroughly—it was the most evident mark of his genius—but he came to his task with the main objectives already determined, and with definite plans for their attainment. He was indeed already an old man of sixty-eight, spare, frail, delicate, but tough beyond all expectation; and destined to live, in constant vital activity, for yet another twenty-five years.

Few popes have begun their reigns so well informed about the nature of the difficulties that faced them as was Leo XIII, and this by his own personal study of the thought of the time, as well as by his close observation of men and events. There had been strong opposition to his election; and there was much criticism, from within, as his policy was revealed. But Leo was ruthless and, all unmoved, he brushed the reactionaries aside. "These men are too old for me," he said. The cheerful *bonhomie* of Pius IX gave place to the steely determination of a pope who seemed pure intelligence, all mind, who could work at his desk ten and twelve hours a day, week in, week out, for years on end; and who took it for granted that the rest of mankind could—and would—do the same in the service of the Church. There were to be no more mistakes of temperament, no sentimental gestures, no reactions from one extreme to the other; a vast information, a cool detached and balanced judgment was to preside for the next generation over the universal Church, a political genius essentially constructive, but whose most striking characteristic perhaps was a deep understanding of the limits of what was immediately possible.

The new policy can be stated very simply. The prelates who grew to maturity in those years of general disaster that followed the events of 1789, and who became the rulers of the Church in the first two-thirds of the nineteenth century, had derived from their personal experiences of the catastrophe such a horror for the principles in whose name the destruction was accomplished, that they could think of no other course, after 1815, but to work for the extirpation of the new Liberalism. But, unhappily for the energy expended—where this generation managed to show itself energetic—Liberalism was too strongly entrenched to be moved; in one form or another it had come to stay: nor, of course, would the destruction of Liberalism necessarily mean a revival of Catholicism. These truths were, however, hidden from the vast majority of ecclesiastics during the early nineteenth century. Hence their persistence in a struggle as long as it was unavailing, and a consequent new bitterness against the Church generated in all the so-called Catholic countries of the world. Hence, too, the almost instinctive willingness of so many of these ecclesiastics to join in the fierce political battles of the time as close allies of the anti-Liberal governments, in support of the Carlists in Spain and the Bourbons in France and the Austrians in Italy. To support such causes was to be everywhere on the beaten side; and so, in Catholic circles, there was, by the time that the long reign of Pius IX came to its end, a general sense of frustration, of the hopelessness of action, and a tendency to waste energy in mere wishful thinking.

Leo XIII was determined to lead the Church out of this blind alley. Liberalism having come to stay, Catholics must be shown how to live in a Liberal world, and yet live by their Catholic principles; they must learn, not only how they could survive in such a world, but how to be active loyal citizens of the Liberal states. The pope would be their teacher. In some way the Church must face the task of adjusting itself to the new political society. It must negotiate with what it can no longer command, and it must devise a new, stronger, spiritual formation for the Catholics who are to live, as Catholics, in this non-religious world. It was one of Leo XIII's greatest merits to have insisted, in season and out of season, to a generation of Catholics inclined to shun all contact with the impious thing in the name of the purity of their faith, that only by living in this new world could the Church, in fact, survive, for to live in that world is the Church's first duty; only by such living contact can she fulfil her mission to convert it.

Still more boldly, the pope proposed to teach the Liberal world also—to show the sincere men in it, the Liberals in good faith that is to say—that Catholicism is the best, nay the sole, guarantee of real liberty. Catholic principles this pope will proclaim no less definitely than his predecessors of the older régime; but the truth of these principles is now argued persuasively, and the witness of history is called in to support the pope's thesis, how it is in the nature of things—and how all past history witnesses to this—that civilisations which turn away from God inevitably perish. And Leo XIII, with many a moving anxious warning about the disaster he foresees to be steadily drawing nearer, offers Catholicism to the rulers and the peoples of the world as their surest guide, their strongest protection. He makes constant appeal to the reasonableness of what the Church claims, when he speaks to the world outside; and to the reasonableness of what it commands, when he is addressing Catholics. Here is a pope with whom no man will be able to pick a quarrel.

The spirit of Leo XIII's action upon the Church may be studied in his great encyclical letters, in the various administrative decrees which modernised the government of the Church, and also in the pope's handling of the many difficulties which came to him as an heritage from the events of the fifty years preceding his election. The three major difficulties were the relations of Catholicism with three new political entities, no one of them as yet, in 1878, ten years old: the kingdom of Italy, the Third French Republic, and the German Empire. Relations with all three were already strained before Leo came into office. He was successful in bringing peace to Germany; but, though hardly from any lack of skill or goodwill, he failed with France; the Italian crisis was, to the end, insoluble.

Bismarck's measures to subject Catholicism in Prussia to the control of the state have been described already, and the persecution of the Catholics which ensued. Their unhappy plight was, seemingly, a main anxiety with the new pope, for it produced from him the first evidence that he meant to rule in the Church—and how—when the very evening of his election he put aside the letter prepared for his signature announcing to the German emperor his election, and set himself to write, in its stead, a personal letter which also expressed his hope for the speedy end of the religious war.

So, by Leo's personal act there began a renewal of contact, and a long diplomatic duel between himself and Bismarck that did not end for nearly ten years. The emperor was by no means hostile to the pope's pleas that the persecuting laws should be rescinded. Bismarck had gained nothing at all by them; but his pride was deeply engaged in the business, and also his deep personal anti-Catholic feelings. And, as the struggle developed, new schemes suggested themselves to him. The Catholics of Germany had shown that there were no limits to what they would suffer rather than yield; they had shown also, in the new Centre Party which they had created, an ability to organise their political independence that was new in Germany. They were, indeed, a power in the Empire. This struggle—now called the *Kulturkampf*—had made them. It occurred to Bismarck that, through the pope, he might find a way to control the new party and make a general use of it in his parliamentary manœuvres. He held out baits to the pope in this sense. But Leo was too loyal to be tempted, and yet too wary to give offence as he side-stepped his adversary. The chancellor's plans to divide the alliance of pope and Catholics failed time and again; and each time Leo gave the leaders of the Centre

Party stronger assurances of his will to see the thing through. When the pope's agent, the then nuncio at Munich, seemed in danger of yielding too much to Bismarck's expert tactics he found himself promoted to Lisbon, and the conduct of the affair was handed over to the nuncio at Vienna, Ludovico Jacobini, one of the ablest of all the counsellors of Leo XIII, and later (1882-1887) his Secretary of State. In his demand that the laws be annulled which subjected the education of the clergy to the government of this Protestant country and which subjected to its courts the Catholic bishops' control of their clergy, the pope remained immovable. On the matter of the government's claim to appoint to certain ecclesiastical offices he was ready to negotiate. But not all the favours which Bismarck offered—the chief of them the re-establishment of a Prussian embassy at the Vatican—could shake the pope from the first point. Improvements of the objectionable code, ameliorations, he merely noted; taking occasion, each time, to explain how radically unacceptable the laws were! And, with supreme skill, Leo XIII managed to do all this without increasing the German Chancellor's hostility—as he also managed to keep on good terms with him without any resulting lack of confidence on the part of the Centre Party and its great leader, Windthorst.

Bismarck was unwilling to go back on laws he had promoted. Leo would not trust anything less than a formal revocation of them. But as the years went by, the Chancellor saw in the growth of Socialism a menace to all he had accomplished. He would one day need the Centre Party as an ally. The settlement of the religious difficulty grew more and more urgently necessary for him—and yet he would not yield. In 1885 he made a great bid for the pope's favour. A dispute had arisen between the new Empire and Spain over the German occupation of the Caroline Islands in the Pacific. Bismarck proposed, with the consent of Spain, that Leo XIII should be asked to mediate between the two powers. The pope accepted, and gave a decision which, most remarkably, satisfied both sides. But the compliments from Berlin that the incident brought him did not for an instant shake his will that the laws of May must be repealed.

The long dispute was finally ended through the diplomatic skill of Mgr. Galimberti, Leo's envoy in 1887 to the celebrations of Wilhelm I's jubilee. In March and April of that year the Prussian diet voted the new laws. Bismarck himself made an eloquent speech in support of them and praised the pope as an agent of peace in the Empire.

The admirable unity of the Catholics of Germany during the long fight was, undoubtedly, a leading element in the pope's success. The bishops were of one mind, they were loyal to the pope's directions; and their people were not only loyal to them but singularly well organised, and led by a politician of genius, Windthorst, who was also an excellent Catholic. The conditions under which Leo XIII had to work in France were very different. Although, here again, it was in one of the new democratic states that religion was to be persecuted—that is to say under a régime where power lay in a parliament elected by popular vote; and here again it was the pope's policy that Catholics should secure justice within the régime, using their rights as citizens.

It was an aim which, in France, Leo pursued for twenty-five years, with a persistence and a patience that no succession of disappointments could exhaust. He did not, however, succeed. The bad will of the enemies of Catholicism was too much for him and also—it needs to be added—the incredibly bitter divisions among the Catholics themselves. These divisions were, in very large part, a legacy from the turbulent course of French history during the nineteenth century, when in less than sixty years there were half a dozen political revolutions. In the pope's own lifetime he had seen France an empire (under Napoleon), a kingdom under the restored Bourbons, a more Liberal monarchy under the Orleanist prince Louis Philippe, a republic, an empire once more (under Napoleon III) and now again a republic, for the third time. Each revolution had left behind a defeated and dispossessed section who looked for the future restoration of the régime they favoured, and for revenge. No one of these régimes, indeed, whatever their professions, had really given Catholicism its lawful place in what was, professedly, a Catholic country. Some had been violently hostile; others had favoured the Church but only as a means to use its prestige for political ends.

By the time of Leo's election there was, then, in France a seething mass of violently discontented politicians of all kinds; and the Catholics were as violently divided as the rest of the country. The new republic was but three years established, and established by a majority of one vote only, almost by accident, under a constitution designed for a restoration of the monarchy. And within this Third Republic a very recent crisis had driven the Conservatives from power—forever as the event was to show—and had brought in the first of those combinations of Radical groups which were thenceforward to dominate the Republic's whole history, until their own chronic internecine strife brought the country to the catastrophe of 1940. One thing alone all these Radical groups had in common, a real hatred and fear of Catholicism; and they had recently come into power, in 1877, under such circumstances that observers could be certain a new concerted attack upon the Church would not be long delayed.

Such was the situation that faced Leo XIII in 1878. The solution he proposed was as simple as it was drastic. The pope considered that the cause of the monarchy was dead. There was just no chance at all that the French people would ever again settle down permanently under another restoration, whether of the Bourbons or of the Orleans princes. Catholics, as sensible men, should accept the *fait accompli* and rally to the Republic, fighting within it by constitutional means for their rights as loyal citizens. Unfortunately, hardly any French Catholics at all were Republicans. The great majority were royalists of the extreme right; and among these were almost all the clergy, the bishops, and what laymen had any place in the public life of the day. The pope had an all but impossible task before him, for he could do no more than urge the wisdom of what he proposed and guarantee its lawfulness. The day had long gone by when it would have been possible to issue commands in the matter, even had the pope wished to do this.

Meanwhile the common enemy was about to deliver his first well planned attack, and the unconcealed opposition of all sections of Catholics to the Republican régime gave him an obvious excuse to cover the illiberal tyranny he was about to exercise.

In March, 1880, new laws deprived of their seats in the *Conseil supérieur de l'Instruction publique* the members nominated by the various religious bodies, and withdrew all recognition of the Catholic universities. Four months later, by a governmental decree, the Jesuits were expelled from France, and their property seized: the other orders were given three months in which to petition for state recognition; those to whom this was refused were to be dissolved. This law affected some 8,000 men and 100,000 nuns. The Catholic reaction was immediate and vigorous; 2,000 lawyers gave a collective opinion that the decrees were illegal, and 400 magistrates resigned rather than enforce them. All to no effect. Another series of laws took all religious instruction out of the schools, the primary schools and the grammar schools; the faculties of Catholic theology in the universities were suppressed, and the chaplaincies in the great écoles normales; the seminaries were subjected to the laws of military service and the army chaplaincies abolished; the nuns were forbidden to serve as nurses in the hospitals, and hospital chaplaincies abolished. A divorce court was set up.

This radical, pitiless secularisation of French life, brought about within a matter of six years, bred a bitterness of feeling hard to exaggerate. But the pope kept his head. His advice to the French Catholics remained the same throughout: to abandon forever the dream of regaining their rights through the overthrow of the Republic; to organize; and to refrain from imprudences which played into the hands of their enemies. It has been urged on behalf of the Catholic irreconcilables that Leo XIII never realised the depth of the anti-religious hatred which inspired those enemies. Nevertheless the policy which the pope recommended was the only possible policy; and whatever the criticisms of it and of its author, no policy could have succeeded in a body whose chiefs so fought and tore one another in public as did the leading Catholics of France in these years. For a long time many of them affected to doubt whether the policy of *ralliement* really was the pope's will. When this was made clearer than clear, by the pope's own declarations, they sulked.

Then, in 1894, came the *affaire Dreyfus*, and to the dismay of the pope the Catholics threw themselves fanatically into the business—and again on the wrong side. Their adversaries saw more clearly the practical wisdom of Leo's policy; it was the last thing they, too, wished to succeed, and they greeted every new advance he made to the Republic with howls of rage.

Towards the end of the pontificate (1899–1903) the active persecution began anew, under the leadership of an ex-seminarist, Emile Combes. The last of the nuns were now expelled from France, their convents and schools were seized. A spy system was established in the army, and officers known to be practising Catholics were harassed and driven out.

All the efforts of Leo XIII, it might seem, had been in vain. To a French cardinal who, to console the pope, said to him some days before his death, "France is not an antireligious country. It's only a small group who are persecutors," Leo replied dryly, "No doubt. But they are the masters; and they are let to do it." But the long patient diplomacy, and the abundance of wise counsel, had been far from wasted. The pope, although he knew it not, had really breathed a new spirit into French Catholicism; his patience had prevented any extension of the breach with the idea of Republican government; it had taught the younger generation of the Catholics that a good Catholic could be a good Republican, and however slowly the lesson had been learned, it had—as events were to show—been well learned; and the pope's persistence had dissipated for ever, in the mind of every honest man, the fiction that Catholicism was bound up with the political arrangements of the *ancien régime;* and finally it had preserved Catholics from the final and fatal gaffe of being the aggressors in a kind of civil war.

Where Leo had sown in tears his successors were to reap one day joyously. But first there would need to come the thunderstorm of the reign of Pius X.

The chances of any pope conciliating the government of the French Republic might have seemed small, to those who knew the spirit which animated the triumphant parties of the Left. Leo's chances with the new power in

Italy were nil. The violent invasion and conquest of the Papal State had had for its complement the notorious Law of Guarantees (1871) which—an extraordinary attempt by the victorious power to win from its victim a tacit abdication of sovereignty—provided a monetary compensation for the spoliation, but avoided all recognition of the pope's character as a sovereign, and treated him as no more than a highly favoured subject of the Sardinian monarchy. There could be but one reply to this; and when Pius IX's determination to refuse all recognition of the *fait accompli* was known, the new government, in order to force his will, began a violent campaign against his religion. The remaining religious orders were dissolved, their monasteries in Rome confiscated and used for state purposes; the clergy were forced into the army as soldiers, the religious oath in the law courts was abolished; religious teaching was banished from the schools; in disregard of its own laws the government allowed newspapers and magazines to circulate filled with anti-Christian blasphemies and outrageous attacks on the pope, and it permitted anti-papal demonstrations beneath the very walls of the Vatican. Also, by a systematic abuse of powers which it usurped, the government hindered the nomination of bishops until more than sixty sees were vacant. "Verius in aliena potestate sumus quam nostra," said Leo XIII in protest.

The insecurity of which he never ceased openly to complain was far from imaginary. One incident after another stands recorded in permanent witness to the reality of the pope's anxiety. There was the attempt of the Italian government to lay hands on the Propaganda funds, the alms sent in from all over the world for the missions to convert the heathen peoples of Africa and the East; and its attempt to confiscate the funds of the Italian Catholic Charities. There were the official celebrations, turned into an orgy of blasphemous anti-religious hate, of such long-past historical events as the burning of Arnold of Brescia (1155) and the Sicilian Vespers (1282). There were the funeral solemnities of Garibaldi. There were the terrible scenes that marked the removal of the body of Pius IX to the cemetery of San Lorenzo when, with the connivance of the government, a mob of the vilest elements set on the cortège and all but succeeded in throwing the dead pope's body into the Tiber. There was—above all—the inauguration of the monument to Giordano Bruno, the spirit of which was revealed by the honours paid to the flags that headed the demonstration, the red flag of revolution, the green flag of the Masons and the black flag of Satan. That terrible day the pope spent in prayer before the Blessed Sacrament exposed.

Leo XIII did not exaggerate—his was not that type of mind. He understood perfectly the forces that fought him, the nature of their hostility and the powerlessness of the successive Italian governments to control the deviltry they had called to their aid. More than once—so close did he feel the pressure of the party to be whose aim was the papacy's destruction—the pope seriously thought of leaving Rome. The hostility towards him never ceased, which had begun on the very day of his election when a government circular forbade officials everywhere to attend the thanksgiving services for the new pope's election. From such a régime it would have been folly to expect fair play. There was nothing to be done but, with all possible patience, carefully to avoid whatever might be taken as a condonation of the Masonic iniquity and, with principles intact, await the better time that must one day come.

It was a leading principle of Leo XIII's long reign, from which no discouragement ever for a moment turned him, and a principle which certainly has permanently characterised all papal action ever since, that the Church should never allow itself to be isolated from the general life of the time; and it was but a necessary consequence of this that the pope strove to bring the papacy into ever closer contact with the day-to-day life of the Church throughout the world. It is now that there begins, for example, not indeed the fashion of pilgrimage to Rome but such an extension and development of it that soon there was hardly a town in the world that had not some Catholics in it who had seen the pope, heard him speak, received his personal blessing. Since Leo XIII's time the reigning pope is a more familiar figure to Catholics in general than, in former ages, their own bishops were to them, only too often.

By the time the invention of wireless telephony arrived to make it possible for the whole Church to hear the very voice of its earthly head, the Church had already become far more familiar with his active, practical direction on all questions of the day than at any time before. Leo XIII did no greater service to the Church than to establish the practice of teaching and guiding it through frequent encyclical letters—veritable treatises on dogma and morals, which applied eternal principles to the ever changing needs of mankind. Here, better perhaps than anywhere else, can the measure be taken of the importance of Leo XIII as the creator of a new age in Catholic history. The great encyclicals are his most enduring memorial. The hostile forces that so often thwarted his action have disappeared: the empire of the Hohenzollerns, the Third Republic, Casa Savoia; and the Catholic kings too, who paid him little better than lip service. Hapsburgs in Austria and Bourbons in Spain. Their very names begin to be archæology. But the encyclicals are as alive, as active, as pertinent as on the day when they were penned. They are more closely studied to-day than ever they were, and the greatest of Leo's successors have had little more to do than build more extensively on the foundations he laid.

Three of these letters must be mentioned here, for they represent the three main influences of Leo XIII upon Catholic thought; and, taken together, they constitute that new orientation which still governs the life of Catholicism. They are the sources of all the best that has happened since, is happening now and is likely to happen in the coming age. To be familiar with their teaching, saturated with their spirit, is to possess the secret of intelligent co-operation with the papal leadership in the most critical age of all. These three letters are the *Aeterni Patris* of August 4, 1879, the *Immortale Dei* of November 1, 1885, and the *Rerum Novarum* of May 15, 1891.

The first of these deals with the restoration to his proper place, as the primate of Catholic philosophy and theology, of St. Thomas Aquinas; it is the source of all that contemporary influence of Catholicism on the thinkers of the day—less known in England than anywhere else in the world, except Russia—which is so novel a feature of the modern world; and the source of such a general revival within the Church of these studies that, in this most important respect, it is probably healthier than at any time since the death of St. Thomas himself. The *Immortale Dei* is the Magna Carta of the Catholic who believes in democracy as the best system of government. It is a compendium of Catholic teaching on the State from the point of view of the whole long controversy between Catholics and the principles of 1789, and it lays down practical principles to guide the Catholic citizen of the new secular states. The third letter, *Rerum Novarum,* is perhaps the best known of all Leo XIII's acts—its subject is *The condition of the Working Classes,* and it is the foundation of all that Catholic action in social matters which had been increasingly, since 1891, the characteristic of twentieth-century Catholicism.

There is not space to do more than catalogue the rest—even the other major acts—of this great reign: the letters *Divinum Illud* on the Holy Ghost, *Mirae Caritatis* on the Holy Eucharist, the fifteen encyclicals on the devotion to the Rosary, the consecration to the Sacred Heart of the whole human race; the institution and development of the Eucharistic Congresses; the extension of the Foreign Missions; the encyclical on Biblical Studies and the establishment of the Biblical Commission; the letter on the duty of Catholics to be wholly truthful historians, and the throwing open to the scholars of the world of the secret archives of the Vatican; the foundation of the new Catholic universities of Fribourg and Washington, and of the Institute of Thomist Philosophy at Louvain; the immense expansion of the hierarchy. But one last point should be mentioned, the pope's rare gift of choosing really great minds as his collaborators. Never since the time of Paul III did the Sacred College, at any one time, number within its ranks such an array of personalities, and among them, created in Leo's first consistory, our own Newman.

Leo XIII died, in his ninety-fourth year, on July 20, 1903.

Cardinal Joseph Sarto, who, as Pius X, was elected to succeed him (August 4) was so different in character that it has been all too easy for the chroniclers [1] to exaggerate the difference between their policies. There was certainly a change in the manner of the papal action, a note that was perhaps Spanish rather than Roman in the diplomacy and in the handling and execution of the measures for the pursuit of the Modernists. But it was not only that *suaviter in modo* had had the fairest of trials, the assault now became so suddenly rude that only a reply that was peremptory could serve. With the heresy itself, and the new heretics, half-measures would not have been possible in any pontificate; and to have acquiesced in the further acts of the anti-Catholic régime in France would have been mere, futile "appeasement."

The French President, in 1904, ignored the protocol that bound the heads of the Catholic states and paid a state visit to the Italian king in Rome—a declaration to the world that France had abandoned the policy followed since 1870, and had accepted the *fait accompli* that the pope was no longer an independent sovereign. When Pius X protested, the French withdrew their ambassador from the Vatican. Soon afterwards when two French bishops, summoned to Rome to answer grave accusations made against them, appealed to the Government, the Prime Minister—Emile Combes—gave the pope an ultimatum. Either the summons to Rome would be withdrawn, or the French Government would consider the Concordat terminated. Meanwhile in France a law was passed declaring the separation of Church and State. Who would now own the churches, schools, rectories, seminaries and other ecclesiastical property? Not the Church, for it no longer existed in the eyes of the law. It was the State which decided the matter, and the State set up as owner a system of committees—the *Associations Cultuelles*. Pius X took a firm line; he refused all recognition to the new system and forbade the Catholics of France to have anything to do with it, and the Catholics of France—although far from happy at his decision—loyally and unanimously obeyed. Rather than consent to a

---

[1] Events are now too close, sources as yet too little accessible for us to be able to speak of what is written about them as history.

system which left the whole life of the Church at the mercy of a fanatically hostile government, they gave up all their property and something like £3,000,000 a year of revenues. *Succisa virescit.* The crisis proved the essential soundness of French Catholicism, and what a virile generation had grown up during the twenty-five years of Leo XIII's reign. Immense sacrifices were now, everywhere, the order of the day; and the fruit was a Catholic revival of a quality, and on a scale, never seen before. From that great moment, French Catholicism has never looked back.

The heresy that goes by the name of Modernism was an attempt to make Catholicism palatable to the thought of the day by repudiating its objective supernatural character, and reducing it to a matter of individual religious psychology. The Modernists were never, indeed, very numerous and Pius X's acts against them—the decree *Lamentabili* in July and the encyclical *Pascendi*, September 1907—were to most Catholics the first news of their existence. But the group occupied important posts in various seminaries and universities, and the danger anticipated was that it would gradually corrupt the faith of the clergy and of the educated laity, perverting theology and philosophy and the whole theory of the spiritual life. The vigorous action of the pope, however, forced the concealed modernists into the open, and within a very short time the Church was rid of them.

These spectacular, indeed dramatic, events were, however—like the politico-religious duels of Leo XIII that have been recounted—distractions, albeit inevitable and necessary, from the real work of Pius X's reign which was eminently constructive, practical and reformatory. No single pope since the Council of Trent brought about so many important, and needed, changes in Catholic life. Even when set down in a mere list their importance is manifest.

At the heart of the life of the Church is the use Catholics make of the sacrament of the Holy Eucharist; and here Pius X initiated a great development. In the first place he settled for ever, authoritatively, the disputes as to the exact meaning of the Council of Trent's direction about the frequent reception of the sacrament; and secondly the pope laid it down that children should be brought to make their first Communion once they are old enough to know (in a manner suited to their years) the truths necessary for salvation and the differences between the Blessed Sacrament and ordinary bread. These two decrees (of June 23, 1905 and August 8, 1910) have slowly revolutionised Catholic piety. As to the Liturgy in general, Pius X first of all restored the music called Plain Chant to its proper primacy in all sacred functions, adopting the scientific researches of the Benedictines of Solesmes and making them the foundation of the new official version of the chant which he published, and establishing in Rome a Pontifical Institute of Sacred Music with power to grant degrees. Then he drastically revised the calendar of feasts, and restored to its old place the cycle of Sunday offices that is so important and systematic a reminder of the basic truths of the Faith. Finally the pope transformed the very heart of the Church's official daily prayer, the Divine Office, when he rearranged the Breviary Psalter, so that the ancient rule now actually obtained that, week by week, the priest should recite the whole book of the Psalms. To better the education of the clergy was a matter that Pius X had always close at heart, and he effected many improvements in the seminaries of Italy. Of his patronage of sacred learning there is not space to do more than mention the still further encouragement given to the revival of Thomistic studies, and the establishment of a commission of Benedictine scholars charged to restore the primitive text of St. Jerome's translation of the Bible—the Vulgate.

Pius X came to the supreme rule of the Church with a personal experience of the actualities of pastoral life all too rare in popes. He had passed through all the stages, curate, parish, priest, seminary professor, and then, for twenty-eight years successively, he was vicar-general and bishop in three of the great Italian sees. One natural consequence of such a career was an appreciation of the weak places in the machinery of the central government of the Church, and under his direction as pope there came about such a rearrangement of offices, duties and procedure as had not been seen since the reign of Sixtus V. And while before all men's eyes the Roman Curia was thus transformed, there was in progress, quietly and out of sight, the mightiest reform of all, one long-needed, indeed, and recognised as such, but spoken of always as impossible, that many popes had attempted in part but none had the courage to face as a whole—the re-codification of the Canon Law. Not since the Middle Ages had any pope dealt with this on such a scale, and the law had long been the labyrinth which the preface to the new code describes. Pius X died as the great work was completed, and it was promulgated by his successor in 1917.

Pius X was a man of most holy life, a model parish priest, a model bishop and a model pope. It is not surprising that, from the moment of his death, there has been a great movement to secure his canonisation. It is hard to exaggerate what the Church owes to the many personal initiatives of his short eleven years' reign.

The next reign was to be shorter still, for Benedict XV (elected September 2, 1914) lasted for little more than seven years. They were the years of what, until recently, was by common consent called the Great War. It had begun in the first days of August 1914, and its outbreak undoubtedly had much to do with the death of Pius X.

All the energy of his successor was conditioned by the war and its sequelae. Never did the papacy set the world a better example of all-embracing charity—and rarely was any pope so reviled on all sides. From the beginning of his reign Benedict XV—a diplomatist trained in the school of Leo XIII and Rampolla—made two things very clear: he would not, in a matter where he had only *ex parte* statements to guide him, pronounce between the contending alliances, say which host was in the right; nor would he determine the question of fact about particular atrocities charged by either side against the other. He would be truly and perfectly neutral, and yet repeat, in season and out of season, that there is a moral law governing the waging of wars; and he would protest whenever acts occurred that undoubtedly were a breach of this law. Sometimes the protests were made in public declarations, more often by diplomatic representations to the heads of the contending nations. The second feature of the pope's programme was that he would show equal charity to all the victims of the war, whatever the side they were on, whatever the misdeeds of their rulers, and—a part of this charity—he would take every opportunity that came to suggest a truce and the re-establishment of peace.

The three classic documents of the peace apostolate of Benedict XV are his inaugural encyclical *Ad Beatissimi* (November 1, 1914), the diplomatic note to the powers at war of August 1, 1917, containing his peace proposals, and the letter *Pacem Dei munus* (May 23, 1919). They have lost none of their actuality, and when, to-day, after a still greater disaster, the heads of states seem about to repeat so many of the mistakes of twenty-five years ago, they make sorrowful reading. The pope, like his Master, has much the same cause to weep as he looks on Jerusalem.

As to the charity of Benedict XV—it is a marvellous story, never really told and already forgotten. There were, for example, the numerous interventions with the belligerent powers: proposals for the mutual exchange of the incurably wounded, for the exchange of certain classes of civilian prisoners, for the transfer to a neutral country of those permanently injured, and of prisoners who were fathers of three or more children. The pope's diplomatic action was also successful in securing from the Central Empires that prisoners of war would not be forced to work on Sundays. We may also note the pope's protestations to Germany against the deportation of French and Belgians to work in Germany; protestations, also to Germany, against reprisals on prisoners of war; to Austria, against the bombardment of open towns, and to Italy against the confiscation of the Roman residence of the Austrian ambassador to the Holy See. And from the *Osservatore Romano* of December 31, 1917, we learn that several times Benedict XV had protested to Germany and Austria against the violation of International Law in methods of warfare.

Much of this diplomatic activity of the Holy See has only been publicly known since the end of the war. Better known—and yet never really well known—was the immense work of charity done to all belligerents, irrespective of nationality or religion. The principal instrument of this work was the Prisoners of War Bureau set up at the Vatican in December, 1914, as a means of communication and relief between the prisoners and their families. Then there were a whole series of letters of sympathy to the bishops and peoples of the various countries, twelve of them to Belgium and twenty-two to France. And, with the letters, went alms on a truly magnificent scale, if the pope's scanty resources be considered. During the war it was to the countries devastated by the German occupation that the alms chiefly went; afterwards to Russia, and to the starving people and children of Central Europe. In the course of the war itself Benedict XV gave away some five-and-a-half million lire from his own purse, and another thirty millions gathered by collections in what Catholic churches he could get in touch with.

The policy of the three pontificates since 1914 has known a continuity rare in papal history. This has been due first to the unusual circumstance that the newly elected Pius XI in 1922 retained in his office the cardinal who had been since 1914 Benedict XV's Secretary of State, Pietro Gasparri; and then, that the same pope appointed to succeed Gasparri his own pupil, Eugenio Pacelli; and finally, on the death of Pius XI, Cardinal Pacelli was himself elected pope, who as Pius XII is still reigning.

How shall we describe, in a summary, the rich, intense, constructive papal activity of these last twenty-five years, the teaching, administration, expansion, reforms? For a beginning we might stress the rare combination of Pius XI's gifts—a strong man, conscious of his strength: his keen intelligence, highly trained; a learned man, first of all, very well educated through forty years of constant, critical studies; with a universal interest in things of the mind, and vast encycyopædic knowledge of the modern world; with an affection, openly expressed, for his own time, and an appreciation of the age of crisis as the age of Catholic opportunity. It was his instinct to plan on the great scale, to give and to do in the grand manner; he was the embodiment of the virtues of liberality, magnanimity and magnificence; there was in him unshakable courage; and he had the capacity to re-state the ancient truths of faith in terms of the apostolate which the needs of the age demand. The seventeen years of his reign

(February 6, 1922—February 10, 1939) were indeed momentous.

In Europe three great empires had recently fallen, and out of the wreckage many new states had emerged. One of the pope's first problems was to concert with these new states treaties which would guarantee to their Catholic citizens the free exercise of their religion. Whence a series of twelve concordats—the most famous of which, in the event, was that with the German Reich, signed on September 18, 1933, and destined to be violated by the Nazis while the ink of their signature was still wet. In France the national peril of the years 1914–18 had burnt up the miserable anti-clericalism of earlier times. Towards the end of the reign of Benedict XV, diplomatic relations were renewed with the Holy See, and in 1924 Pius XI had the satisfaction of negotiating a settlement about ecclesiastical property through a new scheme of *Associations Cultuelles* in which the Church was now officially represented.

The most striking event, however, in this field of politico-religious diplomacy, was the settlement of the Roman Question in 1929. It has been too little noted that what then took place was not merely the diplomatic act by which the Italian state acknowledged fully the sovereign status of the pope, and the sovereign independence of the tiny territory which satisfied him as adequate for the purpose of expressing his sovereign status; there was also a religious act, a true concordat, between the Holy See and the Italian state, that liberated the Church in Italy from a yoke it had had to bear for centuries. It is not too much to say that, for Pius XI, the political treaty's main importance was that it made possible this concordat, "the giving back of Italy to God" in his own words. For the first time for hundreds of years the pope could now appoint bishops to all the sees of the Italian peninsula without let or hindrance from the civil power, and Italian education was definitively centered round the teaching of religion. After nearly a century of anti-religious violence, Catholicism at last gained legal security for its most elementary rights. Needless to say the evil habits of that century were not wiped out immediately. Many ill effects of the long servitude and struggle were bound to survive—time alone, and patience and prudence can efface them; after the great event of 1929 there was more than one crisis. But from the chance that Pius XI so boldly took, and the treaties he so carefully negotiated with Mussolini, a new Catholic Italy is already emerging, and more will be heard of it.

That a pope of such antecedents as Pius XI should do much for the cause of learning and scholarship was only to be expected. New Catholic universities were founded at Milan, in Poland, and in Holland; in Rome itself new Pontifical Institutes for Oriental Studies were created; the standard of studies in the various Roman universities was raised, and the whole system co-ordinated by the great decree *Deus Scientiarum Dominus* of 1930. Here again is one of those measures that will make all the difference as the years go by.

Another important reorganisation took place in the work of the Foreign Missions. The first sign of what the Holy See intended was given in the letter *Maximum Illud* of Benedict XV in 1919. What that pope planned, his successor accomplished. The world-famous society, the *Association for the Propagation of the Faith*, now became, in the reign of Pius XI, an official organ of the Missions, charged with the collection of alms, and its headquarters were transferred from Lyons to Rome. Other auxiliary societies were grouped around it. A great permanent missionary exhibition in the Lateran Palace is the visible sign of the new "science" of "Missiology." It is a sign, too, of the new spirit that has developed, as a thing essential, the missionary's care for the social welfare of the "natives," and that has brought it about that active interest in the Foreign Missions is part of the normal life of every Catholic parish throughout the world.

But the most important feature of the new development is the carrying into execution of the old ideal that the best clergy for any people is a native clergy. For many years, indeed, there had already been native priests, but with Pius XI came a succession of native bishops, and now Pius XII had given the Chinese the first cardinal of their own race. And these last two popes have given the devoted European missionaries in these lands the lesson —hard perhaps for human nature to welcome—that it is one of their principal tasks to train so efficient a native clergy that they may themselves hand over to these the direction of this nascent Catholicism. "It would be a wholly erroneous judgement," said Pius XI, "to class these native races as made up of a lower and weakened kind of humanity." New religious orders are needed too, says that pope, native orders, of nuns especially; and the pope insists that the traditional arts of these countries shall find expression in the churches and schools, and that no longer shall European "styles" be imported and imposed.

Pius XI took up the practice inaugurated by Leo XIII of teaching the Church through frequent encyclical letters, and he developed it. His encyclicals were more frequent; and they are much, very much, longer. They analyse the causes of world unrest, discuss the new development of the authority of states, expound the true nature of Christian education, recall—with the most direct concern about fashionable contemporary aberrations—all that is meant by marriage and by Christian marriage, and they consider, with real interest in the new thing as such, the possibilities for good, and the latent dangers, of an invention that is no less universally powerful than that of printing, the cinema.

But the most celebrated letters of this collection are those which deal with social problems properly so called, with the question of war and peace, and with the development of totalitarianism in Italy, Germany and Russia. The fortieth anniversary of Leo XIII's *Rerum Novarum* was commemorated by a lengthy review of the whole question of Capital and Labour, of the nature and value of Socialism as a remedy for the abuses of Capitalism, of the part Catholics had played—and had failed to play—in the world movement for social betterment; and once more the pope insisted that this complex of problems is, at bottom, a matter not of techniques but of morals.

The most striking feature of world history in the years that followed the war of 1914–18 was undoubtedly the reappearance, naked and unashamed, of the totalitarian state; and its first appearance in the west was in Italy, only a few months after Pius XI's election. It is not surprising that, from the very beginning, the pope watched the Mussolini régime with great anxiety. Year by year he spoke publicly of the dangers bound up with the theory that the state is omnipotent. To some extent the danger may have seemed less to other observers because the Fascist State proved willing to come to an accommodation on the Roman Question. But even in the parliamentary proceedings that ratified the acts of 1929 Mussolini revealed enough of the cloven hoof for Pius XI to risk all by publicly repudiating his ideas as incompatible with Christianity. Two years later, when Mussolini's bravos raided the clubs of the Catholic Youth Movement, and beat up all the personnel they could lay hands on, the storm really broke, and Pius XI in a most powerful letter —*Non Abbiamo Bisogno* (June 29, 1931)—made it clear that no Catholic could be a genuine convinced Fascist. There was no reply to this from the government, and a time of uneasy deadlock followed. Then a *modus vivendi* was arranged.

The Italian version of the absolute state was, however, a poor pale thing indeed compared with that which, ten years later, came into Germany with Hitler's accession to power in 1933. There is no need to expatiate on its peculiar combination of guile and violence and ignore its masterly power of organisation. We all of us—now—know all about this. The first act of the Nazis was to approach the Holy See with an offer to negotiate a concordat for the whole of Germany—an offer which, if genuine, would have ended anxieties that had baffled the popes for fifty years and more. Pius XI accepted, and the negotiations produced the Concordat of 1933. It was no sooner signed than the Nazis began, not so much merely to violate the treaty, but rather to use it as an instrument to fend off the Holy See's efforts to remedy the violation. A slow legal extermination of Catholicism in Germany soon began, all the Nazi technique in full operation and (since it was merely a Christian religion that was the victim) with scarcely any notice from the world outside. The patience of the pope had, finally, to give place to another attitude and in the encyclical *Mit Brennender Sorge,* of March 14, 1937, Pius XI exposed with "shattering force" the Nazi mixture of fraud and cruelty and denounced the whole Nazi conception of life as utterly and, necessarily, anti-Christian.

Neither the Fascists nor the Nazis expected—nor did they receive—from the Catholic Church anything but the bluntest condemnation of their fundamental theories. The basic reason of that condemnation was the simple fact that both systems were a denial of the rights of man as a human person. The State which they had set up was claiming rights that belonged to God alone; and claiming to exercise these rights not as God exercises them, Who works always according to the natures He has created, but in direct violation of the end of man. For the like reason Communism too must be condemned; and Communism, condemned by Leo XIII as far back as 1878, was by this time, like its kindred tyrannies, enthroned as a sovereign state. Pius XI dealt with the problem of Russia in a lengthy encyclical dated five days later than the letter to Germany. It was not the pope's first reference to Russia. That empire had never, indeed, been anything but hostile to Catholicism. The Tsars had persecuted their Polish subjects throughout the nineteenth century; they had persecuted the few Russians who were Catholics, and above all those Russian Catholics who used the same Greek liturgy and rites as their schismatic oppressors. This did not, in any way, prevent the popes, when the terrible famines of the post-war period devastated central and eastern Europe, from despatching to Russia what aid they could in goods and in money. If they did not do more it was chiefly because the Soviets, once securely in power, refused to accept their aid. From about 1920 the persecution began with a new bitterness, not of Catholics alone, whether Latin or Uniate, but of all religions, in the name of a new militant atheism. The total number of the victims still staggers the mind, made now more apt to believe in the reality of wickedness on the great scale by the tale of the later horrors perpetrated by the Nazis. In the end there was but one Catholic priest known to the government and allowed to exist as such, the American chaplain to the French embassy at Moscow. Against the cruelties of the Soviet system the pope did not cease to protest; for its blasphemous anti-God crusade he called on the Catholics of the world to make reparation, and ordered prayers to be said for Russia at the end of every Mass, every day, throughout the world. Finally came the encyclical on *Atheistic Communism* of 1937. This account of Pius XI's reaction to Communism needs, in order to be complete, a reference at least to his several declarations about the persecutions in Spain and in Mexico which also occurred in his reign.

So far it is the external activities of the reign that have been described. As always, the most significant part of the papal action lies elsewhere. The key to the whole of this great pope's effect must be sought in the two themes which he never ceased to develop and to expound through all the seventeen years he ruled the Church: that the only way to peace is through the reign of Christ over all human life, and that to act continuously as a Catholic upon the *milieu* in which God has placed him is, for every Catholic, an elementary apostolic duty. "Christ the King" and "Catholic Action"—here are the leading ideals of the reign, the way of salvation for the whole of our time.

Pius XI died, after a few days' illness, on February 10, 1939—just about midway between the Munich accords and the beginning of the last war. The conclave of 1939 did a most unusual thing. At the first ballot, and unanimously, it elected the late pope's Cardinal Secretary of State. He took the name Pius XII.

Whatever glories or sorrows the future holds in store for a pontificate that is now seven years old, history will always associate the name of the present pope with an immense work for the peace of the world. In the critical seven months between the election and the outbreak of the war, Pius XII made as many as six public appeals to the peoples of the world, reasoned, impassioned, pathetic; the appeals of an experienced statesman and man of affairs, of a mind and heart filled with pity at the thought of what horrors lay before millions of innocent people, appeals that came from the very soul of one to whom the peace-bearing mission of Christ our Lord was dearer than life itself. And through the diplomatic channels open to him the pope was continuously active. But the fate of mankind was, yet once again, at the mercy of the wicked, and the innocent were to pay heavily for the long practical incompetence and the moral indifference of the rulers on both sides. The war came. Pius XII, still consumed by his universal pity for mankind wherever suffering, did not slacken in his great work. In the first sixteen months of the war there were as many as thirty more public appeals of one kind or another.

These appeals—to give them a none too satisfactory generic title—were by no means mere effusions of humanitarian emotion. They were the product of a great intelligence, truly realist, and cast in the mould of a great juridical tradition. Together they constitute the greatest recall of western civilisation to the ideals of Law that has ever been made. The absolute need for the rule of Law, the inalienable rights of man, the rights of nations, however small, the criminal wickedness of the tyrannous state, the nature of true democracy and its rights, the need to exorcise lying—and the half-lie—from public policy, and to recognise the fact that much of this has been based, and is still based, on lies and half-lies—it is with such thoughts as these in his mind, and with a most acute presentation of them all as elements that will make or mar the effort for peace, that Pius XII has carried out his great mission. His effort has brought much condemnation in quarters which, for centuries, have sulked at the very name of pope, and expressions of agreement. From the totalitarian states, whose system of government was, yet once again, the unmistakable target of the papal condemnation there came endless reviling, calumny and abuse and threats—as all this still comes, while these words are written, from the government that holds Russia in thrall.

These war addresses of Pius XII, then, contain an abundance of wise guidance on the most urgent topics of the day. They are a constant, detailed, and explicit statement of Christianity as supplying the sole solution for the problem that underlies all the technique of politics and diplomacy. But, knowing that the Church is set in the world as salt to keep it wholesome, the pope never ceases in his effort that the salt shall not lose its savour. He reminds his own people that these questions of social and international justice are questions of conscience—not mere political idealism. And in such great letters as the *Summi Pontificatus* and *Mystici Corporis Christi* he exhorts and leads them to a stronger and more real practice of Catholicism based on an ever deeper understanding of its meaning. Nor should all mention be omitted of the new charter of Biblical Studies, the encyclical *Divino Afflante*.

Peace can only come through justice, through the triumph of what is just, of what is the right to do—and Catholics above all others, and before all others, need to practise justice. This is the great key principle, it would seem, of Pius XII's crusade for a better world; and in that crusade he invites to stand by his side all men of good will, pledging himself explicitly "to do the work of Truth in Charity." Of this universal charity his own action has been a most striking example, and all the world knows it—the world at any rate, of those ordinary folk of whom, said Lincoln, "God must be very, very fond, seeing He made so many of them."

Chronological Tables [1]

TABLE I

Popes.	Roman Emperors.
St. Peter, 29-67	Tiberius, 14-37
	Caligula, 37-41
	Claudius, 41-54
St. Linus, 67-78	Nero, 54-68
	Galba
	Otho } 68-69
	Vitellius
St. Cletus, 78-90	Vespasian, 69-79
	Titus, 79-81
St. Clement I, 90-100	Domitian, 81-96
	Nerva, 96-98
	Trajan, 98-117
St. Anacletus, 100-112 *	
St. Evaristus, 112-121	Hadrian, 117-138
St. Alexander I, 121-132	
St. Sixtus I, 132-142	Antoninus Pius, 138-161
St. Telesphorus, 142-154	
St. Hyginus, 154-158	
St. Pius I, 158-167	Marcus Aurelius, 161-180
St. Anicetus, 167-175	
St. Soter, 175-182	Commodus, 180-192
St. Eleuterius, 182-193	Septimius Severus, 193-211
St. Victor I, 193-203	
St. Zephyrinus, 203-221	Caracalla, 211-217
St. Callistus I, 221-227	Heliogabalus, 218-223
St. Urban I, 227-233	Alexander Severus, 223-235
St. Pontian, 233-238	Maximin, 235-238
St. Anteros, 238-239	Gordian, 238-244
St. Fabian, 240-250	Philip, 244-249
	Decius, 249-251
St. Cornelius, 251-253	Gallus, 251-253
St. Lucius I, 253-254	Valerian, 253-258
St. Stephen I, 254-257	
St. Sixtus II, 257-258	
St. Denis, 259-268	Gallienus, 260-268
St. Felix I, 269-274	Claudius II, 268-269
St. Eutychian, 275-283	Aurelian, 270-275
	Tacitus, 275-276
	Probus, 276-282
	Caius, 282-284

[1] For the notes to these tables cf. *infra,* p. 314.

TABLE II

Popes.	Eastern Emperors.	Western Emperors.
St. Caius, 283-296	Diocletian, 284-305	Maximian, 286-305
St. Marcellinus, 296-304		
St. Marcellus I, 308-309	Galerius, 305-311	Constantius Chlorus, 305-306
St. Eusebius, 309-310	Licinius, 311-324	Constantine I, 306-337
St. Melchiades, 311-314		Constantine I, sole emperor, 324-337
St. Silvester I, 314-335	Constantius II, 337-361	Constantine II, 337-340
St. Mark, 336		Constans I, 337-350
St. Julius I, 337-352		Constantius II, sole emperor, 350-361
St. Liberius, 352-366		Julian the Apostate, sole emperor, 361-363
		Jovian, sole emperor, 363-364
St. Damasus I,[1] 366-384	Valens, 364-378	Valentinian I, 364-375
St. Siricius, 384-399	Theodosius I, 379-395	Gratian, 375-383
		Valentinian II, 383-392
	Theodosius I, sole emperor, 392-395	
St. Anastasius I, 399-401	Arcadius, 395-408	Honorius, 395-423
St. Innocent I, 401-417	Theodosius II, 408-450	
St. Zozimus, 417-418		
St. Boniface I, 418-422		Valentinian I, 364-375
St. Celestine I, 422-432		
St. Sixtus III, 432-440		
St. Leo I, 440-461	Marcian, 450-457	Avitus, 455-457
	Leo I, 457-474	Majorian, 457-461
St. Hilary, 461-468		Severus, 461-467

Popes.	Eastern Emperors.	Western Emperors.
St. Simplicius, 468-483	Leo II, 474	Anthemius, 467-472
	Zeno, 474-491	Julius Nepos, 472-475
		Romulus (Augustulus), 475-476 [2]
		(Clovis, King of Franks, 481-507)
St. Felix III,[1] 483-492	Anastasius I, 491-518	
St. Gelasius I, 492-496		
St. Anastasius II, 496-498		
St. Symmachus, 498-514		(Theodoric, King of the Ostrogoths, ruler of Italy, 493-526)
St. Hormisdas, 514-523	Justin I, 518-527	
St. John I, 523-526		
St. Felix IV, 526-530	Justinian I, 527-565	

297

TABLE III

Popes.	Roman Emperors.
Boniface II, 530-532	
John II, 532-535	
St. Agapitus I, 535-536	
St. Silverius, 536-537	
Vigilius, 537-555	
Pelagius I, 555-561	
John III, 561-574	Justin II, 565-678
Benedict I, 575-578	Tiberius II, 578-582
Pelagius II, 578-590	Maurice, 582-602
St. Gregory I, 590-604	Phocas, 602-610
Sabinian, 604-606	
Boniface III, 607	
St. Boniface IV, 608-615	Heraclius, 610-641
St. Deusdedit I, 615-619	
Boniface V, 619-625	
Honorius I, 625-638	
Severinus, 638-640	
John IV, 640-642	Constantine III and Heracleonas, 641-642
Theodore I, 642-649	Constans II, 642-668
St. Martin I, 649-655	
St. Eugene I, 654-657	
St. Vitalian, 657-672	Constantine IV, 668-685
Deusdedit II, 672-676	
Donus I, 676-678	
St. Agatho, 678-681	
St. Leo II, 682-683	
St. Benedict II, 684-685	
John V, 685-686	Justinian II, 685-695
Conon, 686-687	
St. Sergius I, 687-701	Leontius, 695-698
John VI, 701-705	Tiberius III, 698-705
John VII, 705-707	Justinian II, 705-711 (restored)
Sisinnius, 708	
Constantine, 708-715	Philip Bardanes, 711-713
	Anastasius II, 713-715

TABLE IV

Popes.	Roman Emperors.	Kings of the Franks.
	Theodosius III, 716-717	Charles Martel, 716-741 [3]
St. Gregory II, 715-731	Leo III, 717-741	
St. Gregory III, 731-741		
St. Zachary, 741-752	Constantine V, 741-775	Pepin the Short, 741-768
Stephen II, 752 ‡		
St. Stephen III, 752-757		
St. Paul I, 757-767		Charlemagne, 768-814
Stephen IV, 768-772		
Adrian I, 772-795		
		Emperors in the West.
	Leo IV, 775-780	
	Constantine VI, 780-797	
Leo III, 795-816	Irene, 797-802	Charlemagne, 800-814
	Nicephorus I, 802-811	
	Michael I, 811-813	
	Leo V, 813-820	Louis the Pious, 814-840
St. Stephen V, 816-817	Michael II, 820-829	
St. Pascal I, 817-824		
Eugene II, 824-827		
Valentine, 827		
Gregory IV, 827-844	Theophilus, 829-842	Lothair I, 840-855
Sergius II, 844-847	Michael III, 842-867	
St. Leo IV, 847-855		
Benedict III, 855-858		Louis the German, 855-875

‡ This pope, who died three days after his election, before being consecrated, is not reckoned in many lists—whence it is his successor who is often counted as Stephen II.

TABLE V

Popes.	Roman Emperors.	Emperors in the West.	English Kings.
St. Nicholas I, 858-867	Basil I, 867-886	Charles the Bald, 875-877	Alfred, 871-901
Adrian II, 867-872		Charles the Fat, 882-887	
John VIII, 872-882			
Marinus I, 882-884			
Adrian III, 884-885			
Stephen VI, 885-891	Leo VI, 886-912		
Formosus, 891-896			
Boniface VI, 896 *			
Stephen VII, 896-897			
Romanus, 897-898			
Theodore II, 898			
John IX, 898-900			
Benedict IV, 900-903			Edward the Elder, 901-925
Leo V, 903			
Christopher, 903-904 *			
Sergius III, 904-911			
Anastasius III, 911-913	Constantine VII, 912-958		
Lando, 913-914	Romanus I, 919-944		
John X, 914-928			Athelstan, 925-940
Leo VI, 928-929			
Stephen VIII, 929-931			
John XI, 931-935			
Leo VII, 936-939		Otto I, 936-973	

300

TABLE VI

Popes.	Roman Emperors.	Emperors in the West.	English Kings.	France.
Stephen IX, 939-942			Edmund the Elder, 940-946	
Martin III,[4] 942-946				
Agapetus II, 946-955			Edred, 946-955	
John XII, 955-964	Romanus II, 958-963		Edwy, 955-959	
	Basil II, 963-1025		Edgar, 959-975	
Benedict V, 964-965	{ Constantine VIII, 963-1028			
John XIII, 965-972	Nicephorus II, 963-969	Otto II, 973-983		
	John I, 969-976			
Benedict VI, 972-973			Edward the Martyr, 975-978	
Donus II, 974 *				Hugh Capet, 987-996
Benedict VII, 974-984				Robert the Pious, 996-1031

Popes.	Roman Emperors.	Emperors in the West.	England.	France.
John XIV, 984-985		Otto III, 983-1002	Ethelred II, 978-1016	
John XV, 985-996 [5]				
Gregory V, 996-999 [g]				
Sylvester II, 999-1003 [F]		St. Henry II, 1002-1024		
John XVII, 1003				
John XVIII, 1003-1009				
Sergius IV, 1009-1012			Canute, 1016-1035	
Benedict VIII, 1012-1024				

TABLE VI—continued

Popes.	Roman Emperors.	Emperors in the West.	England.	France.
John XIX, 1024-1033	Romanus III, 1028-1034	Conrad II, 1024-1039		Henry I, 1031-1060
Benedict IX, 1033-1044	Michael IV, 1034-1041	Henry III, 1039-1056	Harold I, 1035-1040	
	Michael V, 1041-1042		Hardicanute, 1040-1042	
	Constantine IX, 1042-1055			
			St. Edward the Confessor, 1042-1066	
Gregory VI, 1044-1046 ?				
St. Clement II, 1046	Theodora, 1055-1056			
Damascus II, 1048	Michael VI, 1056-1057	Henry IV, 1056-1106		
St. Leo IX, 1049-1054 8	Isaac Comnenus, 1057-1059			
Victor II, 1054-1057				
Stephen X, 1057-1058				
Nicholas II, 1059-1061	Constantine X, 1059-1067			
	Romanus IV, 1067-1071			
Alexander II, 1061-1073	Michael VII, 1071-1078		Harold II, 1066	
			William the Conqueror, 1066-1087	Philip I, 1060-1106
St. Gregory VII, 1073-1085	Nicephorus III, 1078-1081		William II, 1087-1099	

Popes.	Roman Emperors.	Emperors in the West.	England.	France.
B. Victor III, 1087	Alexius I Comnenus, 1081-1118			
B. Urban II, 1088-1099		Henry V, 1106-1125	Henry I, 1099-1135	Louis VI, 1106-1137
Pascal II, 1099-1118				
Gelasius II, 1118-1119	John II Comnenus, 1118-1144			
Calixtus II, 1119-1124		Lothair II, 1125-1137	Stephen, 1135-1154	Louis VII, 1137-1180
Honorius II, 1124-1130		Conrad III, 1137-1152		
Innocent II, 1130-1143				
Celestine II, 1143-1144				
Lucius II, 1144-1145	Manuel Comnenus, 1144-1180			
B. Eugene III, 1145-1153		Frederick I, 1152-1190	Henry II, 1154-1189	
Anastasius IV, 1153-1154				
Adrian IV, 1154-1159 9				
Alexander III, 1159-1181				Philip II, 1180-1223 (Augustus)
Lucius III, 1181-1185	Alexis III, 1195-1203			
Urban III, 1185-1187	Andronicus, 1183-1185			
Gregory VIII, 1187	Isaac II, 1185-1195 (Angelus)			
Clement III, 1187-1191		Henry VI, 1190-1197	Richard I, 1189-1199 (Cœur de Lion)	
Celestine III, 1191-1198	Alexis III, 1195-1203		John, 1199-1216	
Innocent III, 1198-1216	Baldwin I, 1204-1205 †	Otto IV, 1198-1212	Henry III, 1216-1272	
	Henry, 1205-1216 †	Frederick II, 1212-1250		
Honorius III, 1216-1227	Peter, 1216-1219 †			Louis VIII, 1223-1226
	Robert, 1219-1228 †			

TABLE VI—continued

Popes.	Roman Emperors.	Emperors in the West.	England.	France.
Gregory IX, 1227-1241	Baldwin II, 1228-1261 †	Conrad IV, 1250-1254		St. Louis IX, 1226-1270
Celestine IV, 1241				Philip III, 1270-1285
Innocent IV, 1243-1254				
Alexander IV, 1254-1261	Michael VIII, 1261-1282			
Urban IV, 1261-1265 F				
Clement IV, 1265-1268 F				
B. Gregory X, 1271-1276		Rudolf I, 1273-1291 (Hapsburg)	Edward I, 1272-1307	
B. Innocent V, 1276				
Adrian V, 1276				
John XXI, 1276-1277 P				
Nicholas III, 1277-1280	Andronicus II, 1282-1328			
Martin IV, 1281-1285 F				Philip IV, 1285-1314 (The Fair)
Honorius IV, 1285-1287				
Nicholas IV, 1288-1292		Adolf, 1292-1298		
St. Celestine V, 1294				
Boniface VIII, 1294-1303 [10]		Albert I, 1298-1308		
B. Benedict XI, 1303-1304 [11]				

Popes.	Roman Emperors.	Emperors in the West.	England.	France.
Clement V, 1305-1314 F	Andronicus III,	Henry VII, 1308-1314	Edward II, 1307-1327	Louis X, 1314-1316
John XXII, 1316-1334 F	1328-1341	Lewis of Bavaria } -1330	Edward III, 1327-1377	Philip V, 1316-1322
		Frederic of Austria } -1347		Charles IV, 1322-1328
				Philip VI, 1328-1350
				(Valois)
Benedict XII, 1334-	John V, 1341-1391 [12]			
1342 F				
Clement VI, 1342-1352 F		Charles IV, 1347-1378		John II, 1350-1364
Innocent VI, 1352-1362 F				Charles V, 1364-1380
B. Urban V, 1362-1370 F			Richard II, 1377-1399	Charles VI, 1380-1422
Gregory XI, 1370-1378 F				
Urban VI, 1378-1389		Wenceslaus, 1378-1400	Henry IV, 1399-1413	
Boniface IX, 1389-1404	Manuel II, 1391-1425	Rupert, 1400-1410		
Innocent VII, 1404-1406				
Gregory XII, 1406-1415		Sigismund, 1410-1437	Henry V, 1413-1422	
Alexander V, 1409-1410 GK				
	These two popes elected by the self-summoned Council of Pisa.			
John XXIII, 1410-1415				
'Clement VII,' 1378-1394	The French anti-popes of the Great Schism.		Henry VI, 1422-1461	Charles VII, 1422-1461
'Benedict XIII,' 1394-1428				
Martin V, 1417-1431	John VI, 1425-1448			
(Colonna)		Albert II, 1438-1439		

305

TABLE VI—continued

Popes.	Roman Emperors.	Emperors in the West.	England.	Spain.
Eugene IV, 1431-1447 (Condulmare)	Frederick III, 1439-1493			
Nicholas V, 1447-1455 (Parentucelli)	Constantine XI, 1448-1453 Last of the Roman Emperors			
Calixtus III, 1455-1458 s (Borgia)				
Pius II, 1458-1464 (Piccolomini)		Edward IV, 1461-1483	Louis XI, 1461-1483	
Paul II, 1464-1471 (Barbo)				
Sixtus IV, 1471-1484 (della Rovere)		Edward V, 1483 / Richard III, 1483-1485 / Henry VII, 1485-1509	Charles VIII, 1483-1498	Ferdinand & Isabella 1479-1504 († Isabella) 1516 († Ferdinand)
Innocent VIII, 1484-1492 (Cibo)				
	Emperors.		*France.*	
Alexander VI, 1492-1503 s (Borgia)	Maximilian I, 1493-1519		Louis XII, 1498-1515	
Pius III, 1503 (Piccolomini)		*England.*		
Julius II, 1503-1513 (della Rovere)		Henry VIII, 1509-1547		

Popes.	Emperors.	England.	France.	Spain.
Leo X, 1513-1521 (Medici)	Charles V, 1519-1556 (also King of Spain, 1516-1556)		Francis I, 1515-1547	Charles I, 1516-1556
Adrian VI, 1522-1523 (Boyens)				
Clement VII, 1523-1534 (Medici)				
		Mary, Queen of Scots, 1542-1567 († 1587)		
Paul III, 1534-1549 (Farnese)		Edward VI, 1547-1553	Henry II, 1547-1559	
Julius III, 1550-1555 (del Monte)		Mary I, 1553-1558		
Marcellus II, 1555 (Cervini)				
Paul IV, 1555-1559 (Carafa)	Ferdinand I, 1556-1564	Elizabeth, 1558-1603	Francis II, 1559-1560	Philip II, 1556-1598
Pius IV, 1559-1565 (Medici)			Charles IX, 1560-1574	
St. Pius V, 1566-1572 (Ghislieri)	Maximilian II, 1564-1576			
Gregory XIII, 1572-1585 (Buoncompagni)	Rudolf II, 1576-1612		Henry III, 1574-1589	
Sixtus V, 1585-1590 (Peretti)			Henry IV, 1589-1610	
Urban VII, 1590 (Castagna)				

TABLE VI—continued

Popes.	Emperors.	England.	France.	Spain.
Gregory XIV, 1590-1591 (Sfondrati)				Philip III, 1598-1621
Innocent IX, 1591 (Fachinetti)				
Clement VIII, 1592-1605 (Aldobrandini)		James I, 1603-1625		
Leo XI, 1605 (Medici)				
Paul V, 1605-1621 (Borghese)	Mathias, 1612-1619		Louis XIII, 1610-1643	
	Ferdinand II, 1619-1637			Philip IV, 1621-1665
Gregory XV, 1621-1623 (Ludovisi)				
Urban VIII, 1623-1644 (Barberini)	Ferdinand III, 1637-1658	Charles I, 1625-1649		
Innocent X, 1644-1655 (Pamfili)		The Commonwealth, 1649-1660	Louis XIV, 1643-1715	
Alexander VII, 1655-1667 (Chigi)	Leopold I, 1658-1705	Charles II, 1660-1685		Charles II, 1665-1700
Clement IX, 1667-1669 (Rospigliosi)				
Clement X, 1670-1676 (Altieri)		John Sobieski, King of Poland, 1674-1696		

Popes.	Emperors.	England.	France.	Spain.
Ven. Innocent XI, 1676-1689 (Oderscalchi)		James II, 1685-1688		
Alexander VIII, 1689-1691 (Ottobuoni)		William III, 1689-1702 & Mary II, 1689-1694		
Innocent XII, 1691-1700 (Pignatelli)			Peter the Great, 1689-1725, of Russia	
Clement XI, 1700-1721 (Albani)	Joseph I, 1705-1711	Anne, 1702-1714		Philip V, 1700-1724
Innocent XIII, 1721-1724 (Conti)	Charles VI, 1711-1740	George I, 1714-1727	Louis XV, 1715-1774	Luis, 1724-1725
Benedict XIII, 1724-1730 (Orsini)		George II, 1727-1760		Philip V, 1725-1746
Clement XII, 1730-1740 (Corsini)			Frederick the Great, 1740-1786, of Prussia	
Benedict XIV, 1740-1758 (Lambertini)	Charles VII, 1740-1745 Francis I, 1745-1765 (husband of Maria Teresa)			Ferdinand VI, 1746-1759
Clement XIII, 1758-1769 (Rezzonico)	Joseph II, 1765-1790	George III, 1760-1820		Charles III, 1759-1788
Clement XIV, 1769-1774 (Ganganelli)			Catharine the Great, 1762-1796, of Russia	
Pius VI, 1775-1799 (Braschi)	Leopold II, 1790-1792 Francis II, 1792-1806		Louis XVI, 1774-1792 Republic, 1792	Charles IV, 1788-1808

TABLE VII

Popes.	Austria.	England.	France.
Pius VII, 1800-1823 (Chiaramonti)			Napoleon, 1799-1814
	Francis I, 1806-1835		Louis XVIII, 1814-1824
		George IV, 1820-1830	
Leo XII, 1823-1829 (della Genga)			Charles X, 1824-1830
Pius VIII, 1829-1830 (Castiglioni)		William IV, 1830-1837	Louis Philippe, 1830-1848
Gregory XVI, 1831-1846 (Cappellari)	Ferdinand, 1835-1848		
		Victoria, 1837-1901	
Pius IX, 1846-1878 (Mastai-Ferretti)	Francis Joseph, 1848-1916		Republic, 1848-1852

	Italy.	France.
	Victor Emmanuel II, K. of Sardinia, 1848-1861 K. of Italy, 1861-1878	Napoleon III, 1852-1870
		Republic
		Thiers, 1871-1873 McMahon, 1873-1879
	Umberto I, 1878-1901 Victor Emmanuel III, 1901-1946 Umberto II, 1946	
Leo XIII, 1878-1903 (Pecci)		Grévy, 1879-1887

TABLE VII—*continued*

Spain.	Prussia.	Russia.	U.S.A.
	Frederick William III, 1797-1840		Washington, 1789-1797
			Adams, 1797-1801
		Alexander I, 1801-1825	Jefferson, 1801-1809
Ferdinand VII, 1808-1833			Madison, 1809-1817
			Monroe, 1817-1825
		Nicholas I, 1825-1855	J. Q. Adams, 1825-1829
Isabella II, 1833-1868			Jackson, 1829-1837
			Van Buren, 1837-1841
	Frederick William IV, 1840-1861		Harrison, 1841
			Tyler, 1841-1845
			Polk, 1845-1849
			Taylor, 1849-1850
			Fillmore, 1850-1853
		Alexander II, 1855-1881	Pierce, 1853-1857
			Buchanan, 1857-1861
	William I, 1861-1888		Lincoln, 1861-1865
Republic, 1868-1870	German Empire.		Johnson, 1865-1869
Amadeus, 1870-1873	William I, 1871-1888		
Republic, 1873-1874			
Alfonso XII, 1874-1885			
		Alexander III, 1881-1894	Grant, 1869-1877
			Hayes, 1877-1881
			Garfield, 1881

TABLE VII—continued from page 310

Popes.	Austria.	England.	France.
			Carnot, 1887-1894
			Casimir-Perrier, 1894-1895
			Faure, 1895-1899
			Loubet, 1899-1906
		Edward VII, 1901-1910	
Pius X, 1903-1914 (Sarto)			
		George V, 1910-1936	Fallières, 1906-1913
Benedict XV, 1914-1922 (della Chiesa)			Poincaré, 1913-1920
		Charles, 1916-1918	
			Deschanel, 1920-1921
Pius XI, 1922-1939 (Ratti)	Republic, 1918-1938		Millerand, 1921-1924
			Doumergue, 1924-1931
		Edward VIII, 1936	Doumer,
		George VI, 1936	Lebrun, 1931-1934
			1934-1940
Pius XII, 1939 (Pacelli)	Republic, 1946		

TABLE VII—*continued from page 311*

Spain.	Germany.	Russia.	U.S.A.
			Arthur, 1881-1885
Alfonso XIII, 1886-1931			Cleveland, 1885-1889
	Frederick III, 1888		B. Harrison, 1889-1893
	William II, 1888-1918		Cleveland, 1893-1897
		Nicholas II, 1894-1917	
			McKinley, 1897-1901
			T. Roosevelt, 1901-1909
			Taft, 1909-1913
			Wilson, 1913-1921
		Republic, 1917	
	Republic, 1918		Harding, 1921-1923
			Coolidge, 1923-1929
			Hoover, 1929-1933
Republic, 1931	Hitler, 1933-1945	Stalin, 1924	F. D. Roosevelt, 1933-1945
Franco, 1938			Truman, 1945

NOTES

[1] Some lists insert a Felix II, pope from 355.

[2] This emperor's abdication marks the end of the line of Roman Emperors in the West.

[3] Charles Martel was never, of course, King of the Franks in name, nor was his son Pepin until 751.

[4] Marinus I, 882-884, is reckoned as Martin II, and, in some lists, Martin III is styled Marinus II.

[5] Some lists insert a John XV, pope for a few weeks in 985, and reckon the pope called in this list John XV as John XVI.

[6] Some lists reckon as pope from 997-998 a John XVII; he was in reality an anti-pope.

[7] Some lists insert a Sylvester III, 1045, before Gregory VI.

[8] Leo VIII, 963-965, was not the lawful pope.

[9] The solitary English pope, Nicholas Brakespear.

[10] Boniface VII, 984, was an anti-pope.

[11] Benedict X, 1058, was an anti-pope.

[12] John III, 1222-1254, and John IV, 1258-1261, reigned at Nicea during the Latin occupation of Constantinople.

* Popes marked thus are not found in all the lists. It should perhaps be stated that there is no general agreement as to the dates of the popes of the first three centuries.

† These are the Latin Emperors in Constantinople.

The family names of the popes are given in parentheses from the time of Martin V, 1417-1431.

The nationality of the non-Italian popes is shown from the time of the first German and French popes (Gregory V, 996-999; Silvester II, 999-1003) down to Adrian VI, 1522-1523—since whom all the popes have been Italian—by the letters F (French), G (German), S (Spanish), D (Dutch), P (Portuguese), GK (Greek).

Index

Abelard, 118
Acacius, 51-2, 54, 61
Adoptionists, 22
Aelia, 29
Africa, 30, 55, 57, 60, 68, 76, 92
Aistulf, 96
Alaric, 75-76
Albigenses, 22, 128, 177
Alcuin, 90
Alexander Severus, emperor (223–235), 32
Alexandria, 25, 27, 29, 39, 47, 63, 66, 93
Allen, Cardinal, 264
Alsace, 84
Anagni, 148
Anastasius I, emperor (491–518), 52
Anne, Queen of England, 267
Antioch, 28, 46-8, 53, 63, 66, 93, 122
Antipopes:
 Benedict XIII (1394–1424), 157-61
 Clement III (1080), 110
 Clement VII (1378–1394), 157
 Felix V (1440), 163
 Nicholas V (1328), 151
Apollinaris of Laodicea, 44
Apologists, 15, 23-4, 139
Apostolicum, bull (1765), 226
Arabia, 58, 92
Arians, 36, 38, 39, 72, 82, 85
Asia Minor, 13, 29, 33, 63
Aristotle, 117, 140-42
Arius, 39
Arles, 30
Augustinus, the, 211
Ausculta Fili, bull (1302), 147
Australasia, 263
Austria, 30
Averroës, 117, 141
Avicenna, 117, 141
Avignon, 144, 145, 149, 153, 155, 162

Baius, Michael, 211
Balkans, the, 68
Bangor, 83
Barbarians, 74-5
Barnabites, 199
Basiliscus, emperor (477), 50
Bavaria, 30
Belgium, 84
Benedictines, 163, 238, 255
Bithynia, 32
Black Death, 152-53

Blessed Sacrament, Company of the, 210
Bobbio, 84
Bohemia, 120, 165
Book of Common Prayer, 264
Bourges, Pragmatic Sanction of (1438), 164
Britain, 13, 33, 60, 68, 76, 79, 87-91
Bulgaria, 113-14

Cajetan, Cardinal, 177
Calvin, John, 178
Calvinism, 207-8
Camaldolesi, 104, 195
Canada, 263
Canossa, 110
Canterbury, 89
Capuchin Franciscans, 199
Cardinals, College of, 147, 149, 154, 164, 168, 182, 189, 194, 254
Carmelites, 199
Carthage, 26, 30
Carthusians, 195
Catharine de Medici, Queen of France, 208
Cavour, 254
Centre Party, 251
Cerularius, Michael, 114
Chapters, The Three, 56-7
Charity, Sisters of, 210
Charlemagne, king and emperor (768–814), 82, 95, 97-9
Charles IV, emperor (1347–1378), 151
Charles V, emperor (1519–1556), 55, 174, 185, 188, 189, 191, 203, 258
Charles I, King of England, 265
Charles II, King of England, 265
Charles III, King of Spain (1759–1788), 226-7
Charles Martel, 90, 93, 95
Chartreux, 118
China, 21, 261-2
Cid, the, 121
Cistercian Order, cf., Citeaux
Citeaux, 118, 119, 120, 130
Civil Constitution of the Clergy, 243
Clement of Alexandria, 27-8
Clericis Laicos, bull (1296), 147
Clovis, 82
Cluny, 103-4
Commodus, emperor (180–192), 32
Concordat of 1516, 174

315

Concordat of Worms (1122), 112, 116, 121
Conrad II, emperor (1024–1039), 102
Conradin, 138
Consalvi, Cardinal, 252
Consolamentum, 128
Constans I, emperor (337–350), 41
Constans II, emperor (642–688), 59
Constantine the Great (306–337), 29, 33, 35, 36, 40, 69, 98
Constantine IV, emperor (668–685), 60
Constantine V, emperor (741–775), 94
Constantinople, 43, 44, 49, 92
Constantinople II, emperor (337–361), 36, 41
Contarini, Cardinal, 187, 189
Councils, General:
  Basle (1431–1449), 162-3
  Chalcedon (451), 38, 45, 49–50
  Constance (1414), 160, 256
  Constantinople I (381), 42
  Constantinople II (553), 57
  Constantinople III (680), 60
  Constantinople IV (869), 113
  Ephesus (431), 44-7
  Ferrara (1438), 163
  Florence (1438–1440), 115
  Lateran I (1123), 121
  Lateran III (1179), 125
  Lateran IV (1215), 135
  Lateran V (1512–1517), 143
  Lyons I (1245), 138
  Lyons II (1274), 115, 143
  Nicea I (325), 40, 41, 42
  Nicea II (787), 94
  Siena (1423), 162
  Trent (1545–1563), 181, 186-92, 197, 202, 213, 228
  Vatican (1869–1870), 241
Councils, Local:
  Arles (34), 30
  Clermont (1095), 111, 122
  Constantinople (861), 114
  Constantinople (879), 114
  Ephesus (499), 48
  Hieria (753), 94
  in Trullo (692), 61
  Lateran (649), 60
  Latrocinium (449), 49
  Orleans (511), 82
  Pavia (1423), 162
  Pisa (1409), 159
  Pisa (1511), 173
  Rimini-Seleucia (359), 42
  Rome (1059), 107
  Sutri (1046), 101, 105
  Toledo (589), 85
  Whitby (664), 89
Counter-Reformation, 180-204
Cromwell, Oliver, 267
Crusades, 111, 115, 122-4

Decius, emperor (249–51), 31
Decretum of Gratian, 117

Defensor Pacis, 151
Deism, 206, 221-2
Diamper Synod, 260
Diocletian, emperor (284–305), 33
Dioscoros, 47, 50
Dominus ac Redemptor, brief, 228
Domitian, emperor (81–96), 31
Donatism, 68-9
Douai College, 264

Edward VI, of England, 180
Egypt, 13, 25, 29, 49, 54, 57, 62, 92
Elizabeth, Queen of England, 180, 198, 264
Ems, Protestation of, 231
Encyclion, 51
Erasmus, 166
Eusebius of Nicomedia, 39, 40, 42
Eutyches, 47-8

Febronius, 228-9
Fénelon, 219
Ferdinand II, emperor (1619–1637), 204
Francis I, King of France (1515–1547), 207
Franciscans, cf., Friars Minor
Franks, 82
Frederick I, Barbarossa, emperor (1152–1190), 111, 124-5
Frederick II, emperor (1212–1250), 134-5
Freemasonry, 206, 252
Freising, 84
Friars Minor, 124, 131, 132-4
Frisia, 91
Fulda, 91

Gallicanism, 215-16, 224, 241-2, 243-4
Gallienus, emperor (260–268), 32
Garibaldi, 254
Gaul, 13, 30, 33, 60, 68, 76, 82-4, 87, 91, 95
German Theology, The, 166
Germany, 13, 60, 90-1, 98-9, 108, 110-11, 121, 126, 203-4
Gerson, 158
Gnosticism, 16-19
Gnostics, 139
Golden Bull, 152
Görres, 249
Goths, 74-5
Gratian, emperor (375–383), 37, 117
Greece, 13, 29, 68
Guéranger, Dom, 255
Guyon, Mme., 218-19

Hadrian, emperor (117–138), 29
Henoticon, 52
Henry III, emperor (1039–1056), 105
Henry IV, emperor (1056–1106), 102, 109-10
Henry VI, emperor (1190–1197), 127

Henry VII, emperor (1308–1314), 150
Henry VIII, of England, 126, 179, 187, 202
Henry IV, of France (1586–1610), 208
Heraclius, emperor (610–641), 57
Hildebrand, 108-10
Hirschau, 104
Holland, 90
Honorius, condemnation of Pope, 60
Honorius, emperor (395–423), 69, 75
Hormisdas, Formula of Pope, 53-4
Hosius of Cordova, 40
Hubert, of Moyenmoutier, 106
Hungary, 30, 78, 163
Huns, 74
Hus, John, 165
Ibas, of Edessa, 56
Iconoclasts, 93-4, 112
Ignatius of Constantinople, Patriarch, 112-13
Illyricum, 113-14

Imitation of Christ, 163
Inquisition, 129-30, 194, 217
Introducion à la Vie Devote, 208
Iona, 89
Ireland, 78, 79-80
Irene, empress regent (780), 94
Islam, 58, 92-3, 98, 100, 121-23, 162

James II, of England, 266
Jandel, Pére, 255
Jansenism, 210-16, 219-21, 224, 243
Jansenius, 212
Japan, 260
Jerusalem, 29, 49, 53, 122
Jesuits, 190, 195, 199-200, 206, 210, 212, 213, 217, 223-28, 240, 258, 260, 261-62, 263, 265
Jewish Christians, 29
John of Jandun, 150
Joseph II, emperor (1765–1790), 228, 230-32, 253
Jugo-Slavia, 68
Julian the Apostate, emperor (361–363), 36-7, 42
Justin I, emperor (518–527), 53
Justinian I, emperor (527–565), 55-7
Justinian II, empreror (685–711), 61

Ketteler, von, 250
Knights Hospitallers, 123
Knights Templars, 123, 149
Korea, 262
Kubla Khan, 261
Kulturkampf, 271

La Mennais, 247
Leo III, emperor (717–741), 93

Leovigild, 84-5
Lérins, 79
Lewis of Bavaria, emperor (1314–1347), 150
Licinius, emperor (311–324), 34, 35, 36
Lindisfarne, 89
Lollards, 165
Lombards, 87, 96
Lombardy, 84
London, 88
Lorraine, 84
Lothair, King of Lorraine (863), 102
Louis the Pious, emperor (814–840), 99
Louis XIV, of France (1643–1715), 206, 216-17, 220, 262
Louis XV, of France (1715–1774), 224-25
Louis XVI, of France (1774–1793), 242, 243
Lourdes, 256
Lucian, 40
Luther, 143, 166, 174, 175-78, 180
Luxembourg, 84
Luxeuil, 84
Lyons, 30

Macedonia, 29
Mahometans, 58, 92-3, 98, 121-23, 162, 168, 171
Mainz, Pragmatic Sanction of (1439), 164
Manfred, King of Sicily, 138
Manichees, 21-2, 128
Marcian, emperor (450–457), 48
Marcionism, 19-20, 36
Marcus Aurelius, emperor (161–180), 31
Marmoutier, 78
Marsilio of Padua, 150
Matilda, Countess, 110
Maximin, emperor (235–238), 32
Mary, Queen of England (1553–1558), 180
Metternich, 253
Milan, 34, 35
Missions, Foreign, 210
Modernism, 221
Möhler, 249
Molinos, Michael, 217-18
Monarchians, 22-23
Mongols, 261
Monophysites, 46, 50-60
Monothelism, 59-60
Montanism, 19, 36
Morocco, 21
Morone, Cardinal, 187

Napoleon I, 56, 245-46
Nazareans, 29
Nero, emperor (54–68), 26, 31
Nestorius, 44-46
Newman, Cardinal, 238, 239
Northmen, 100

Occam, William of, 150
Odoacer, 77
Olier, Jean Jacques, 209
Oratorians, 200
Oratory of Divine Love, 198
Origen, 28, 65, 72
Osrhoene, 29
Otto I, emperor (936–973), 102
Otto III, emperor (983–1002), 102

Palestine, 29, 45, 63, 92
Papal State, the, 95-7, 162, 167, 170, 172, 251-54
Paraguay, 223, 259
Paris, University of, 140
Pelagianism, 71, 79
Pepin the Short, 95
Persia, 21, 92
Persons, Robert, 265
Peter the Lombard, 117
Philip the Arab, emperor (244-249), 32
Philip IV of France, the Fair (1285–1314), 147-8
Philip II of Spain (1556–1598), 196, 202-3
Photius, 61, 102, 112-14
Pistoia, Synod of, 228, 232
Pliny the Younger, 32
Poitiers, 95
Poland, 121, 178
Pole, Cardinal, 188
Pombal, 223
Pompadour, Mme. de, 224
Popes:
    Adrian I, 94, 97
    Adrian II, 113
    Adrian IV, 124
    Adrian VI, 167, 183-84
    Alexander II, 108
    Alexander III, 111, 125-27, 137
    Alexander IV, 138, 146
    Alexander V, 137, 159
    Alexander VI, 172, 185
    Alexander VII, 202, 205, 215
    Benedict VIII, 105
    Benedict IX, 105
    Benedict XI, B., 149
    Benedict XIV, 223
    Benedict XV, 256, 284-85
    Boniface VIII, 147, 152
    Calixtus II, 112
    Calixtus III, 167
    Celestine III, 127
    Clement I, S., 26
    Clement IV, 138, 144
    Clement V, 145, 149, 152
    Clement VI, 151
    Clement VII, 179, 184-85, 199
    Clement VIII, 203, 210
    Clement IX, 215, 219
    Clement XI, 220
    Clement XIII, 224-27, 234
    Clement XIV, 206, 227, 229
    Constantine, 97
    Damasus, S., 42, 73
    Denis, S., 26

Eugene IV, 161, 162-63
Gregory the Great, S., 80, 86
Gregory II, S., 62, 90, 96
Gregory III, S., 91
Gregory VII, S., 108-10, 121, 145, 152, 231
Gregory IX, 125, 129, 133, 136, 141
Gregory XI, 155
Gregory XII, 157-61
Gregory XIII, 181, 198, 202
Gregory XVI, 242, 253
Honorius I, 58-9
Honorius III, 136
Hormisdas, S., 53
Innocent III, 127-32, 134-35, 154
Innocent IV, 137, 146, 261
Innocent VI, 155
Innocent VIII, 170-71, 173, 185
Innocent X, 202, 204, 215
Innocent XI, 216, 217
Innocent XII, 217
John VII, 61
John VIII, 101, 114
John XII, 102, 104
John XXII, 150-51
John XXIII, 159-60
Julius II, 170, 172-73
Julius III, 181, 188, 191-92
Leo the Great, S., 47-49, 77
Leo III, 99
Leo IX, 105, 111, 115
Leo X, 169, 174, 179, 182, 198
Leo XII, 242, 246, 253
Leo XIII, 242, 247, 256, 264, 269-80
Liberius, 67, 72
Lucius III, 127
Martin I, S., 59
Martin V, 161-62
Nicholas I, S., 101, 113
Nicholas II, 106, 107
Nicholas V, 161, 167
Pascal II, 111
Paul I, 97
Paul II, 168
Paul III, 181, 185-90, 198, 242, 258
Paul IV, 181, 196-97
Paul V, 202, 210
Pius II, 167
Pius IV, 181, 197
Pius V, S., 181, 197, 202, 264
Pius VI, 229, 231, 237, 243
Pius VII, 56, 238, 240, 245-46
Piux IX, 242, 247, 254-56
Pius X, 256, 281-84
Pius XI, 256, 286-92
Pius XII, 286, 292-93
Sergius I, S., 61
Sixtus IV, 168
Sixtus V, 181, 198, 202
Stephen III, 96
Stephen X, 107
Urban II, B., 108, 122
Urban IV, 138, 146
Urban V, B., 155

Popes—cont'd
  Urban VI, 156
  Urban VIII, 202, 215
  Victor I, S., 26
  Victor II, 107
  Victor III, B., 111
  Vigilius, 56-57
Portugal, 122
Praemunire, 154
Prague, 121
Preachers, Order of, 124, 129-30,
  133, 163, 210, 255
Premonstratensian Order, 118,
  119, 120-21, 130-31
Propagation of the Faith, Associa-
  tion for the, 263
Provence, 129
Provisors, Statute of, 154
Prussia, 121
Pulcheria, empress, 48

Quesnel, Pasquier, 220
Quietism, 217-19, 234

Ransom, Order of, 134
Ravenna, 76
Reccared, 85
Reims, 30
Rerum Novarum, 250
Revolution, French, 206, 232, 237,
  240, 242-45, 266
Ricci, Matteo, 261
Risorgimento, The, 252-54
Rome, Church of, 26-27, 29-30,
  40, 42, 43, 44-45, 47-48, 51,
  58, 60, 106-7
Romulus Augustulus, emperor
  (475-476), 77
Roncaglia, 124
Roumania, 29
Rousseau, Jean Jacques, 223
Russia, 29

St. Bartholomew, Massacre of,
  208
St. Cyran, 211
St. Sulpice, Company of, 209
Sacred Heart, Devotion to, 233
Saints and Beati:
  Aidan, 89
  Albert the Great, 141
  Alcantara, Peter of, 199
  Alphonsus Liguori, 232, 235
  Amand, 84
  Ambrose of Milan, 37
  Anselm, 117
  Antony of Egypt, 63
  Athanasius, 41, 65
  Augustine of Hippo, 22, 28,
    70-72, 74, 176, 211, 212
  Basil of Cappadocia, 42, 63, 65
  Bede, 89-90
  Bellarmine, Robert, 200
  Benedict, 80-82
  Benet Biscop, 89
  Bernadette, 256
  Bernard, 118, 123
  Bernardine of Siena, 163

Bonaventure, 141-42
Boniface, 83, 90-91, 95
Bridget of Sweden, 155
Cajetan, 190, 194
Caesarius of Arles, 82
Carthusian Martyrs, BB., 179
Catherine of Siena, 155
Charles Borromeo, 197, 213
Clement Hofbauer, 236
Colombière, Claude de la, B.,
  233-34
Columba, 80, 88
Columbanus, 80, 82, 83-84
Corbinian, 84
Cuthbert Mayne, B., 264
Cyprian, 26
Cyril of Alexander, 44-47, 50,
  56, 66-7
Denis of Alexandria, 26
Dominic, 129-31
Edmund Campion, B., 265
Edwin, 88
Eloy, 84
Flavian of Constantinople,
  47-48
Francis of Assisi, 132
Francis de Sales, 208-9
Francis of Solano, 258
Francis Xavier, 200
Gabriel of the Sorrows, 256
Germanus of Auxerre, 79
Gregory of Nazianzen, 65
Gregory of Nyssa, 65
Gregory of Tours, 82
Gregory the Wonderworker, 29
Henry II, emperor (1002-1024),
  105
Hermenegild, 85
Hilary of Arles, 79
Hilary of Poitiers, 78
Ignatius of Antioch, 26
Ignatius Loyola, 200
Irenaeus, 18, 26
Isidore of Seville, 86
Jean Marie Vianney, 255-6
Jerome, 39, 73
Joan of Arc, 153
John the Apostle, 18
John Bosco, 256
John Chrysostom, 43, 66
John of the Cross, 199
John Fisher, 179
John Gualbert, 104
Joseph Cottolengo, 256
Justin Martyr, 27
Killian, 84
Leander of Seville, 85
Leger, 84
Leonard of Porto Maurizio, 234
Louis IX, King of France
  (1226-1270), 137, 138
Louise de Marillac, 210
Margaret Mary, 232
Martin of Braga, 84
Martin de la Porres, B., 259
Martin of Tours, 78
Methodius of Constantinople,
  94

Saints and Beati—cont'd
Norbert, 119
Omer, 84
Oswald, 88
Patrick, 79-80
Paul, 14, 19, 29, 30
Paul of the Cross, 232, 234
Paul of Thebes, 62
Peter Canisius, 200
Peter Damian, 106, 111
Philip Neri, 200, 213
Polycarp, 18
Rémy, 82
Romuald, 104
Rose of Lima, 259
Sophronius, 58
Stephen Harding, 118
Teresa, 199
Theodore of Tarsus, 89
Thomas Aquinas, 141, 142, 143, 165
Thomas More, 179, 189
Toribio de Mogrovejo, 258
Vincent Ferrer, 165
Vincent de Paul, 210
Virgil, 84
Willibrord, 90
Zaccaria, Anthony, 199
Salzburg, 84
Saxons, 98
Scandinavia, 120
Scotland, 80
Septimius Severus, emperor (193-211), 31
Sergius of Constantinople, 58, 60
Severus of Antioch, 53, 54
Somaschi, 199
Spiritual Exercises, The, 200
Spain, 13, 30, 33, 60, 68, 75, 84, 85, 92, 121
Spirituals, Franciscan, 150
Subordinationism, 22
Suevi, 84
Summa Theologica, 142
Switzerland, 84, 178
Syncretism, 15
Syria, 29, 45, 49, 53, 57, 92

Tabennisi, 63
Tertullian, 20
Theatines, Order of, 190, 194, 198
Theodora, empress regent (842), 94

Theodore of Mopsuestia, 56
Theodoret of Cyrrhus, 45, 46-47, 48, 49
Theodoric the Ostrogoth, 77
Theodosius the Great, emperor (379-395), 37, 41
Theodosius II, emperor (408-450), 46, 48
Theophilus of Alexandria, 43, 50
Theophylact, 101
Thirty-Nine Articles, 264
Thomas à Kempis, 163
Thuringia, 90
Toulouse, 30
Traité sur l'amour de Dieu, 209
Trajan, emperor (98-117), 31, 32
Trèves, 30
Trinity, Order of, 134
Truce of God, 120
Turks, 121
Type, The, 59

Unam Sanctam, bull (1303), 148
Unigenitus, bull, 220
Universities, Catholic, 238-39
Ursuline nuns, 190
U.S.A., 232, 263
Utrecht, 90

Valens, emperor (364-378), 37, 42
Valentinian III, emperor (425-455), 77
Valerian, emperor (253-258), 32
Vandals, 69, 74, 76
Vincentians, 210, 262
Visigoths, 84
Vittoria, Francis de, 258
Voltaire, 222, 223, 224, 225

War, Hundred Years', 153
War, Thirty Years', 204
Wars of Religion, 208
Westphalia, Treaties of, 204-5, 241
William III, King of England, 267
Würzburg, 84
Wycliffe, John, 165

York, 88

Zeno, emperor (474-491), 51, 77